The Future of Global Currency

Can the euro challenge the supremacy of the U.S. dollar as a global currency? From the time Europe's joint money was born, many have predicted that it would soon achieve parity with the dollar or possibly even surpass it. In reality, however, the euro has remained firmly planted in the dollar's shadow. The essays collected in this volume explain why. Because of America's external deficits and looming foreign debt, the dollar can never be as dominant as it once was. But Europe's money is unable to mount an effective challenge. The euro suffers from a number of critical structural deficiencies, including an anti-growth bias that is built into the institutions of the monetary union and an ambiguous governance structure that sows doubts among prospective users. As recent events have demonstrated, members of the euro zone remain vulnerable to financial crisis. Moreover, lacking a single voice, the bloc continues to punch below its weight in monetary diplomacy. The world seems headed toward a leaderless monetary order, with several currencies in contention but none clearly dominant.

This collection distills the views of one of the world's leading scholars in global currency, and will be of considerable interest to students and scholars of international finance and international political economy.

Benjamin J. Cohen is Louis G. Lancaster Professor of International Political Economy at the University of California, Santa Barbara. A specialist in the political economy of international money and finance, he is the author of twelve previous books, including most recently *Global Monetary Governance* (Routledge, 2008).

Jerry Cohen is the authoritative commentator on key currencies in the global monetary system. This collection of essays on the subject is knowledgeable, insightful, and extraordinarily timely.

Andrew Walter, *London School of Economics, UK*

The international monetary system is currently being transformed dramatically by a complicated array of economic and political pressures. Jerry Cohen remains the best guide to understanding how that system, and its key European component, is likely to evolve in coming years. The clarity of his prose matches the brilliance of his many insights. This volume deserves a prominent place on undergraduate and graduate student reading lists, but its contents will enlighten any interested reader.

Louis W. Pauly, *University of Toronto, Canada*

Benjamin Jerry Cohen learned international economics from me. I have learned international political economy from him. You will too by reading the excellent collection of papers in this volume.

Peter B. Kenen, *Princeton University, USA*

The Future of Global Currency

The euro versus the dollar

Benjamin J. Cohen

Routledge
Taylor & Francis Group

LONDON AND NEW YORK

To my "fire friends," with deepest gratitude

First published 2011
by Routledge
2 Park Square, Milton Park, Abingdon, Oxon, OX14 4RN

Simultaneously published in the USA and Canada
by Routledge
711 Third Avenue, New York, NY 10017

Routledge is an imprint of the Taylor & Francis Group, *an informa business*

© 2011 Benjamin J. Cohen

The right of Benjamin J. Cohen to be identified as author of this work has
been asserted by him in accordance with the Copyright, Designs and Patent
Act 1988.

Typeset in Times New Roman by Taylor & Francis Books

British Library Cataloguing in Publication Data
A catalogue record for this book is available from the British Library

Library of Congress Cataloging in Publication Data
Cohen, Benjamin J.
The future of global currency : the euro versus the
dollar/Benjamin J. Cohen.
    p. cm.
Includes bibliographical references and index.
1. Euro. 2. Dollar. 3. International finance. 4. European Union
countries–Foreign economic relations. 5. United States–Foreign economic
relations. I. Title.
HG925.C629 2010
332.4'94–dc22   2010027714

ISBN: 978-0-415-78149-7 (hbk)
ISBN: 978-0-415-78150-3 (pbk)
ISBN: 978-0-203-83380-3 (ebk)

Contents

Preface   vii
Acknowledgments   viii

Introduction   1

PART I
The global currency system   7

1   Life at the top: international currencies in the
    twenty-first century   9

2   The euro and transatlantic relations   37

PART II
The euro challenge   53

3   EMU and the dollar: who threatens whom?   55

4   Global currency rivalry: can the euro ever
    challenge the dollar?   59

5   Enlargement and the international role of the euro   74

6   The euro in a global context: challenges and capacities   98

7   Dollar dominance, euro aspirations: recipe for discord?   114

PART III
Glimpses of the future   135

  8 A one-and-a-half currency system, *with Paola Subacchi*   137

  9 Toward a leaderless currency system   148

 10 The international monetary system: diffusion
     and ambiguity   167

     Notes   183
     Bibliography   185
     Index   197

Preface

In November 2008, my home in Santa Barbara burned down in a wildfire. Everything I owned was destroyed, including my professional library. All my books and papers, accumulated over half a century, were lost.

Almost immediately, friends and colleagues around the academic world began sending me replacements. Soon books began to arrive on an almost daily basis—dozens, scores, ultimately hundreds. The list of my "fire friends," as I came to call them, eventually grew to more than fifty. I cannot begin to express how grateful I am to them all.

This book is dedicated to all my fire friends, whose generosity continues to astonish me. With apologies for any names I may have inadvertently omitted, they are: Jonathan David Aronson, Aaron Belkin, Bill Bernhard, Jacqueline Best, Kerry Chase, Christian Chavagneux, Cornell University Press (Roger Haydon), Bob Cox, Beth DeSombre, Peter Dombrowski, Jeff Frieden, Randy Germain, Peter Gourevitch, Joanne Gowa, Rodney Bruce Hall, Jeffrey Hart, Virginia Haufler, Eric Helleiner, *International Affairs* (Caroline Soper), *International Organization* (Emanuel Adler, Lou Pauly), Miles Kahler, Saori Katada, Peter Katzenstein, Peter Kenen, Bob Keohane, Jonathan Kirshner, David Lake, Kathryn Lavelle, Peter Loedel, Sophie Meunier, Ron Mitchell, James Morrisson, Layna Mosley, Craig Murphy, *New Political Economy* (Nicola Phillips), John Odell, Peterson Institute of International Economics (Randy Henning, Ted Truman, and others), Jon Pevehouse, Princeton University Press (Chuck Myers), *Review of International Political Economy* (Kate Weaver, Mark Blyth), Routledge Publishers (Craig Fowlie), Nita Rudra, Herman Schwartz, Beth Simmons, David Stasavage, Michael Tomz, University of Pennsylvania Department of Political Science (Ed Mansfield and others), Robert Wade, Andrew Walter, and Hubert Zimmermann.

My thanks also to Craig Fowlie, for suggesting that I put this collection of essays together, and to Tabitha Benney, for her able assistance in getting the job done.

Acknowledgments

The essays in this volume have been only lightly edited and are little changed from the original. Chapter 1 first appeared as Princeton Essay in International Economics No. 221 (International Finance Section, Department of Economics, Princeton University, December 2000), reprinted with permission. Chapter 2 was included in *Hard Power, Soft Power and the Future of Transatlantic Relations*, ed. Thomas L. Ilgen (Burlington, VT: Ashgate, 2006), reprinted with permission. Chapter 3 was published in the *Swiss Political Science Review* 2 (1996), reprinted with permission. Chapter 4 first appeared in the *Journal of Common Market Studies* 41 (2003), reprinted with permission. Chapter 5 was published in the *Review of International Political Economy* 14 (2007), reprinted with permission. Chapter 6 was included in *The Euro at Ten: Europeanization, Power, and Convergence*, ed. Kenneth Dyson (Oxford: Oxford University Press, 2008), reprinted with permission. Chapter 7 appeared in the *Journal of Common Market Studies* 47 (2009), reprinted with permission. Chapter 8 was published in the *Journal of International Affairs* 62 (2008), reprinted with permission. Chapter 9 was included in *The Future of the Dollar*, ed. Eric Helleiner and Jonathan Kirshner (Ithaca, NY: Cornell University Press, 2009), reprinted with permission. Chapter 10 appeared in *International Affairs* 84 (2008), reprinted with permission.

Introduction

The day of the dollar is over, the era of the euro has begun—such was the view of many well-informed observers when Europe's new joint currency was born back in 1999. America's faltering greenback, long the dominant currency in the world economy, now faced a potent new rival. It was only a matter of time until the euro would achieve parity with the greenback as a global currency or possibly even surpass it. Typical was Nobel Prize laureate Robert Mundell, often hailed as the father of the euro, who boldly asserted that Europe's money "will challenge the status of the dollar and alter the power configuration of the system."

As Mundell's wording suggested, much was at stake. An international currency bestows considerable benefits on its issuer; material capabilities may be greatly enhanced. For decades, the United States had exploited the global acceptability of the greenback to promote America's foreign policy objectives. In effect, Washington was free to spend money around the world virtually without limit in support of its military, diplomatic, and economic programs— an advantage that Charles de Gaulle roundly criticized as an "exorbitant privilege." But why shouldn't Europeans enjoy an exorbitant privilege, too? With the creation of the euro, it was widely believed, the balance of power in monetary affairs would soon tip in Europe's direction.

Not everyone agreed, however—and among the skeptics I may count myself. From the time the Maastricht Treaty was signed in 1992, setting the European Union (EU) on the way to its Economic and Monetary Union (EMU), I had my doubts, first expressed in print as early as 1996. Yes, EMU had much going for it, including a thriving economy as large as that of the United States and an array of world-class financial markets. No one could deny the new currency's strengths. But there were weaknesses too, structural and deep, that in my opinion were bound to limit the euro's appeal outside the EU's immediate neighborhood. The euro, I believed, would never be able to topple the dollar from its perch as the world's preeminent global currency. Little that has happened in the period since the euro's birth has persuaded me to think otherwise.

In many respects, of course, the euro must be rated as an historic achieve-ment. To merge the separate monies of some of the biggest economies in the world was certainly no small deed. Technically, the euro's birth proved to be remarkably smooth, quickly relegating EMU's so-called "legacy" currencies to the dustbin of history. The new European Central Bank (ECB) experienced few difficulties taking over management of monetary policy for the group as a whole. Membership of the euro zone expanded from its initial eleven countries to, at last count, sixteen. And for the first time since the era of the classical gold standard, participants no longer had to worry about the risk of exchange-rate disturbances in their corner of the world. In place of distinct national currencies, each vulnerable to the dangers of market speculation, they could all enjoy the equivalent of irrevocably fixed exchange rates with their neighbors—the hardest of "hard" pegs.

On the broader world stage, however, accomplishments have been rather more modest. The dollar's status has not, in fact, been challenged. To be sure, international use of the euro did grow in the currency's first years, particularly in bond markets. In short order, Europe's money successfully established itself as second only to the greenback in global finance. But after an initial spurt of enthusiasm for the new currency, internationalization soon leveled off and has since been confined largely to a limited range of market sectors and regions. Overall, sometime around EMU's fifth birthday, the euro's trajectory effectively stalled. A ceiling appears to have been reached, leaving Europe's money firmly planted in the dollar's long shadow.

Not even the global crisis that began in mid-2007, triggered by the subprime mortgage collapse in the United States, was able to elevate the euro's fortunes. By 2008 the soundness of the world's entire monetary structure had been thrown into question. If ever there was a moment when the euro might have been expected to come into it own, this was it. American financial enterprises were clearly to blame for the troubles. Why not turn to EMU instead? Yet in fact the reverse occurred. Even at moments of greatest panic, market actors looked to the greenback, not the euro, for safety. Global demand for dollar-denominated assets accelerated sharply, while euro claims were abandoned.

Worse, by the early months of 2010 doubts began to be expressed about the viability of the euro itself. The catalyst was Greece, whose mushrooming sovereign debt problems threatened to overwhelm EMU's governing institutions. Exchange-rate disturbances may no longer be a risk within the euro zone, but that did not rule out market speculation against a weak and vulnerable economy. In the EU's own version of a Greek tragedy, policymakers bickered publicly over what to do to help Athens—a process described by one journalist as "an exercise in cat-herding." Ultimately, with the help of the International Monetary Fund (IMF), an unprecedented "stabilization mechanism" worth nearly $1 trillion was cobbled together to stave off the possibility of default by Greece or other euro-zone countries. But by then the damage was done. Confidence in EMU was at a low ebb.

Some sources even went so far as to declare that Europe's experiment in monetary union had now failed. In a well-publicized speech in London in mid-May, Paul Volcker—former chair of the Federal Reserve and now an influential White House adviser—dramatically warned of the "potential disintegration of the euro." German Chancellor Angela Merkel went even further, telling her parliament that the euro-zone crisis was the greatest test for the EU since its creation. "It is a question of survival," she said. "The euro is in danger. If the euro fails, then Europe fails." Never had Europe's money looked less like a contender for global status.

As this book went to press in mid-2010, the fate of the euro seemed to be hanging in the balance. My own view, which I have often expressed to my students and others, is that over the long term the euro will not succeed—but neither will it fail. It will not fail because the political commitment to its survival, in some form, simply runs too deep across the EU. Like Mark Twain, Europeans may rightfully feel that reports of the death of their currency have been greatly exaggerated. But neither will the euro truly succeed, because its deficiencies also are too deep. In some sense, the euro's fate will always be hanging in the balance.

One thing seems certain. As an international currency, the euro is unlikely to break through the ceiling that it reached after its first few years. Parity with the dollar will not be attained. The reasons for my judgment are spelled out in the essays collected together in the pages of this volume. The essays in this book, all but one written during the lifetime of the euro, divide into three groups. The two essays in Part I set the stage, describing the wider contexts in which the bilateral rivalry between Europe's money and the greenback was to be played out. Part II focuses more narrowly on the rivalry itself and, in particular, on the deficiencies of the euro that in my view severely constrain its prospects as a global currency. Finally, the three essays in Part III look more to the future, contemplating what the global monetary system might look like further down the road following the stalled challenge of the euro.

Chapter 1, published in the millennium year of 2000, takes a broad perspective on the monetary system as a whole, laying out long-term prospects for global currencies in the twenty-first century. Particular emphasis is placed on what I call the Big Three—the dollar, euro, and Japanese yen—the three most widely used monies of their day. The essay explores how relative standing among the Big Three may be influenced by a trio of key considerations: the logic of market competition, the strategic preferences of national governments, and prospective technological developments. Analysis suggests little near-term threat to the predominance of the Big Three, although relative standing could be substantially altered by market competition, which in turn could lead to intensified policy competition among issuing authorities. Over the longer term, technological developments could lead to the development of entirely new rivals to today's top currencies, thereby transforming the geography of money virtually beyond recognition.

Chapter 2, in turn, narrows the focus to the bilateral relationship between the United States and Europe. How, the essay asks, will the euro's challenge to the dollar affect transatlantic relations? Could monetary rivalry spill over into a broader geopolitical confrontation between historical allies? Much depends, I contend, on how vigorously the nations of Europe choose to promote their currency's internationalization. Europeans may certainly be expected to do whatever they can to reinforce the market appeal of the euro. But would they go further, to seek formation of an organized monetary bloc with foreign governments—a move that would almost certainly provoke determined resistance from Washington? I find little evidence to believe that Europe is prepared to push currency competition with the United States to the point where it might jeopardize more vital political and security interests. Mutual restraint, I argue, is the much more likely scenario.

What, then, can be said about the prospective market appeal of the euro? That is the central question addressed in the next five chapters, beginning in Chapter 3 with a brief early comment of mine published not long after the Maastricht Treaty was signed. In response to those predicting a bright global future for Europe's new money, I advised a note of caution. The greenback would not be so easily displaced, I warned. On the contrary, even within the European region itself the euro could find itself on the defensive, given the dollar's continuing attractiveness for many international uses. It would not be easy to overcome the greenback's entrenched advantages.

A few years later, in 2003, I spelled out my argument more fully in the third *Journal of Common Market Studies*—European Union Studies Association Lecture, presented at the eighth biennial international conference of the European Union Studies Association. Reproduced here as Chapter 4, the lecture outlines four reasons why, in my opinion, the euro is fated to remain a distant second to the dollar. First is the persistent inertia of monetary behavior in general, owing to what economists call "network externalities"— essentially, the natural advantage that an incumbent currency has in offering an already well-established transactional domain. The greenback's network externalities can be counted on to inhibit any rapid switch to Europe's money. Second is the cost of doing business in euros, which is unlikely to decline substantially below transactions costs for the dollar. Third is an anti-growth bias that I argue is built into the institutions of EMU, tending to limit returns on euro-denominated assets. And fourth is the ambiguous governance structure of the monetary union, which sows doubt among prospective euro users. Even under the best of circumstances, the chapter concludes, the euro is fighting a distinctly uphill battle.

Would enlargement make a difference? That is the question taken up in Chapter 5. We know that the monetary union's membership will continue to grow, since eventual adoption of the joint currency is a legal obligation for all of the twelve countries added to the EU since the euro's birth, as well as for any future entrants. More members will mean an even broader transactional domain, increasing exponentially the potential for network externalities to offset the natural incumbency advantages of the dollar. But outweighing that gain, I suggest, would be a distinctly negative impact on the governance structure of EMU, which can be expected to sow even greater doubts among prospective euro users. From the start, internationalization of the euro has been retarded by a lack of clarity about the delegation of monetary authority among governments and EU institutions. In effect, no one knows who really is in charge. The addition of a diverse collection of new members, with significantly different interests and priorities, can only make the challenge of governance worse, exacerbating ambiguity at the expense of transparency and accountability. Enlargement, I contend, will diminish, not enhance, the euro's appeal as a rival to the greenback. New governance issues are also addressed in Chapter 6, which focuses on how the creation of the euro has affected the power of participating states to cope with external challenges. Overall, the essay suggests, EMU has signally failed to enhance the group's autonomy or influence in monetary affairs. Despite the elimination of any risk of exchange-rate disturbances within the euro zone, members remain vulnerable to fluctuations of the euro vis-à-vis outside currencies; and, as the Greek episode in 2010 made vividly clear, the bloc has become, if anything, even more exposed to threats of financial instability. Likewise, lacking a single voice, the group continues to punch below its weight in monetary diplomacy. The fundamental problem, I argue, lies in the mismatch between the domain of the monetary union and the jurisdiction of its participating governments. The euro is a currency without a country—the product of an interstate agreement rather than the expression of a single sovereign power. Hence EMU's power to cope with external challenges is structurally constrained.

The consequences of all these deficiencies are evident in Chapter 7, which reviews available statistical information on the actual performance of the euro as an international currency over its first decade. The numbers clearly confirm the failure of the euro's challenge to the dollar. Overall, Europe's money has done little more than hold its own as compared with the past global market shares of EMU's legacy currencies. After a fast start, international use broadly leveled off by 2004 and has shown little growth since then. Moreover, increases have been uneven across both functional categories and regions. The expansion of usage has been most dramatic in the issuance of debt securities; there have also been some modest increases in the euro's share of trade invoicing and central bank reserves. But in other categories, such as foreign-exchange trading or banking, the dominance of the greenback remains as great as ever. Likewise, in regional terms, it is evident that internationalization has been confined mostly to countries with close geographical and/or institutional links to the euro zone—what might be considered EMU's natural hinterland in the periphery of Europe, the Mediterranean littoral, and parts of Africa. Elsewhere, again, the dollar continues to cast a long shadow.

Can Europe do anything about the euro's deficiencies? Some suggestions are offered in Chapter 8, co-authored with Paola Subacchi, director of international economic studies at the Royal Institute for International Affairs (otherwise known as Chatham House, London). As matters stand now, the essay asserts, the world can expect to continue living for some time in a "one-and-a-half currency system," with Europe's money playing at best a subordinate role as compared to the dollar. To enhance the euro's role, Subacchi and I argue, a determined reform of EMU's governance structure is imperative, with emphasis on two issues in particular—exchange-rate management and institutional representation. On the one hand, Europe needs more proactive management of the euro's exchange rate, to reduce the bloc's vulnerability to fluctuations vis-à-vis outside currencies, coupled with better coordination and surveillance of fiscal policies at the national level. On the other hand, it also needs to consolidate euro-zone representation in relevant international bodies and forums such as the IMF and Group of 20 if it is to be able to function as a monetary heavyweight comparable to the United States. Without such reforms to help project power more effectively, we suggest, Europe will never be ready for prime time.

Extending the perspective and time horizon, Chapter 9 moves beyond the euro alone to consider the wider array of potential future challengers to the dollar. These include not only Europe's money but also, possibly, a revived yen or even, in the longer term, an emergent Chinese yuan. The essay accepts that the global position of the greenback may be weakening under the burden of America's external deficits and looming foreign debt. The dollar can never be as dominant as it once was. But neither is there any obvious new leader lurking in the wings, just waiting to take center stage. The weaknesses of the euro are by now obvious. Other potential challengers have deficiencies, too, which are likely to limit their appeal as well. Most probable, therefore, is the gradual emergence over time of a fragmented global order, with several monies in contention but none clearly in the lead. We are heading, I contend, toward a *leaderless* currency system.

Finally, in Chapter 10, I reflect on implications of global currency rivalries for the broader international monetary order. The trend toward a leaderless currency system is just one signal among many that the distribution of power in monetary affairs is changing, with significant implications for the management of global finance in the future. More and more states are gaining a degree of insulation from outside pressures, enhancing their ability to act autonomously; yet few are yet able to exercise greater authority to shape events or outcomes. Leadership, therefore, is being dispersed rather than relocated and monetary power is steadily diffusing, generating greater ambiguity in prevailing governance structures. Increasingly, governance is coming to rely not on formal negotiation but, rather, on informal custom and usage to define standards of behavior. The result over time will be an ever greater level of uncertainty about the prevailing rules of the game. If instability and crisis are to be avoided, I suggest, a change of bargaining strategy among governments will be needed to conform more comfortably to the new distribution of power.

Part I
The global currency system

1 Life at the top

International currencies in the twenty-first century

One of the most remarkable developments in global monetary relations at century's end is the rapid acceleration of cross-border competition among currencies—a spreading, market-driven phenomenon that I have elsewhere called the deterritorialization of money (Cohen 1998). Circulation of national currencies is no longer confined within the territorial frontiers of nation-states. A few popular currencies, most notably the U.S. dollar and German Deutschmark (DM) (now being succeeded by the euro), have come to be widely used outside their country of origin, vying directly with local rivals for both medium-of-exchange and investment purposes. Competition is intense and, as in most competitions, success is largely a matter of survival of the fittest.

The result of this phenomenon has been a fundamental transformation of the geography of money, the broad configuration of global currency space. Where once existed a familiar landscape of relatively insular national monetary systems—in effect, a simple map of neatly divided territorial currencies—monies have now become both more entangled and more hierarchical. My image for this new geography is the Currency Pyramid: narrow at the peak, where the strongest currencies dominate, and increasingly broad below, reflecting varying degrees of competitive inferiority. A few monies enjoy the power and prestige of high rank; more constrained policy options are available to the issuers of many others. The highest standing is enjoyed by the dollar, the use of which predominates for most, if not all, cross-border purposes. Closest competition comes currently from the euro—newly created by Europe's Economic and Monetary Union (EMU)—and the Japanese yen, although neither currency can as yet claim anything like the universal appeal of America's greenback.

What are the prospects for today's top international currencies in the twenty-first century? The purpose of this essay is to take an objective new look at this critical question, giving particular emphasis to the factors most likely to influence the rivalry and rank of the top currencies over time. To put the discussion in perspective, I begin with a few basic statistics on cross-border currency use. I then explore the way in which the future of the top currencies may be influenced by the logic of market competition, the strategic preferences of national governments, and prospective technological developments. Analysis suggests little near-term threat to the predominance of today's top currencies, although relative standing could be substantially altered by market competition, which in turn could lead to intensified policy competition among issuing authorities. Over the longer term, however, stretching further into the next century, technological developments could lead to the creation of entirely new rivals to today's top currencies, thereby transforming the geography of money virtually beyond recognition.

International currencies

Currencies may be employed outside their country of origin for either of two purposes: for transactions between nations or for transactions within foreign states. The former purpose is conventionally referred to as "international" currency use, or currency "internationalization"; the latter is described as "currency substitution" and can be referred to as "foreign-domestic use." The top international monies are widely used for both purposes.

Both currency internationalization and currency substitution are products of intense market rivalry—a kind of Darwinian process of natural selection, driven by the force of demand, in which some monies, such as the dollar, Deutschmark, and yen, come to prevail over others for various commercial or financial purposes. Although cross-border use is known to be accelerating rapidly, its full dimensions cannot be measured precisely in the absence of comprehensive statistics on global currency circulation. Partial indicators, however, may be gleaned from a variety of sources to underscore the impressive orders of magnitude involved.

The clearest signal of the rapid growth of currency internationalization is sent by the global foreign-exchange market where, according to the Bank for International Settlements (1999), average daily turnover has accelerated from $590 billion in 1989 (the first year for which such data are available) to $1.5 trillion in 1998—a rate of increase in excess of 25 percent per annum. Even allowing for the fact that much of this activity is accounted for by interdealer trading, the pace of expansion is impressive. The dollar is the most-favored vehicle for currency exchange worldwide, appearing on one side or the other of some 87 percent of all transactions in 1998 (little changed from its 90 percent share in 1989); the Deutschmark appeared in 30 percent of transactions and the yen in 21 percent. The dollar is also the most-favored vehicle for the invoicing of international trade, where it has been estimated to account for nearly half of all world exports (Hartmann 1998)—more than double America's actual share of world exports. The Deutschmark share of invoicing in recent years was 15 percent (roughly equal to Germany's proportion of world exports); the yen's share was 5 percent (significantly less than Japan's proportion of world exports).

A parallel story is evident in international markets for financial claims, including bank deposits and loans as well as bonds and stocks, all of which have grown at double-digit rates for years. Using data from a variety of sources, Thygesen and the ECU Institute (1995) calculated what they call "global financial wealth," the world's total portfolio of private international investments. From just over $1 trillion in 1981, aggregate cross-border holdings quadrupled, to more than $4.5 trillion, by 1993—an expansion far greater than that of world output or trade in goods and services. Again, the dollar dominated, accounting for nearly 60 percent of foreign-currency deposits and close to 40 percent of international bonds. The Deutschmark accounted for 14 percent of deposits and 10 percent of bonds; the yen, for 4 percent of deposits and 14 percent of bonds. More recently, the International Monetary Fund ([IMF] 1999) put the total of international portfolio investments (including equities, long- and short-term debt securities, and financial derivatives) at just over $6 trillion in 1997.

The clearest signal of the rapid growth of currency substitution is sent by the rapid increase in the physical circulation of these same currencies outside their country of origin. For the dollar, an authoritative Federal Reserve study (Porter and Judson 1996) puts the value of U.S. banknotes in circulation abroad in 1995 at between 55 and 70 percent of the total outstanding stock—equivalent to perhaps $250 billion in all. The same study also reckons that as much as three-quarters of the annual increase of U.S. notes now goes directly abroad, up from less than one-half in the 1980s and under one-third in the 1970s. Appetite for the dollar appears to be not only strong but growing. Using a comparable approach, Germany's Deutsche Bundesbank (1995) has estimated Deutschmark circulation outside Germany, mainly in East-Central Europe and the Balkans, at about 30–40 percent of total stock at end-1994, equivalent to some 65–90 billion DM ($45–$65 billion). The Deutschmark's successor, the euro, is confidently expected to take over the Deutschmark's role in foreign-domestic use, once euro notes enter circulation in 2002, and perhaps even to cut into the dollar's market share. Similarly, on the other side of the world, Bank of Japan officials have been privately reported to believe that of the total supply of yen banknotes, amounting to some $370 billion in 1993, as much as 10 percent was located in neighboring countries (Hale 1995). Combining these diverse estimates suggests a minimum total foreign circulation of the top currencies in the mid-1990s of at least $300 billion—by no means an inconsiderable sum and, judging from available evidence, apparently continuing to rise rapidly.

The evidence also suggests that a very wide range of countries is affected by this phenomenon, even if the precise numbers involved remain somewhat obscure. According to one authoritative source (Krueger and Ha 1996), foreign banknotes accounted for 20 percent or more of the local money stock during the mid-1990s in as many as three dozen nations inhabited by at least one-third of the world's population. The same source also suggests that, in total, as much as 25–33 percent of the world's circulating currency was recently located outside its country of issue.

These numbers clearly confirm the growing importance of both international and foreign-domestic use of the top international currencies for both medium-of-exchange and store-of-value purposes. Most prominent, obviously, is the dollar, which remains by far the world's most popular choice for both currency internationalization and currency substitution. In effect, the dollar's domain spans the globe, from the Western Hemisphere to the former Soviet bloc and much of the Middle East; in all these regions, dollars circulate widely as a *de facto* parallel currency. Next is the Deutschmark, now being replaced by the euro, which is preeminent in monetary relations in much of the European neighborhood. In third place is the yen, albeit at some distance behind the first two. At the peak of the Currency Pyramid today, these three monies—the Big Three—plainly dominate.

Market competition

But what of tomorrow? Will the Big Three continue to dominate, or can significant changes be expected? Broadly speaking, life at the top will be influenced most by three key considerations: the logic of market competition, the strategic preferences of national governments, and prospective technological developments. All three factors suggest that substantial new transformations in the geography of money are in the making.

Consider, first, the logic of market competition. Today's Big Three dominate, first and foremost, because they are (or have been) attractive to market participants for a variety of monetary purposes. If we learn anything from the history of money, however, it is that monetary attractiveness can change—and, with it, the relative standing of individual currencies. The past is littered with the carcasses of currencies that once dominated international commerce, from the Athenian drachma and Byzantine solidus (the bezant) to Florence's florin, Spain's (later Mexico's) silver peso and, most recently, Britain's pound sterling. Shakespeare's words are as apt for money as they are for monarchs: "Uneasy lies the head that wears the crown." What does the logic of market competition tell us about who is likely to wear the crown tomorrow?

Attributes of success

What makes a money attractive in the first place? The principal attributes required for competitive success in the international marketplace are familiar to specialists and are uncontroversial. Three features stand out.

The first requirement, at least during the initial stages of a currency's cross-border use, is widespread confidence in a money's future value backed by political stability in the country of origin. Essentially, this means a proven track record of relatively low inflation and inflation variability. High and fluctuating inflation rates increase the cost of acquiring information and performing price calculations. No currency is apt to be willingly adopted for international or foreign-domestic use if its purchasing power cannot be forecast with some degree of assurance.

Second are two qualities that I have elsewhere referred to as "exchange convenience" and "capital certainty" (Cohen 1971), a high degree of transactional liquidity and reasonable predictability of asset value. The key to both is a set of well-developed financial markets, sufficiently open so as to ensure full access by nonresidents. Markets must not be encumbered by high transactions costs or formal or informal barriers to entry. They must also be broad, with a large assortment of instruments available for temporary or longer-term investment, and they must be deep and resilient, with fully operating secondary markets for most, if not all, financial claims.

Finally, and most important of all, a money must promise a broad transactional network, because nothing enhances a currency's acceptability more than the prospect of acceptability by others. Historically, this has usually meant an economy that is large in absolute size and well integrated into world markets. A large economy creates a naturally ample constituency for a currency; economies of scale are further enhanced if the issuing country is also a major player in world trade. No money has ever risen to a position of international preeminence that was not initially backed by a leading economy. The greater the volume of transactions conducted in or with a given country, the greater are the potential network externalities to be derived from use of its money.

Reiteration of these essential attributes permits two broad inferences. First, among currencies in circulation today, there seems to be no candidate with even the remotest chance in the foreseeable future of challenging the top rank currently enjoyed by the dollar, euro, and yen. Second, among the Big Three, there seems a very real chance of significant shifts in relative market standing.

No new challengers

The first inference follows logically from observable fact. We know that there is a great deal of inertia in currency use that can slow the transition from one equilibrium to another. Recall, for instance, how long it took the dollar to supplant the pound sterling at the top of the Currency Pyramid even after America's emergence a century ago as the world's richest economy. As Paul Krugman (1992: 173) has commented: "The impressive fact here is surely the inertia; sterling remained the first-ranked currency for half a century after Britain had ceased to be the first-ranked economic power." Similar inertias have been evident for millennia, as in the prolonged use of such international moneys as the bezant and silver peso long after the decline of the imperial powers that first coined them. It has also been evident more recently in the continued popularity of the dollar despite periodic bouts of exchange-rate depreciation. Such inertia seems very much the rule, not the exception, in currency relations.

Inertia is promoted by two factors. The first is the preexistence of an already well-established transactional network, which confers a natural advantage of incumbency. Once a particular money is widely adopted, not even a substantial erosion of its initial attractions—stable value, exchange convenience, or capital certainty—may suffice to discourage continued use. That is because switching from one currency to another necessarily involves an expensive process of financial adaptation. Considerable effort must be invested in creating and learning to use new instruments and institutions, with much riding on what other market agents may be expected to do at the same time. As attractive as some new contender may seem, adoption will not prove cost-effective unless other agents appear likely to make extensive use of it too. The point is well put by Kevin Dowd and David Greenaway:

> Changing currencies is costly—we must learn to reckon in the new currency, we must change the units in which we quote prices, we might have to change our records, and so on. ... [This] explains why agents are often reluctant to switch currencies, even when the currency they are using appears to be manifestly inferior to some other.
>
> (Dowd and Greenaway 1993: 1180)

The second factor is the exceptionally high level of uncertainty that is inherent in any choice among alternative moneys. The appeal of any money, ultimately, rests on an intersubjective faith in its general acceptability—something about which one can never truly be sure. Uncertainty thus encourages a tendency toward what psychologists call "mimesis": the rational impulse of risk-averse actors, in conditions of contingency, to minimize anxiety by imitative behavior based on past experience. Once a currency gains a degree of acceptance, its use is apt to be perpetuated—even after the appearance of powerful new challengers—simply by regular repetition of previous practice. In effect, a conservative bias is inherent in the dynamics of the marketplace. As one source has argued, "imitation leads to the emergence of a convention [wherein] emphasis is placed on a certain 'conformism' or even hermeticism in financial circles" (Orléan 1989: 81–83).

Because of this conservative bias, no new challenger can ever hope to rise toward the top of the Currency Pyramid unless it can first offer a substantial margin of advantage over existing incumbents. The dollar was able to do that in relation to sterling, once New York overtook London as the world's pre-eminent source of investment capital—although even that displacement, as Krugman notes, took a half century or more. Today, it is difficult to find any money anywhere with a comparable promise of competitive advantage with respect to the present Big Three.

Some sources suggest a possible future role for China's yuan, given the enormous size of the Chinese economy (already, by some measures, the second largest in the world) and its growing role in world trade. However broad the yuan's transactional network may eventually become, though, the currency's prospects suffer from the backwardness of China's financial markets and still lingering uncertainties about domestic political stability—to say nothing of the fact that use of the yuan continues to be inhibited by cumbersome exchange and capital controls. Similar deficiencies also rule out the monies of other large emerging markets, such as Brazil or India. Conversely, the still-independent currencies of some economically advanced countries, such as Switzerland or Canada, or even Britain, are precluded, despite obvious financial sophistication and political stability, by the relatively small size of the economies involved (Britain's pound, in any event, is expected eventually to be absorbed into Europe's monetary union). Nowhere, in fact, does there seem to be any existing money with a reasonable chance of soon overcoming the powerful forces of inertia favoring today's incumbents. For the foreseeable future, the dominance of the Big Three seems secure.

Relative shifts

Continued collective dominance, however, does not exclude the possibility of significant shifts in relative standing among the Big Three. At the top of the Currency Pyramid, the dollar today reigns supreme. But might that change? Could the dollar's market leadership be challenged anytime soon by either the euro or the yen?

Less probability may be attached to a successful challenge by the yen than by the euro, despite Japan's evident strengths as the world's top creditor nation and its enviable record of success in controlling inflation and promoting exports. Cross-border use of the yen did accelerate significantly in the 1980s, during the glory years of Japanese economic expansion. Internationalization was particularly evident in bank lending and in securities markets, where yen-denominated claims were especially attractive to investors. But the yen never came close to overtaking the popularity of the dollar, or even the Deutschmark, and it was little used for either trade invoicing or currency substitution. Its upward trajectory, moreover, was abruptly halted in the 1990s, following the bursting of Japan's "bubble economy," and there seems little prospect of resumption in the near term so long as Japanese domestic stagnation persists. In fact, use of the yen abroad in recent years has, in relative terms, decreased rather than increased, mirroring Japan's economic troubles at home. These difficulties include not only a fragile banking system but also a level of public debt, relative to gross domestic product (GDP), that is now the highest of any industrial nation. Japanese government bonds have already been downgraded by rating agencies, discouraging investors. The decline of foreign use of the yen has been most striking in neighboring Asian countries, where bank loans and other Japanese investments have been rolled back dramatically. "The country's financial muscle in Asia is waning," reports the *New York Times*, "Japanese investment in the region may never be the same" ("Japan's Light Dims in Southeast Asia," December 26, 1999).

The biggest problem for the international standing of the yen is Japan's financial system, which despite recent improvements, has long lagged behind American and even many European markets in terms of openness or efficiency. Indeed, as recently as two decades ago, Japanese financial markets remained the most tightly regulated and protected in the industrial world, preventing wider use of the yen. Strict exchange controls were maintained on both inward and outward movements of capital; securities markets were relatively underdeveloped; and financial institutions were rigidly segmented. Starting in the mid-1970s, a process of liberalization began, prompted partly by a slowing of domestic economic growth and partly by external pressure from the United States. Exchange controls were largely eliminated; new instruments and markets were developed; and institutional segmentation was relaxed—all of which did much to enhance the yen's exchange convenience and capital certainty. Most dramatic was a multiyear liberalization program announced in 1996, dubbed the "Big Bang" in imitation of the swift deregulation of Britain's financial markets a decade earlier.

The reform process, however, is still far from complete and could take many years to come even close to approximating market standards in the United States or Europe. One recent study applauds the prospective shakeout of the Japanese banking sector but admits that the transition is unlikely to be fully executed for at least another decade (Hoshi and Kashyap 2000). Other sources are even less encouraging, questioning whether Japan's public authorities have the political will needed to overcome determined resistance from powerful vested interests. Both Ito and Melvin (2000) and Schaede (2000) emphasize the extent to which the success of the Big Bang will depend on completion of complementary reforms in tax codes, regulatory processes, and the institutions of law enforcement and legal recourse—initiatives that would require fundamental changes in the way business is done in Japan. Tokyo's politicians have so far shown little enthusiasm for such radical transformation. Yet, without further progress, the yen will remain at a competitive disadvantage relative to both the dollar and the euro. International traders and investors will have little incentive to bear the costs and risks of switching from either of the other top currencies to the yen. Indeed, the trend is more likely to continue moving the other way, toward a gradual erosion of the yen's relative standing in a manner reminiscent of sterling's long decline in an earlier era.

More probability, by contrast, can be attached to a successful challenge by the euro, which started life in January 1999 with most of the key attributes necessary for competitive success already well in evidence. Together, the eleven current members of EMU—familiarly known as "Euroland"—constitute a market nearly as large as that of the United States, with extensive trade relations not only in the European region, but also around the world. The potential for network externalities is considerable. Euroland also starts with both unquestioned political stability and an enviably low rate of inflation backed by a joint monetary authority, the European Central Bank (ECB), that is fully committed to preserving confidence in the euro's future value. Much room exists, therefore, for a quick ascendancy for the euro as an international currency, just as most observers predict (for example Bergsten 1997; Hartmann 1998; Portes and Rey 1998). The new currency has already begun to surpass the past aggregate share of the Deutschmark and other EMU currencies in foreign trade and investment. The only question is how high the euro will rise and how much business it will take from the dollar.

As with the yen, the answer rests first and foremost on prospective developments in financial markets. Even with the euro's promise of broad economies of scale and stable purchasing power, the dollar will be favored by the natural advantages of incumbency unless euro transactions costs, which historically have been higher than those on the more widely traded dollar, can be lowered to more competitive levels. The level of euro transactions costs will, in turn, depend directly on what happens to the structure of Europe's financial markets as the merger of Euroland currencies proceeds. Without sustained improvements in market efficiency and openness, it will be difficult for the euro to overcome the forces of inertia characteristic of international currency use. Richard Portes and Hélène Rey (1998: 308) put the point most succinctly: "The key determinant of the extent and speed of internationalization of the euro will be transaction costs in foreign exchange and securities markets."

In fact, prospects for the structural efficiency of Europe's financial system seem good. On a purely quantitative basis, introduction of the euro will eventually create the largest single-currency financial market in the world. The aggregate value of Euroland financial claims (bonds, equities, and bank loans) is already almost as large as that of the United States and will undoubtedly keep growing in the future. Beyond that, there are bound to be significant qualitative improvements in market depth and liquidity, as previously segmented national markets are gradually knitted together into one integrated whole. The elimination of exchange risk inside EMU has already intensified competition between financial institutions, particularly in such hotly contested activities as bond underwriting and syndicated bank lending, encouraging cost-cutting and innovation. Over the longer term, harmonization of laws and conventions and the development of new cross-border payments systems will enhance the marketability of assets of all kinds. Progress to date has been swiftest in money markets and the corporate bond market, where instruments and procedures are already largely standardized. Primary equity markets have also expanded rapidly, along with efforts to merge national stock exchanges. Although a projected merger of the Frankfurt and London exchanges failed to materialize, a successful partnership has been created by the bourses of Paris, Amsterdam, and Brussels under the label "Euronext." Full consolidation of markets for government bonds, it is expected, will take longer, owing to the persistence of differential credit and liquidity risk premiums between countries.

There is little reason to doubt that these improvements will have a substantial effect on international investment practice. Curiously, foreign savers and portfolio managers have been slower than anticipated to add to their holdings of euro-denominated assets, as compared with investments in EMU currencies in the past, despite the greater depth and liquidity on offer. Most likely, the comparatively low demand has been due to uncertainties about the euro's exchange rate, which has declined throughout the currency's first two years in existence. But the impact of EMU is already clearly evident on the borrowing side, where nonresidents have been attracted by the opportunity to tap into a much broader pool of savings. In bond and money markets, new foreign issues jumped sharply after the euro's introduction. Indeed, in the second half of 1999, euro-denominated international bond and notes issuance actually exceeded dollar issuance for the first time. Equity issues also grew substantially, and the euro share of international bank lending rose by several percentage points. Comprehensive surveys of the euro's first year (Danthine *et al.* 2000; Detken and Hartmann 2000) agree that major changes are occurring in the European financial landscape.

Yet, the question remains: Will Europe's structural improvements lower euro transactions costs enough to overcome the powerful conservative bias inherent in the dynamics of the marketplace? About that, legitimate doubts remain. Certainly, much of the increase of business in euros will come at the expense of the dollar, reducing the dollar's present margin of leadership. But it seems equally certain that anticipated efficiency gains in Europe's financial markets, although substantial, are unlikely on their own to suffice to displace the dollar from top rank. Neither Danthine *et al.* (2000) nor Detken and Hartmann (2000) find much evidence of reduced transactions costs to date. In any event, no one expects that market spreads for the euro will ever decline to a level significantly below those currently quoted for the dollar. Spontaneous market developments will therefore almost surely have to be reinforced by deliberate policy actions for the crown to pass securely to the euro. Again, Portes and Rey (1998: 310) put the point most succinctly: "If they wish to promote the emergence of the euro as an international currency, European authorities must make the domestic euro financial markets more efficient, more integrated and cheaper for participants."

In short, the logic of market competition tells us that, in all likelihood, the only serious challenge to the dollar in coming years will be from the euro— not from the yen and, most certainly, not from any other existing national currency. Even for the euro, however, success will be determined not just by market developments, but also by official policy actions. This brings us to the subject of the strategic preferences of governments.

Government preferences

No discussion of currency relations can ignore government preferences. States have long placed a high value on control of the issue and management of money—commonly referred to as "national monetary sovereignty." We know, of course, that in a number of countries, private monies exist, sometimes in fairly sizable numbers (L. D. Solomon 1996). But we also know that all such monies remain deliberately local, circulating on a very restricted scale. The currencies that really matter in today's world are state currencies: the progeny of independent national governments (or several governments acting collectively in a monetary union). Currency outcomes, as a consequence, are inherently political, not just economic. The future of national currencies, including the Big Three, will depend not only on the logic of market competition but also on the nature of state behavior.

From monopoly to oligopoly

National policy choices were relatively simple when money was largely territorial. Currency domains could be assumed to coincide precisely with the political frontiers of states. Governments could legitimately aspire to exercise a monopoly control within their own jurisdiction over the issue and management of money.

It is easy to see why a monetary monopoly might be highly prized by governments. Genuine power resides in the command that money represents. A strictly territorial currency confers four main benefits: a potent political symbol to promote a sense of national identity; a potentially powerful source of revenue, seigniorage (otherwise known as the "inflation tax"), to underwrite public expenditures; a possible instrument to manage the macroeconomic performance of the economy; and a practical means to insulate the nation from foreign influence or constraint. Absolute monetary sovereignty clearly privileges the interests of government in relation to societal actors—a privilege that, over time, has been wisely used by some and badly abused by many others.

A map of neatly divided territorial currencies is still the geography that most people think of, insofar as they think about currency space at all. It is also the geography that most people think has prevailed for all time, as if monetary relations could never be configured in any other way. In fact, nothing is further from the truth. Monetary geography is not written in stone, and territorial currencies are, in historical terms, of quite recent origin. Prior to the 1800s, no government even thought to claim a formal monopoly over the issue and use of money within its political domain. Cross-border circulation of currencies was not only accepted but widespread and commonplace. The notion of absolute monetary sovereignty began to emerge only in the nineteenth century, with the formal consolidation of the powers of nation-states in Europe and elsewhere, and reached its apogee only in the middle of the twentieth century. Since then, the tide has clearly reversed— all part of the broadening globalization of the world economy that has been going on since World War II. Driven by the pressures of competition and technological innovation, national financial and monetary systems have become increasingly integrated, effectively widening the array of currency choice for many transactors and investors. As a result, strictly territorial currencies are fast disappearing in most parts of the world. Today, as we enter the twenty-first century, money is becoming increasingly deterritorialized.

Currency deterritorialization poses a new and critical challenge to policymakers. No longer able to exert the same degree of control over the circulation of their monies, governments are driven to compete, inside and across borders, for the allegiance of market actors—in effect, to fight for market share, much as rival firms in an oligopolistic industry compete. Their targets are the users of money, at home or abroad. Their aim is to sustain or enhance a currency's appeal, almost as if monies were goods to be sold under registered trademarks. As Robert Aliber (1987: 153) has quipped, "the dollar and Coca-Cola are both brand names. ... Each national central bank produces its own brand of money. ... Each national money is a differentiated product. ... Each central bank has a marketing strategy to strengthen the demand for its particular brand of money." Monopoly, in short, has yielded to some thing more like oligopoly, and monetary governance is rapidly being reduced to little more than a choice among marketing strategies designed to shape and manage demand. The management of money, at its most basic, has become a political contest for market loyalty.

Furthermore, all states must be considered part of the oligopolistic struggle, no matter how competitive or uncompetitive their respective currencies may be. Rivalry is not limited merely to the trio of monies at the peak of the Currency Pyramid, as is sometimes suggested (de Boissieu 1988). That would be so only if cross-border competition were restricted to international use alone—if the Big Three currencies, along with a few minor rivals (for example sterling and the Swiss franc), were vying for shares of private investment portfolios or for use in trade invoicing. Deterritorialization, however, extends to foreign-domestic use as well—to currency substitution as well as currency internationalization—thus involving all national currencies, in direct competition with one another to some degree, the weak as well as the strong. Money's oligopoly is truly global.

The question is, in this new oligopolistic setting driven by the logic of market competition, how can governments be expected to respond to emerging rivalries at the peak of the Currency Pyramid? Outcomes will be determined jointly by two sets of state actors—those at the peak of the pyramid (the United States, Euroland, and Japan) and those below. I shall examine each group in turn.

Leadership rivalries

At the peak of the Currency Pyramid, anticipated shifts in relative standing among the Big Three currencies will almost certainly trigger enhanced policy competition across both the Atlantic and the Pacific. The reason is simple.

Much is at stake, and the benefits of market leadership will not be conceded without a struggle.

Although minimized by some (for example Wyplosz 1999: 97–100), the benefits of market leadership can be considerable. Most discussion focuses primarily on seigniorage: the implicit transfer, equivalent to a subsidized or interest-free loan, that goes to a country when its money is widely used and held abroad. Seigniorage income, on its own, is unlikely to be large enough to spark significant policy conflict. This fact, however, ignores two other material gains that, although less easily quantified, are apt to be considered much more important. One is the increased flexibility of macroeconomic policy that is afforded by the privilege of being able to rely on domestic currency to help finance external deficits. The other is the political power that derives from the monetary dependence of others. Not only is the issuing country better insulated from outside influence or coercion in the domestic policy arena. It is also better positioned to pursue foreign objectives without constraint or even to exercise a degree of influence or coercion internationally. Political power may be employed bilaterally or, alternatively, through the mechanisms of a multilateral agency such as the IMF, where market leaders are bound to have disproportionate sway. As much was admitted to me once by a highly placed U.S. Treasury official, who confided that in Washington policy circles, the IMF was viewed as "a convenient conduit for U.S. influence" (Cohen 1986: 229).

To this list, some would also add the international status and prestige that goes with market leadership. Widespread circulation of a currency is a constant reminder of the issuing country's elevated rank in the community of nations. Certainly, foreign publics cannot help but be impressed when another nation's money successfully penetrates the domestic financial system and gains widespread acceptance. "Great powers have great currencies," Robert Mundell (1996: 10) once wrote. Although policymakers may be loath to admit it, such reputational considerations are apt to be given some importance too.

Admittedly, there are limits to most of these benefits. All are likely to be greatest in the early stages of cross-border use, when confidence in a money is at a peak. Later on, as external liabilities accumulate, increasing supply relative to demand, gains may be eroded, particularly if there is an attractive alternative available. Foreigners may legitimately worry about the risk of future devaluation or even restrictions on the usability of their holdings. Thus, the market leader's policy behavior may eventually be constrained, to a degree, by a need to discourage sudden or substantial conversions through the exchange market. Both seigniorage income, on a net basis, and macroeconomic flexibility will be reduced if a sustained increase of interest rates is required to maintain market share. Similarly, overt exploitation of political power will be inhibited if foreigners can switch allegiance easily to another currency. Even admitting such limits, however, numerous sources acknowledge that these are advantages worth fighting for (see, for example, Portes and

Rey 1998: 308–10). There is more than enough incentive here to motivate policymakers. Enhanced competition among the Big Three should therefore come as no surprise.

Consider Europe, for example, whose new monetary union creates a golden opportunity to bid for higher market standing. Officially, European aspirations remain modest. According to an authoritative statement by the ECB (1999: 31), the development of the euro as an international currency—if it happens at all—will be mainly a market-driven process, simply one of many possible byproducts of EMU. Euro internationalization "is not a policy objective [and] will be neither fostered nor hindered by the Eurosystem. ... The Eurosystem therefore adopts a neutral stance" (ECB 1999: 45). But these carefully considered words may be dismissed as little more than diplomatic rhetoric, revealing nothing. Behind the scenes, it is known that there is considerable disagreement among policymakers, with the eventual direction of policy still unsettled. Many in Europe are indeed inclined to leave the future of the euro to the logic of market competition. But many others, aware of the strong incumbency advantages of the dollar, favor a more proactive stance to reinforce EMU's potential. EMU has long been viewed in some circles, particularly in France, as the European Union's best chance to challenge the long-resented hegemony of the dollar.

Much more revealing, therefore, is not what the ECB says, but what it does. Especially suggestive is the bank's controversial decision to plan issues of euro notes in denominations as high as 100, 200, and 500 euros—sums far greater than most Eurolanders are likely to find useful for everyday transactions when euro bills and coins begin to circulate in 2002. Why issue such notes? Informed sources suggest that the plan may have been decided in order to reassure the German public, fearful of losing their beloved Deutschmark, that notes comparable to existing high-denomination Deutschmark bills would be readily available. But that is hardly the whole story. As knowledgeable experts like Kenneth Rogoff (1998) and Charles Wyplosz (1999) observe, it is also likely that the decision had something to do with the familiar phenomenon of dollarization: the already widespread circulation of large-denomination dollar notes, especially $100 notes, in various parts of the world. Dollarization translates conservatively into an interest saving for the U.S. government, a form of seigniorage earnings, of at least $15 billion a year (Blinder 1996)—not a huge profit, but nonetheless enough, apparently, to persuade EMU's authorities to plan on offering a potentially attractive alternative. As Rogoff (1998: 264) has written: "Given the apparently overwhelming preference of foreign and underground users for large-denomination bills, the [ECB's] decision to issue large notes constitutes an aggressive step toward grabbing a large share of developing country demand for safe foreign currencies."

How will Washington react? Officially, the U.S. remains unconcerned. "The emergence of the euro as an international currency should not be viewed with alarm," writes the president's Council of Economic Advisers (1999: 297). "It is unlikely that the dollar will be replaced anytime soon." Policy statements regarding the prospective challenge of the euro have been studiously neutral, asserting that EMU is Europe's business, not America's. But these words, too, may be dismissed as diplomatic rhetoric, concealing as much as they reveal. As Portes (1999: 34) writes: "It is difficult to believe that the American authorities are indifferent." In fact, in Washington, as in Europe, there is still much disagreement behind the scenes about the eventual direction of policy, and, especially in the Congress, there is much pressure to respond to the Europeans in kind. Already a proposal to offer a $500 note to rival the ECB's large-denomination bills has been circulated on Capitol Hill (Makinen 1998: 5). Legislation has even been introduced to encourage developing countries to adopt the dollar formally as a replacement for their own national currencies—official dollarization, as the idea has come to be known. As an incentive, Washington would offer a specified share of the resulting increase in U.S. seigniorage earnings. Policy support for official dollarization is being actively promoted by the Joint Economic Committee of the U.S. Congress (1999).

More generally, given the considerable benefits of market leadership, there seems every reason to expect Euroland and the United States to compete vigorously to sustain or promote demand for their respective currencies. Many Europeans clearly wish to see the euro established on a par with the dollar as an international currency. What more can Europe do, apart from issuing high-denomination notes? International investments in euro bonds and stocks, which, as indicated, have lagged until now, might be encouraged with selected tax incentives, including abolition of any withholding or reporting requirements. Likewise, cross-border use of the euro as a vehicle currency might be underwritten with targeted subsidies for European banks, lowering the cost of commercial credit for third-country trade. In so doing, however, Euroland would also put itself on track for open confrontation with the United States. Aggressive policy initiatives from one side of the Atlantic will almost certainly provoke more retaliatory countermeasures from the other side, along lines already being mooted in Washington. Competition is likely to be intense and possibly nasty.

The same can be expected across the Pacific as well, where Japan has given every indication that it, too, intends to stay in the fray, actively battling to preserve as much as possible of the yen's currently fragile international role—in East Asia at least, if not beyond. One straw in the wind came in 1996, when Japan signed a series of agreements with nine neighboring countries to lend their central banks yen if needed to help stabilize exchange rates. Informed sources had no doubt that these pacts were deliberately designed to increase Japanese influence among members of an eventual yen bloc. "It's a manifest attempt to take leadership," said one bank economist in Tokyo (*New York Times*, April 27, 1996). And an even stronger indicator came in 1997, after the first shock waves of the Asian financial crisis, when Tokyo seized upon the occasion to propose a new regional financial facility—quickly called the Asian Monetary Fund (AMF)—to help protect local currencies against speculative attack. The AMF proposal was by far the most ambitious effort yet by Japan to implement a strategy of market leadership in Asian finance. Tokyo's initiative was successfully blocked by the United States, which publicly expressed concern about a possible threat to the central role of the IMF. Privately, it was clear that Treasury officials were even more concerned about a possible threat to the dominance of the dollar in the region. Nonetheless, the idea continues to attract favorable interest (Bergsten 1998).

Moreover, despite economic troubles at home and the steady repatriation of private investments from abroad, Tokyo has persisted in seeking new ways to promote its monetary role in the region (Hughes 2000). In October 1998, Finance Minister Kiichi Miyazawa offered some $30 billion in fresh financial aid for Asia in a plan soon labeled the "New Miyazawa Initiative." Two months later, he made it clear that Japan had every intention of reviving its AMF proposal when the time seemed right (*Financial Times*, December 16, 1998). Similarly, in late 1999, Japanese authorities floated a plan to drop two zeros from the yen (which is currently valued at near 100 yen for either the dollar or the euro) in order to facilitate its use in foreign transactions. Simplifying the currency's denomination, said one official, "might have a positive effect in that the yen would be more internationally easy to understand" (*New York Times*, November 19, 1999). Commented a foreign banker in Tokyo: "If there's a liquid market in dollars and a liquid market in euros, there's a risk of Japan becoming a sort of second-string market. ... They don't want the yen to become the Swiss franc of Asia" (*New York Times*, November 19, 1999). Most recently, in May 2000, Tokyo engineered an agreement among thirteen regional governments on a new network of swap arrangements centered on the yen (*The Economist* 2000a: 76–77). Clearly, Tokyo does not intend to allow further erosion of its currency's standing without a fight.

But here too, as in Europe, aggressive policy initiatives will almost certainly put the Japanese on track for confrontation with the United States. Even a yen-bloc enthusiast like David Hale (1995: 162) acknowledges that "there is also a risk that [such measures] will be interpreted as a threat by some Americans [and] could intensify the economic conflicts that are already straining U.S.–Japan relations." Yen competition with the dollar is likely to be no less heated than the expected dollar–euro rivalry, and could be even nastier. Market leadership will continue to be the strategic preference of proponents for all the Big Three currencies.

Follower options

But will other currencies follow? For countries lower down in the Currency Pyramid, fallout from intensified rivalry among the Big Three will be unavoidable. Governments across the globe will be compelled to reconsider their own strategic preferences. Outcomes, however, are likely to be far less uniform than many predict.

Most common is the prediction that growing currency deterritorializat-ion and heightened competition for market leadership will encourage the emergence of two or three large monetary blocs centered on the dollar, euro and, possibly, the yen (Eichengreen 1994; Beddoes 1999; Hausmann 1999). Governments will seek to shelter themselves from possible currency turmoil by subordinating their monetary sovereignty to one of the top international currencies by way of a firm exchange-rate rule—in effect, a strategy of market "followership" (analogous to passive price followership in an oligopoly). Linkage could take the form of a tight single-currency peg or, more radically, could be implemented by means of an ostensibly irrevocable currency board or even official dollarization ("euroization?" "yenization?").

Market followership would naturally be attractive to countries that have particularly close economic or political ties to one of the dominant financial powers. These might include many of the states of Latin America, ever in the shadow of the United States, states from the former Soviet bloc, or states in the Mediterranean basin or sub-Saharan Africa that have close ties to Europe. The dollar already serves as nominal anchor for a number of smaller countries in the Caribbean and Pacific, as well as in scattered locations else-where. The euro does the same for several currency boards in East-Central Europe as well as in the CFA franc zone, having seamlessly assumed the role in francophone Africa previously played by the French franc. Patrick Honohan and Philip Lane (1999) suggest that more African currencies will soon be tied to the euro. Other sources confidently predict that pegs to the euro will soon be adopted by many Mediterranean countries as well (Bénassy-Quéré and Lahrèche-Révil 1999). The debate has also been reopened in Latin America about closer ties to the dollar (Dornbusch 1999; Hausmann *et al.* 1999; Levy Yeyati and Sturzenegger 2000).

In the past, such ideas might have been dismissed as politically naive. All kinds of problems could be cited, from the loss of a lender of last resort under a currency board to the loss of seigniorage with dollarization. But that was before Argentina which, despite a well-known history of the most intense nationalism, successfully opted for a dollar-based currency board in 1991—and whose former president, before leaving office late last year, even proposed replacing Argentina's peso altogether with the dollar. In the context of the coming rivalry among the Big Three, the Argentine case is now considered instructive. A strategy of irrevocable market followership no longer seems a fantasy. As Rudiger Dornbusch (1999: 8) puts the point, with characteristic flair: "The lesson is obvious: Europe's periphery should adopt the Euro on a currency board basis or fully. And in the same spirit, Latin America should follow the Argentine example of a currency board on the U.S. dollar or out-right dollarization." In January 2000, Ecuador became the first to follow Dornbusch's advice, announcing plans to replace its national currency with the dollar; several other Latin American governments were reported to be considering similar initiatives.

But what of countries that might prefer not to be dominated, whether by the United States or by Europe (or Japan)? Not all governments can be expected to acquiesce willingly in a passive strategy of market followership. Other options exist, from free floating to various contingent exchange-rate rules, such as a loose single-currency peg or basket peg, a crawling peg, or target zones of one kind or another. There is every reason to believe that governmental preferences are likely to be correspondingly diverse.

Opinions differ on whether the full range of these options is actually available in practice. According to some observers, neither free floating nor irrevocably fixed rates can be regarded as truly viable options. Fixed rates, we are told, are too rigid, creating the risk of prolonged misalignments and payments disequilibria, and flexible rates are too volatile and prone to speculative pressures. The only real choices are intermediate regimes that promise a degree of adaptability without generating undue uncertainty—"stable but adjustable rates," to borrow a phrase from an earlier era. "Quite the contrary," retort others, who insist that it is the intermediate choices that are discredited, not the extreme "corner solutions," owing to the great increase of international capital mobility in recent decades. This view is rapidly gaining popularity among specialists today. The middle ground of contingent rules has in effect been "hollowed out," as Barry Eichengreen (1994) memorably put it.

In reality, however, neither corner solutions nor contingent rules are discredited, for the simple reason that in an imperfect world there is no perfect choice. All such views rest on implicit—and questionable—political judgments about what tradeoffs may or may not be tolerable to policymakers. Eichengreen's hollowing-out hypothesis, for example, clearly assumes that governments will be unwilling to pay the price of coping with occasional speculative crises. Defenders of contingent rules, conversely, assume that governments will naturally prefer to avoid absolute commitments of any kind—whether to an irrevocable exchange rate or to market determination of currency values—whatever the cost. The reality, as Jeffrey Frankel (1999) has persuasively argued, is that such tradeoffs are made all the time when exchange-rate regimes are decided. No option is ruled out a priori.

The political dimension of exchange-rate choice tends to be discounted in conventional economic models, where policymakers are assumed to be concerned more or less exclusively with maximizing output and minimizing inflation in the context of an open economy subject to potentially adverse shocks. In fact, political factors enter in two ways. First, the calculus is affected by domestic politics: the tug and pull of organized interest groups of every kind. The critical issue is the familiar one of whose ox is gored. Who wins and who loses? The material interests of specific constituencies are systematically influenced by what a government decides to do with its money. Policy design and implementation are bound to be sensitive to the interplay among domestic political forces.

Second, the utility function of policymakers includes more than just macroeconomic performance. As a practical matter, sovereign governments worry about other things, too—not least, about their own policy autonomy, their scope for discretion to pursue diverse objectives in the event of unforeseen developments, up to and including war. Key in this regard is the domestic seigniorage privilege—called by one source a state's "revenue of last resort" (Goodhart 1995: 452). The more tightly a currency is pegged, the less room policymakers have to resort at will to inflationary money creation to augment public spending when deemed necessary. Monetary firmness is gained, but at a loss of fiscal flexibility. Certainly, it is not wrong to attach importance to a reduction of exchange-rate uncertainty, which can promote trade and investment and squeeze out risk premiums in interest rates. But in an insecure world, governments may be forgiven for attaching importance to currency flexibility, too, as a defense against political uncertainty. Policy design and implementation are bound to be sensitive to the interplay among such considerations as well.

For all these reasons, therefore, strategic preferences are apt to vary considerably, depending on the unique circumstances of each country. Although followership may be attractive to some, a more neutral stance will appeal to states with more diversified external relations, political as well as economic. Such states might include those in Japan's neighborhood in East Asia, which trade as much with the United States, and nearly as much with Europe, as they do with Japan, and which prefer to maintain equally cordial ties with all three centers of the industrial world. Indeed, such countries are actually well placed to take advantage of the coming competition among the Big Three to play off one reserve center against another, bargaining for the best possible terms on new debt issues or for a formal share of international seigniorage revenues.

Neutrality in exchange-regime choice can take the form of a floating rate, the current policy in a sizable number of countries, or it can be implemented as a basket peg, with appropriate weights assigned to each of the Big Three currencies, as well as possibly to others. Floating offers the obvious advantage of adaptability to changing circumstances. Stung by the financial crisis that erupted in 1997, which most analysts attribute at least in part to the dollar-dominated pegs that East Asian governments had tried vainly to defend against unrelenting speculation, many states today are attracted by the alternative of no peg at all—a kind of default strategy that relieves them of any formal obligation to intervene in currency markets. But floating is hardly an all-purpose panacea, as informed observers are now beginning to acknowledge (Cooper 1999; Hausmann 1999). In countries where financial markets are still much thinner than in the advanced industrial nations, even small movements into or out of a currency can spell massive exchange-rate volatility. Not all governments may be prepared to live forever with persistent and often arbitrary currency swings. For many, an appropriately weighted basket might not look so bad after all. The pros and cons of basket pegging have long been debated in the formal literature, going back to early contributions by William Branson and Louka Katseli-Papaefstratiou (1980, 1982).

As a device to preserve a degree of currency neutrality as well as stability, basket pegging has recently been forcefully advocated as an alternative to floating, especially for the Asia-Pacific region (see, for example, Williamson 1999).

There is also the option of monetary union—in effect, a strategy of market "alliance" (analogous to a tacit or explicit cartel in an oligopoly). On the model of EMU, local currencies could be merged into one regional money, subordinate to none of the Big Three. Is such an option feasible? Although ardently advocated by some (for example Walter 1998), the possibility of monetary union in East Asia or Latin America has been dismissed by others as impractical on economic grounds (for example, Eichengreen and Bayoumi 1999; Hausmann *et al.* 1999; Levy Yeyati and Sturzenegger 2000). Neither East Asians nor Latin Americans, we are told, come even close to approximating an optimum currency area (OCA). In particular, economic shocks tend to be highly asymmetric, threatening to make management of a single monetary policy in either region highly difficult. Until more of the criteria of OCA theory are satisfied, therefore, governments supposedly will hesitate to take the plunge.

Such arguments, however, are deficient in at least three respects. First, much depends on whether divergences among economies are to be regarded as exogenous or endogenous. A celebrated study by Frankel and Rose (1997) shows, for a large sample of countries, a strong positive relation between bilateral trade intensity and the correlation of business cycles, suggesting that monetary union, by promoting higher volumes of trade, might lead to a significant reduction of asymmetric shocks. Separately, Rose (2000) has established that a common currency may increase trade among partner countries by as much as a factor of three.

Second, much also depends on whether the standard conditions identified in OCA theory are, in fact, the most relevant economic variables to consider. Buiter (2000) makes a strong case for the view that conventional OCA theory seriously misleads by assuming that the exchange rate effectively clears the trade balance. In effect, this presupposes a world without financial capital mobility—a world that is obviously at variance with the reality confronting most governments in East Asia and Latin America.

Finally, such arguments again discount the political dimension which, in the history of monetary unions, has been central. In fact, among all cases of currency unification in the last two centuries, it is impossible to find a single example that was motivated exclusively, or even predominantly, by the concerns highlighted in OCA theory. Political objectives have always predominated. Today, one relevant political objective could well be to avoid dependence on larger outsiders. For this reason alone, the plausibility of the market-alliance option should not be underestimated. Even Mundell (1998), the father of OCA theory, acknowledges that when it comes to a merger of national monetary sovereignties, politics trumps economics.

In short, below the peak of the Currency Pyramid, outcomes will defy easy generalization. Although some states no doubt will be attracted by the security of a followership strategy, sheltering under the wing of one of the Big Three, many others are more likely to prefer to preserve for themselves some room for maneuver in the event of unanticipated circumstances—some more palatable compromise between a government's desire to reduce exchange-rate uncertainty and its legitimate determination to guard against political uncertainty. Many national monies will continue to fight for their own market share, even while others may join together in regional unions or in broader monetary blocs. The geography of money in coming decades will be anything but simple.

Technological developments

Finally, we have to take into consideration one last factor, prospective technological developments, which over the longer term could add even more complexity to tomorrow's monetary landscape. Today's world, I have noted, is still dominated by state currencies. But that will not be so forever. Assuming that current technological trends persist, it is only a matter of time before various innovative forms of money based on digital data—collectively known as "electronic money"—begin to substitute in one way or another for banknotes and checking accounts as customary means of payment. A century from now, electronic money could be in wide circulation, commanding the same general acceptability currently enjoyed by conventional currencies. Once that happens, the geography of money will be even more fundamentally transformed, with currency domains then defined exclusively in the virtual landscapes of cyberspace. Governments will be obliged to compete not only with one another, but also with an increasingly diverse range of private issuers of money. Implications for life at the top of the Currency Pyramid will be truly profound.

From deterritorialization to denationalization

The issue may be simply stated. Even with currency deterritorialization, states today still dominate the supply side of the market, retaining jurisdiction over the issue of the monies that most people continue to use. Governments may no longer be able to enforce an exclusive role for their own currency within established political frontiers; that is, they may no longer be able to exercise the monopoly control they once claimed over demand. As the main source of the supply of money, however, they are still in a favored position (like oligopolists) to influence demand insofar as they can successfully compete inside and across borders for the allegiance of market agents. To the extent that user preferences can be swayed, therefore, governments retain some measure of power.

Even that limited measure of power, however, can be retained only so long as states collectively remain dominant on the supply side of the market. Significantly, voices have long been heard opposing even that much government "interference," preferring, instead, to leave money creation solely in the hands of private financial institutions in a world of truly unrestricted currency competition. Envisioned is a system of effectively deterritorialized money shaped exclusively by market forces—denationalized money, as the idea was called by its best-known advocate, the late Friedrich von Hayek (1990). Although Hayek's influential laissez-faire views have been echoed by other economists in both Europe and the United States, however, they have thus far failed to enter the mainstream of professional thinking on monetary management. A variety of denationalized currencies already exist, both domestically and internationally, to rival the official issue of central banks, but none has as yet had any but a marginal impact on state dominance of the supply side.

At the domestic level, as already observed, diverse private monies circulate in a number of countries. Such currencies, however, are little different from institutionalized systems of multilateral barter, and none trades across national frontiers. At the international level, private substitutes for state monies have long existed in the form of so-called "artificial currency units" (ACUs)—nonstate alternatives designed to perform one or more of the conventional roles of money. Traditionally, though, most ACUs have functioned mainly as a unit of account or store of value, rather than as a medium of exchange, thus posing little direct threat to government dominance of supply. In recent years, the only nonstate form of money that has been used to any substantial degree in international markets is a pool of privately issued assets denominated in European currency units (ECUs), the European Union's old currency unit that came into existence with the European Monetary System in 1979 (now replaced by EMU). Despite having attained limited success in global financial markets, however, the ECU was never widely accepted for private transactional purposes. The IMF's Special Drawing Rights (SDRs) are also a form of artificial currency unit, but for official use only, to be traded among governments or between governments and the IMF.

Electronic money

But now consider electronic money, a technological breakthrough that many specialists think is only a matter of time in coming, given the rapid growth of commerce across the Internet and World Wide Web. Around the globe, entrepreneurs and institutions are racing to develop effective means of payment for the expanding realm of cyberspace. The aim is to create units of purchasing power that are fully usable and transferable electronically: virtual money that can be employed as easily as conventional money to acquire real goods and services. If and when some of these experiments succeed, governments will face a competitive challenge unlike any in living memory—full-bodied ACUs beyond their individual or even collective control—in short, genuinely denationalized monies to rival existing national currencies. When that occurs, dominance of the supply side, not just demand, will be lost.

Hayek's vision of a world of unrestricted currency competition will, like it or not, be realized, and the much-anticipated rivalry of the Big Three could turn out to be little more than a sideshow.

Electronic money (also variously labeled "digital currency," "computer money," or "e-cash") comes in two basic forms, smart cards and network money. Both are based on encrypted strings of digits—information coded into series of zeros and ones—that can be transmitted and processed electronically. Smart cards, a technological descendant of the ubiquitous credit card, have an embedded microprocessor (a chip) that is loaded with a monetary value. Versions of the smart card (or "electronic purse") range from simple debit cards, which are typically usable only for a single purpose and may require online authorization for value transfer, to more sophisticated stored-value devices that are reloadable, can be used for multiple purposes, and are off-line capable. Network money stores value in computer hard drives and consists of diverse software products that allow the transfer of purchasing power across electronic networks.

Both forms of electronic money are still in their infancy. The earliest versions, going back a half decade or more, aimed simply to facilitate the settlement of payments electronically. These included diverse card-based systems with names like Mondex and Visa Cash as well as such network-based systems as DigiCash, CyberCash, NetCash, and First Virtual. Operating on the principle of full prepayment by users, each functioned as not much more than a convenient proxy for conventional money—something akin to a glorified travelers check. The velocity of circulation was affected, but money supply was not. None of these systems caught on with the general public, and most have already passed into history (*The Economist* 2000b: 67).

More recent versions, mostly network-based, have been more ambitious, aspiring to produce genuine substitutes for conventional money. Most widely advertised in the United States (using Whoopie Goldberg as a spokesperson) is Flooz, a form of gift currency that can be used for purchases from a variety of web sites. Other examples include Beenz, Cybergold, and (in Britain) iPoints. All can be obtained by means other than full prepayment of conventional money, usually as a reward for buying products or services from designated vendors. Like the green stamps or plaid stamps of an earlier era or the frequent-flyer miles of today's airline industry, each can be held more or less indefinitely as a store of value and then eventually employed as a medium of exchange.

Although none of these experimental units has yet been adopted widely, smart cards and network money clearly have the capacity to grow into something far more innovative, given sufficient time and ingenuity. Certainly the incentive is there. Electronic commerce is growing by leaps and bounds, offering both rising transactional volume and a fertile field for experimentation. The stimulus for innovation lies in the promise of seigniorage. Money can be made by making money. This motive alone should ensure that all types of enterprises and institutions—nonbanks as well as banks—will do everything they can to promote new forms of e-currency wherever and whenever they can. As one source puts it: "The companies that control this process will have the opportunity to make money through seigniorage, the traditional profit governments derived from minting money. Electronic seigniorage will be a key to accumulating wealth and power in the twenty-first century" (Weatherford 1997: 245–46).

Central will be the ability of these companies to find attractive and, more importantly, credible ways to offer smart cards or network money on credit, denominated in newly coined digital units like Flooz or Beenz, in the same way that commercial banks have long created money by making loans denominated in state-sanctioned units of account. The opportunity for "virtual" lending lies in the issuers' float: the volume of unclaimed e-money liabilities. Insofar as claimants choose to hold their e-money balances for some time as a store of value, rather than cash them in immediately, resources will become available for generating yet more units of effective purchasing power. Moreover, as general liabilities of their issuers, these new virtual monies could circulate freely from user to user without requiring settlement through the commercial-banking system (that is, without debiting or crediting third-party accounts). "Circling in cyberspace indefinitely," as Elinor Solomon (1997: 75) puts it, electronic money would thus substitute fully for existing national currencies. At that point, the infant will have reached maturity.

Maturation will not happen overnight, of course—quite the contrary. The process is apt to be slow and could take most of the next century to be completed. To begin, a number of complex technical issues will have to be addressed, including, inter alia, adequate provisions for security (protection against theft or fraud), anonymity (assurance of privacy), and portability (independence of physical location). None of these challenges is apt to be resolved swiftly or painlessly.

Even more critical is the issue of trust: how to command confidence in any new brand of money, given the inertias that generally typify currency use. The conservative bias of the marketplace is a serious obstacle but not an insuperable one. As the volume of electronic commerce grows, it seems almost inevitable that so, too, will brand-name recognition and trust. Another lesson from monetary history is that, even if adoption begins slowly, once a critical mass is attained widespread acceptance will follow. The success of any new brand of currency will depend first and foremost on the inventiveness of its originators in designing features to encourage use. These "bells and whistles" might include favorable rates of exchange when amounts of electronic money are initially acquired, attractive rates of interest on unused balances, assured access to a broad network of other transactors and purveyors, and discounts or bonuses when the electronic money, rather than more traditional currency, is used for purchases or investments. Sooner or later, at least some of these efforts to whet user appetite are bound to achieve success.

Most critical of all is the question of value, how safely to preserve the purchasing power of electronic money balances over time. Initially at least, this is likely to require a promise of full and unrestricted convertibility into more conventional legal tender—just as early paper monies first gained wide acceptance by a promise of convertibility into precious metal. But just as paper monies eventually took on a life of their own, delinked from a specie base, so, too, might electronic money be able to dispense with all such formal guarantees one day as a result of growing use and familiarity. That day will not come soon, but, given current trends, it seems the most plausible scenario for the more distant future. As *The Economist* once wrote,

> [Over the long term,] it is possible to imagine the development of e-cash reaching [a] final evolutionary stage ... in which convertibility into legal tender ceases to be a condition for electronic money; and electronic money will thereby become indistinguishable from—because it will be the same as—other, more traditional sorts of money.
>
> (*The Economist* 1994: 23)

When that day finally dawns, perhaps one or two generations from now, we could find a monetary landscape literally teeming with currencies in competition for the allegiance of transactors and investors. In the words of banker Walter Wriston:

> The Information Standard has replaced the gold-exchange standard. ... As in ancient times, anyone can announce the issuance of his or her brand of private cash and then try to convince people that it has value. There is no lack of entrants to operate these new private mints ranging from Microsoft to Mondex, and more enter every day.
>
> (Wriston 1998: 340)

How many currencies?

How many currencies might eventually emerge? Almost certainly, it will not be the "thousands of forms of currency" predicted by anthropologist Jack Weatherford (1998: 100), who suggests that "in the future, everyone will be issuing currency—banks, corporations, credit card companies, finance companies, local communities, computer companies, Net browsers, and even individuals. We might have Warren Buffet or William Gates money." Colorful though Weatherford's prediction may be, it neglects the powerful force of network externalities in monetary use, which dictates a preference for fewer, rather than more, monies in circulation. No doubt, there will be much market experimentation, and thousands of forms of e-currency might indeed be tried. But after an inevitable sorting-out process, the number of monies that actually succeed in gaining some degree of general acceptance is sure to be reduced dramatically. Many currencies, unable to compete effectively, will simply disappear.

But neither is it likely that the number of monies will be reduced to as few as one, as Roland Vaubel has contended, exclusively stressing the power of economies of scale. In Vaubel's words (1977: 437, 440): "Ultimately, currency competition destroys itself because the use of money is subject to very sizable economies of scale. ... The only lasting result will be ... the survival of the fittest currency." In fact, economies of scale are not the only consideration that matters, as modern network theory teaches. Of equal importance are considerations of stability and credibility, which suggest that the optimal number of monies in a world of unrestrained currency competition will actually be significantly greater than one (Thygesen and the ECU Institute 1995: 39–45).

In network theory, two distinct structures are recognized in the configuration of spatial relations: the "infrastructure," which is the functional basis of a network, and the "infostructure," which provides needed management and control services. Economies of scale, by reducing transactions costs, promote a consolidation of networks at the level of infrastructure, just as Vaubel argues. At the infostructure level, by contrast, the optimal configuration tends to be rather more decentralized and competitive, in order to maximize agent responsibility. Some finite number of rival networks will counter the negative effects of absolute monopoly, which frequently leads to weakened control by users and diluted incentives for suppliers. Thus, a rational tradeoff exists for market agents, an impulse for some degree of diversification that will most likely result in an equilibrium outcome short of complete centralization. In the monetary geography of the future, a smallish population of currencies is far more probable than a single universal money.

Implications for the Big Three

Where will all this leave today's Big Three? Until now, the top international currencies have enjoyed something of a free ride—all the benefits of competitive success abroad without the corresponding disadvantages of a threat to monetary monopoly at home. In these economies, there has not yet been any real erosion of monetary powers. For them, therefore, the advent of electronic money will represent an unprecedented challenge. Once e-monies begin to gain widespread acceptance, the market leaders, too, like countries further down the Currency Pyramid, will face genuine currency competition on their own turf.

Indeed, the challenge of electronic money is likely to be felt by the market leaders first, even before its impact spreads to countries with less competitive currencies. The reason is evident. It is the Big Three that are most "wired," the most plugged in to the new realm of electronic commerce. Thus, if electronic money is to gain widespread acceptance anywhere, it will most probably happen initially in the United States, Europe, and Japan. It is no accident that Flooz, Beenz, and most other early experiments have originated in the world's most advanced economies, which are both financially sophisticated and computer literate. It is precisely these economies that are likely to be the most receptive to innovative new means of payment that can be used and transferred electronically.

Domestically, the effect will be a significant erosion in the effectiveness of monetary policy. Each of the Big Three central banks—the Federal Reserve, the ECB, and the Bank of Japan—may still be able to exercise a degree of control over monetary aggregates denominated in the economy's own currency unit. But with new electronic monies also in use, variations in the supply of commercial-bank reserves will have correspondingly less influence on the overall level of spending. As other countries with less competitive monies have already discovered, substitute currencies mean alternative circuits of spending, affecting prices and employment, and alternative settlement systems that are not directly affected by the traditional instruments of policy. As Benjamin Friedman (1999: 335) puts the point, "currency substitution opens the way for what amounts to competition among national clearing mechanisms, even if each is maintained by a different country's central bank in its own currency." Electronic money, Friedman (1999: 321) continues, will have the same effect. Monetary policy could become little more than a device to signal the authorities' preferences. The central bank would become not much more than "an army with only a signal corps."

Externally, the effect could be a substantial reshuffling of standing in the Currency Pyramid. Even a small population of currencies will continue to display characteristics of hierarchy, reflecting varying degrees of competitive strength. The currencies that disappear, including many of the newer e-monies as well as older national currencies, will be those that cannot survive the Darwinian process of natural selection. There is no reason to believe that the dollar, euro, and yen will be unable to compete effectively even far into the next century.

There is also no reason to believe, however, that in that more distant future the Big Three will continue to monopolize the peak of the Currency Pyramid. There may be no serious challengers to their dominance among currencies in circulation today, which are all state currencies, but there could well be serious challengers among the electronic monies of tomorrow, which will be largely private. Microsoft money could, in time, become more popular than dollars. As the deputy governor of the Bank of England (*New York Times*, December 20, 1999) has suggested, "the successors to Bill Gates [could] put the successors to Alan Greenspan out of business." Otmar Issing of the ECB puts the point even more harshly. In a world of electronic money, Issing (1999: 21) asks, "would the familiar existing units of account, the euro, the US dollar, the pound sterling, etc., continue to mean anything?" By the end of the twenty-first century, life at the top might look very different indeed.

Conclusion

The conclusions of this essay can be summarized briefly. Prospects for the top international currencies differ considerably, depending on the time horizon in question. In the near term, the position of the Big Three at the peak of the Currency Pyramid looks secure, with no immediate challenger in sight. Relative standings could shift substantially, however, with the euro gaining on the dollar in market competition and the yen possibly fading to an even more distant third place. As a result, policy rivalry among the market leaders will almost certainly intensify, in turn compelling governments elsewhere to reconsider their own strategic preferences. Some countries will undoubtedly opt to tie their currencies closely to one of the Big Three, promoting the coalescence of two or possibly three large monetary blocs. Many others will choose to remain more neutral, however, and some may be tempted by the precedent of EMU to try merging their currencies into regional monetary unions in order to sustain or promote user loyalty.

Beyond the near term, by contrast, the position of the Big Three looks less secure, not because any existing national currency will pose a challenge, but because future private monies are likely to develop in the virtual world of cyberspace. The twenty-first century will introduce the era of electronic monies—monies that are not only deterritorialized but denationalized as well. Some of these new monies may eventually hold more market appeal than any of today's top international currencies.

2 The euro and transatlantic relations

How will the euro affect transatlantic relations? Even while partners in a political and military alliance, Europe and the United States have long been rivals in monetary affairs. Until recently, however, it was a rather one-sided contest, since Europe had no currency—not even the fabled Deutschmark (DM)—that could effectively match the U.S. dollar as international money. Now Europe has the euro, which many have predicted will quickly emerge as a potent competitor to America's greenback. Could growing rivalry between the dollar and the euro endanger the larger European–American partnership?

The dollar today is the only truly global currency, used for all the familiar purposes of money—medium of exchange, unit of account, and store of value. Resentment has long simmered among Europeans sensitive to the inordinate power that the greenback gives the United States—America's "exorbitant privilege," in Charles de Gaulle's memorable phrase. The European Union (EU) is the equal of the United States in economic output and trade. Why should it not be America's equal in monetary matters, too? For many Europeans, this is the "hidden agenda" of the Economic and Monetary Union (EMU). Some degree of monetary conflict, therefore, would seem inevitable. In turn, monetary conflict could spill over into a broader geopolitical confrontation.

Can the dominance of the dollar be challenged? The answer to this critical question comes first by looking at the logic of market competition and second by examining government preferences. Treating the logic of market competition alone, the answer is clear. Despite its recent travails in the exchange markets, the dollar will continue to prevail as the world's only truly global currency. The euro will of course dominate monetary relations within the European region and may even extend its influence to some neighboring areas, such as the Mediterranean littoral or sub-Saharan Africa. But elsewhere, for the foreseeable future, Europe's new money is fated to remain a distant second to the greenback, however much many Europeans would prefer otherwise.

Once we factor in government preferences, however, the outlook becomes cloudier. The Europeans can be expected to make every effort to promote the market appeal of their new currency. The greenback's global dominance will not go unchallenged. But will Europe go further, to seek formation of an organized monetary bloc with foreign governments? That is less certain. At the present time, there seems little reason to believe that Europeans are prepared to push currency confrontation with the United States to the point where it might jeopardize more vital political and security interests. The risk of a serious collision, accordingly, appears low. Mutual restraint, I argue, is the much more likely scenario.

The stakes

What is at stake? Broadly speaking, currencies may be employed outside their country of origin for two purposes—for transactions between nations and within foreign states. The former is conventionally referred to as international currency use or currency internationalization; the latter goes under the label currency substitution and can be referred to as foreign-domestic use. For both purposes America's greenback today is indisputably the global leader, privileging the United States both economically and politically. The stakes, in fact, are considerable. Four distinct benefits may be cited.

Most familiar is the potential for seigniorage. International use of a national money generates the equivalent of a subsidized or interest-free loan—an implicit transfer that represents a real-resource gain for the issuing economy. Consider, for example, the widespread foreign circulation of Federal Reserve notes, which are a form of non-interest-bearing liability. Authoritative studies put the value of all Federal Reserve notes in circulation abroad at between 50 and 70 percent of the total outstanding stock—equivalent at the turn of the century to between $275 billion and $375 billion in all (Porter and Judson 1996; United States Treasury 2000). Estimates also suggest that as much as three-quarters of the annual increase of U.S. notes now goes directly abroad, up from less than one-half in the 1980s and under one-third in the 1970s. Updating earlier estimates, current interest savings from foreign circulation of the greenback may be conservatively calculated at $16–22 billion a year (Frankel 1995; Blinder 1996). To this may be added a saving of interest payments on U.S. government securities, which are uniquely attractive to foreign holders because of their greater liquidity. Economists Richard Portes and Hélène Rey (1998: 309) call this an "often neglected source of seigniorage to the issuer of the international currency." In their words: "This international currency effect reduces the real yields that the United States government has to pay"—a "liquidity discount" that they suggest could amount to at least $5–10 billion a year. Put these numbers together and, paraphrasing former Republican Senator Everett Dirksen's celebrated remark about the Federal budget, we are beginning to talk about real money.

A second gain is the increased flexibility of macroeconomic policy that is afforded by the privilege of being able to rely on one's own currency to help finance foreign deficits. Expanded cross-border circulation reduces the real cost of adjustment to payments imbalances by internalizing through credit what otherwise would be external transactions requiring scarce foreign exchange. In effect, it reduces the role of the balance of payments as a constraint on policy formulation and implementation. How else could the United States have run current-account deficits for so long without any noticeable impact on domestic monetary or fiscal policy? Increased macroeconomic flexibility makes it easier for Washington to pursue strategic goals abroad, whether economic or political, without worrying about where the money is coming from.

Third, and more psychological in nature, is the gain of status and prestige that accompanies market dominance. Money, as I have written elsewhere, has long played a key symbolic role for governments, useful—like flags, anthems, and postage stamps—as a means to cultivate a unique sense of national identity (Cohen 1998). But that critical role is eroded to the extent that a local currency is displaced by a more popular foreign money, especially a money like the dollar that is so widely used. Through its use, foreign publics are constantly reminded of America's elevated rank in the community of nations. "Great powers have great currencies," Nobel laureate economist Robert Mundell (1993: 10) once wrote. In effect, the dollar has become a potent symbol of American primacy—an example of what Joseph Nye (1990) calls "soft power," defined as the ability to exercise influence by shaping beliefs and perceptions. Though obviously difficult to quantify, the role of reputation in geopolitics should not be underestimated.

Finally, there is the gain of "hard" power that derives from the monetary dependence of others. On the one hand, an issuing country is better insulated from outside influence in the domestic arena. On the other hand, it is also better positioned to pursue foreign objectives without constraint or even to exercise a degree of coercion internationally. As political scientist Jonathan Kirshner (1995: 29, 31) reminds us: "Monetary power is a remarkably efficient component of state power ... the most potent instrument of economic coercion available to states in a position to exercise it." Money, after all, is simply command over real resources. If a country can be denied access to the means needed to purchase vital goods and services, it is clearly vulnerable in political terms. Kirshner lists four ways in which currency dependence can be exploited: (1) enforcement—the manipulation of standing rules or threats of sanctions; (2) expulsion—the suspension or termination of privileges; (3) extraction—the use of the relationship to extract real resources; and (4) entrapment—the transformation of a dependent state's interests. The dollar's widespread use puts all of these possibilities in the hands of Washington policymakers.

Admittedly, there are limits to these benefits, as the United States has been reminded lately. Swelling U.S. payments deficits have put the greenback under great strain, risking an erosion of America's privileges. The risk has grown with the creation of the euro, which makes it easier for market actors to switch allegiance. In the first years of the new millennium, the greenback has lost roughly a quarter of its overall value in exchange markets; against the euro alone, the drop has been closer to half. The longer the dollar's depreciation continues, the greater will be the pressure on Washington to address it. In economic terms, this could mean higher interest rates, reducing both seigniorage income, on a net basis, and macroeconomic flexibility. In political terms, both the prestige of the dollar and America's hard power abroad could gradually suffer. But even admitting such limits, there seems little doubt that on balance there are advantages here of considerable significance. The stakes are high indeed.

The logic of market competition

Can the euro challenge the dominance of the dollar? Many have predicted that Europe's new currency will quickly match, and perhaps even surpass, the dollar's global popularity. But the logic of market competition, I contend, suggests otherwise. In pursuit of their own interests, market actors will continue to give a distinct preference to the dollar, current strains notwithstanding.

Barriers to displacement

Displacement of a dominant international money is not easy, for two reasons: first, because the qualities required for competitive success are highly demanding; and, second, because of inertia, a conservative tendency characteristic of monetary behavior.

Fundamentally, currency choice in the global marketplace is shaped by three sets of attributes. First, at least during the initial stages of a money's cross-border use, is widespread confidence in its future value. This confidence derives in large measure from a history of political stability in the country of origin. Second are the qualities of "exchange convenience" (a high degree of transactional liquidity) and "capital certainty" (reasonable predictability of asset value). The key to both these qualities is a set of well-developed financial markets, sufficiently open to ensure full access by nonresidents. Markets must not be encumbered by high transactions costs or formal and informal barriers to entry. They must also be broad, with a large assortment of instruments available for temporary or longer-term forms of investment. And they must be resilient, with fully operating secondary markets for most, if not all, financial claims. Third, a money must promise a broad transactional network, since nothing enhances a currency's acceptability more than the prospect of acceptability by others. Historically, this requirement has usually meant an economy that is large in absolute size and well integrated into world markets. The greater the volume of transactions conducted in or with a country, the greater are the potential network externalities to be derived from the use of its money. Few currencies meet all these demanding conditions.

Moreover, even with the requisite attributes, displacement is difficult because of inertia in currency choice. The principle source of inertia is the preexistence of already well-established transactional networks, which generate a well-documented stickiness in user preferences—what specialists call "hysteresis" or "ratchet effects." In effect, prior use confers a certain natural advantage of incumbency. Switching from one money to another requires expensive financial adaptation. Considerable effort must be invested in creating and learning to use new instruments and institutions, with much riding on what other market agents may be expected to do at the same time. As attractive as a given money may seem, therefore, adoption will not prove cost-effective unless others also appear likely to make extensive use of it.

Inertia is also promoted by the exceptionally high level of uncertainty that is inherent in any choice between alternative moneys. Uncertainty encourages what psychologists call "mimesis," the rational impulse of risk-averse actors, in conditions of contingency, to minimize anxiety by imitative behavior based on past experience. Once a currency gains a degree of acceptance, its use is apt to be perpetuated even after the appearance of powerful new competitors. In effect, a conservative bias regarding currency choice is inherent in the dynamics of the marketplace.

The salience of inertia is well illustrated by the dollar's own experience when it first began to rival the pound sterling, the dominant currency of the nineteenth century. Even after America's emergence as the world's richest economy, it took decades for the greenback to ascend to top rank among currencies. As Paul Krugman (1992: 73) has commented, "the impressive fact here is surely the inertia; sterling remained the first-ranked currency for half a century after Britain had ceased to be the first-ranked economic power." Similar dynamics have been evident for millennia in the prolonged use of such international moneys as the Byzantine solidus (otherwise known as the bezant) or the Spanish silver peso (later known as the Mexican silver dollar) long after the decline of the imperial powers that first coined them (Cohen 1998). Such inertias are very much the rule, not the exception, in global currency relations.

Exceptional or not, even the most stubborn inertias can in time be overcome, as these historical examples also illustrate. But to defeat the conservative bias in market behavior, a new contender must do more than merely match the attributes of the existing incumbent. It must be able to offer substantial advantages over its established rival. The dollar was able to do that in relation to sterling once New York overtook London as the world's preeminent source of investment capital. The problem for the euro is that for the foreseeable future it cannot realistically hope to offer comparable advantages in relation to the dollar.

In principle, prospects for the euro should be bright, particularly following its rapid recent appreciation in exchange markets. Europe's new currency started life in January 1999 with many of the attributes necessary for competitive success already well in evidence. Together, the twelve current members of the Economic and Monetary Union—familiarly known as the euro area or euro zone—constitute an economy nearly as large as that of the United States, with extensive trade relations not only in the European region but around the world. The potential for network externalities is considerable. Likewise, the euro zone started with both unquestioned political stability and an enviably low rate of inflation, backed by a joint monetary authority, the European Central Bank (ECB), that is fully committed to preserving confidence in the euro's future value. Much room exists, therefore, for a quick ascendancy, as frequently predicted. Typical is the attitude of Robert Mundell (2000: 57), who expresses no doubt that the euro "will challenge the status of the dollar and alter the power configuration of the system." In the oft-quoted words of Jacques Delors, former head of the European Commission, "le petit euro deviendra grand."

In practice, however, the outlook for the euro is anything but rosy, despite the currency's recent appreciation. Short-term movements of exchange rates should not be confused with longer-term trends in use for investment or transactional purposes. With each passing year, it becomes increasingly clear that serious obstacles lie in the path of the euro's ascent as an international currency. Within the European region, of course, the euro will dominate easily, and its influence may soon extend to some neighboring areas around the Mediterranean and to sub-Saharan Africa. In these nearby locales the euro is the natural currency of choice given Europe's long history of colonial and post-colonial economic involvement. As one European economist has remarked, "This is the euro's turf" (Wyplosz 1999: 89). But that appears to be as far as the new money's domain will expand due to market forces alone. Virtually all the growth of cross-border use of the euro since its introduction has occurred within the euro's immediate neighborhood (European Central Bank 2003b). Elsewhere, left to the logic of market competition, the currency seems fated to remain a distant second to the greenback. In a recent analysis, I spell out three critical reasons for this negative assessment of the euro's prospects (Cohen 2003).

Transactions costs

The first reason is the cost of doing business in euros, which directly affects the currency's attractiveness as a vehicle for foreign-exchange transactions or international trade. Euro transactions costs, as measured by bid–ask spreads, are historically higher than those on the more widely traded dollar. Whether they can be lowered to more competitive levels will depend directly on what happens to the structural efficiency of Europe's financial markets. On the face of it, prospects for euro transactions costs look good. In purely quantitative terms, the introduction of the euro promises to create the largest single-currency capital market in the world; and that expansion, in turn, should trigger major qualitative improvements in depth and liquidity as previously segmented national markets are gradually knitted together into an integrated whole. As a practical matter, however, progress to date has been disappointing, owing to stubborn resistance to many market-opening measures. Consequently, it is not at all clear that the euro's promise in this respect can ever be fully realized. As a recent EU report on Europe's financial markets, the so-called Lamfalussy Report, firmly insisted: "The European Union has no divine right to the benefits of an integrated financial market. It has to capture those benefits" (European Union 2001: 8). So far, at least, the EU has not done a very good job of doing so.

In certain key respects the dollar's advantages will persist no matter what the EU does. Most important is the lack of a universal financial instrument in Europe to rival the U.S. Treasury bill for liquidity and convenience. This deficiency will be difficult, if not impossible, to rectify so long as the Europeans, with their separate national governments, lack a counterpart to the Federal government in Washington. Full consolidation of the euro zone's markets for public debt is stymied by the persistence of differential credit and liquidity risk premiums among participating countries as well as by variations in legal traditions, procedures, issuance calendars, and primary dealer systems. Market segmentation has also been prolonged by intense competition among governments to establish their own issues as EMU benchmarks.

It is unlikely, therefore, that anticipated efficiency gains, though substantial, will soon suffice on their own to drive the dollar from top rank. To date, there is little evidence of reduced transactions costs for Europe's new money. Indeed, for some transactions bid–ask spreads actually increased after the introduction of the euro, relative to earlier spreads for the Deutschmark, Europe's most widely traded currency prior to EMU (Detken and Hartmann 2002; Hau *et al.* 2002a, 2002b). No one expects that euro transactions costs will ever decline to a level substantially below those presently quoted for the dollar.

Anti-growth bias

A second critical factor is a serious anti-growth bias that appears to be built into the institutional structure of EMU. By impacting negatively on yields on euro-denominated assets, this structural bias directly affects the currency's attractiveness as a long-term investment medium. When EMU first came into existence, eliminating exchange risk within the European region, a massive shift was predicted in the allocation of global savings toward holdings of European assets. In fact, however, international portfolio managers have been slow to move into the euro (European Central Bank 2003b; Geis *et al.* 2004). Liquid funds have been attracted, of course, by the prospect of short-term appreciation. But underlying investor preferences have barely budged, in good part because of doubts about prospects for longer-term growth. In turn, one of the main causes of such doubts seems to lie in the core institutional provisions of EMU that govern monetary and fiscal policy, the key determinants of macroeconomic performance. In neither policy domain is priority attached to promoting real production. Rather, in each, the main emphasis is on other considerations that can be expected to limit opportunities for future expansion, imparting a distinct anti-growth bias to the economy of the euro zone as a whole.

On the monetary policy side, the European Central Bank, unlike many other monetary authorities, was created with the single policy mandate to maintain price stability. Moreover, the ECB is formally endowed with absolute independence, largely insulating it from political influence. Legally, the ECB is free to focus exclusively on fighting inflation, even if over time this might be at the cost of stunting real growth. In practice, naturally, the ECB is not wholly insensitive to growth concerns. Nonetheless, the overall orientation of ECB priorities is clear. From the start, EMU monetary policy has been biased toward restraint, not expansion.

Likewise, with fiscal policy, euro-zone governments have formally tied their own hands with their controversial Stability and Growth Pact (SGP) that mandates a medium-term objective of fiscal balance in all participating economies as well as a strict cap on annual budget deficits. These fiscal restraints make it exceedingly difficult for elected officials to use budgetary policy for contracyclical purposes or to offset the anti-growth bias of monetary policy. Here too, we know, practice has increasingly diverged from principle, and new loopholes have been added to the SGP that effectively ratify larger budget deficits. Many specialists in Europe have called for revision or repeal of the Pact's principle provisions. Until now, however, such appeals have made little headway. So long as the SGP remains formally binding on all euro-zone governments, an anti-growth bias will be perpetuated in fiscal policy, too.

Governance

Finally, there is the governance structure of EMU, which may be the biggest obstacle of all for the euro's prospects as an international currency. The basic question is: Who is in charge? The answer, regrettably, has never been clear. From the start, there has been much confusion concerning the delegation of authority among governments and EU institutions. The Maastricht Treaty, which brought EMU into existence, embodies a variety of artful compromises and deliberate obfuscations in provisions for the political management of the euro, resulting in a high level of ambiguity. Prospective users of the new currency, therefore, may be excused for hesitating to commit themselves to what amounts to a pig in a poke, even if in fact transactions costs could be lowered to competitive levels and rewards to European capital could be improved significantly.

Three key provisions are at issue. First is the governance of EMU's core institution, the European Central Bank. Immediate operational control of monetary policy lies in the hands of the ECB's Executive Board, made up of the president, vice-president, and four other members. Ultimate authority, however, is formally lodged in the Governing Council which, in addition to the six-member Executive Board, includes heads of central banks of the participating states—a number seemingly greater than is consistent with efficient collective decision-making. Sooner or later, therefore, as so often happens in large multinational institutions, real power will have to devolve to a smaller "inner" group formally or informally charged with resolving differences on critical issues. But who will be allowed to join this exclusive club? Will it be the members of the Executive Board, who might be expected to take a broad approach to the euro zone's needs and interests? Or will it be a select coterie of central-bank governors, whose views could turn out to be more parochial? For the moment, no one knows.

Second is the critical matter of exchange-rate policy. Under the Maastricht Treaty, the ECB is assigned day-to-day responsibility for the euro's external value. Authority over the more general orientation of policy, however, is uneasily shared with both the Council of Ministers, representing national governments, and the European Commission in Brussels. Plainly, power over exchange rates was meant to be shared in some form of consensual process. However, efforts to reach agreement over these provisions could result in political deadlock and drift. Again, no one knows.

Finally, there is the issue of external representation. Who is to speak for the euro zone on broader macroeconomic issues such as policy coordination, crisis management, or reform of the international financial architecture? Here there is no answer at all, leaving a vacuum at the heart of EMU. Unlike in trade and the World Trade Organization, no single body or person is designated to represent EMU, whether at the International Monetary Fund or in other monetary forums. Instead, the Maastricht Treaty simply lays down a procedure for resolving the issue at a later date, presumably on a case-by-case basis. At a minimum, this compounds confusion about who is in charge. At worst, the vacuum condemns the euro zone to lasting second-class status by limiting its ability to project power in international negotiations. As one source warns:

> As long as no "single voice" has the political authority to speak on behalf of the euro area, as the U.S. Secretary of the Treasury does for the American currency, the pre-eminence of the US in international monetary matters, as in other realms, is likely to remain unchallenged.
>
> (McNamara and Meunier 2002: 850)

Government preferences

But is Europe really likely to accept such an unappealing outcome? Whatever the logic of market competition, the Europeans can hardly be expected to leave market actors entirely to their own devices, particularly if that means passively submitting to the continued dominance of the dollar. Currency rivalries, in practice, reflect the influence of government preferences as well as market forces. Once we introduce government preferences, the future of the Atlantic currency rivalry becomes considerably cloudier.

A critical distinction

One thing is certain. A strategy to maintain or enhance the market position of the euro will be Europe's preferred choice. Rational policymakers are unlikely to turn their back on the considerable benefits that may be derived from broader circulation of their currency. Given this preference, some level of friction in Atlantic currency relations is inevitable. But following a suggestion I have made elsewhere, a critical distinction must be drawn between two different kinds of monetary conflict: informal and formal (Cohen 2004).

Given the stakes involved, there seems little doubt that the Europeans will do all they can to promote the attractiveness of the euro, with the objective of cultivating widespread use by market actors. Rivalry for market use, what I call informal conflict, is natural between major currencies. It is less evident, however, whether Europe will be motivated to go a step further, to seek to influence the behavior of state actors by sponsoring the formation of an organized currency bloc, what I call formal conflict. Within the European neighborhood, a bloc can be expected to form more or less naturally. That is uncontroversial. What is less clear is whether Europeans will offer direct inducements to encourage greater use of the euro by governments beyond the European neighborhood. About this prospect there is more uncertainty, not least because the balance of benefits and costs implied by that extra step is not at all clear.

What is clear is that whatever Europe does is sure to be closely watched by Washington. Any move to promote an organized euro bloc outside the European neighborhood would, by definition, transform the low politics of market competition into the high politics of diplomatic confrontation. The risk is that policy maneuvering could lead to increased political tensions, particularly if monetary initiatives are perceived to be encroaching on America's established regional relationships, say in Latin America or Southeast Asia.

Precisely for that reason, it is more likely that Europe will act with restraint to avoid a direct confrontation with the United States that could jeopardize more vital political and security interests. While some Europeans might relish the prospect of a blunt challenge to the world's "last remaining superpower," others will not—including, in particular, most of the EU's newest members, whose history and geography provide strong motivation for maintaining close ties to Washington. A European consensus in favor of an open break with the United States is difficult to imagine. The safest bet, therefore, is that currency rivalry will be restricted mainly to the realm of market transactions. The one exception could be in the Middle East, where rivalry for the monetary favor of OPEC governments could initiate serious conflict.

Informal conflict

Although Europe has an obvious incentive to promote the attractiveness of the euro, officially aspirations remain modest. According to authoritative statements by the European Central Bank, the development of the euro as international money—to the extent that it happens—will mainly be a market-driven process, simply one of many possible byproducts of EMU. Europe, says the ECB (2002: 11), "does not pursue the internationalisation of the euro as an independent policy goal. ... It neither fosters nor hinders this process." These carefully considered words, however, may be dismissed as little more than diplomatic rhetoric, revealing nothing. Behind the scenes it is known that there is considerable sentiment for a much more proactive stance.

More revealing, therefore, is not what the ECB says but what it does. Especially suggestive is the bank's controversial decision to issue euro notes in denominations as high as 100, 200, and 500 euros—far greater than most Europeans are likely to find useful for everyday transactions. Why issue such large notes? Informed sources suggest that the plan may have been decided in order to reassure the German public, fearful of losing their beloved Deutschmark, that notes comparable to existing high-denomination DM bills would be readily available. But that is hardly the whole story. It is also likely that the decision had something to do with the familiar phenomenon of currency substitution: the already widespread circulation of large-denomination dollar notes, especially $100 bills, in various parts of the world. In the words of one knowledgeable source: "Given the apparently overwhelming preference of foreign and underground users for large-denomination bills, the [ECB's] decision to issue large notes constitutes an aggressive step toward grabbing a large share of developing country demand for safe foreign currencies" (Rogoff 1998: 264). Europeans who favor more widespread use of the euro have openly applauded the plan. Writes one: "The United States is able to obtain goods and services by simply giving foreigners pieces of green paper that cost pennies to print. ... There is no reason why the United States should monopolize these benefits" (Hüfner 2000: 25).

What more could Europe do, apart from issuing high-denomination notes? The answer lies in the three reasons for the euro's sluggish ascent to date. More could be done to lower transactions costs for nonresidents in European financial markets. International investments in euro bonds and stocks might be encouraged with selected tax incentives, including abolition of any withholding or reporting requirements. Similarly, broader use of the euro for vehicle purposes could be underwritten with targeted subsidies for European banks, lowering the cost of commercial credit for third-country trade. More could also be done to reverse the anti-growth bias built into EMU's institutional structure and to clarify the governance structure of EMU. As indicated, much room exists for policy actions to make the euro more appealing to market actors.

How will Washington react to such competition? Publicly, the United States remains unconcerned. Policy statements regarding a prospective challenge from the euro have been studiously neutral, avoiding provocation. But such words too may be dismissed as diplomatic rhetoric, concealing as much as they reveal. As Richard Portes (1999: 34) observes: "It is difficult to believe that the American authorities are indifferent." In fact, in Washington too there is considerable sentiment behind the scenes in favor of a more proactive stance designed to respond in kind to any direct threat to the dollar. Introduction of the ECB's large-denomination bills, for example, quickly generated counterproposals to issue a rival $500 Federal Reserve note, designed to preserve America's seigniorage earnings abroad. In sum, the probability is that aggressive policy measures from Europe will ultimately provoke countermeasures from Washington, with both sides doing what they can to maximize market use.

Formal conflict?

This does not mean, however, that Europe must necessarily go the next step, to seek to influence state behavior. As compared with the benefits of extensive market use, the additional gains from sponsoring a formal currency bloc could be considerable. But so too could be the costs, political as well as economic, which might discourage new initiatives. Prediction, therefore, is chancy. The Europeans, as indicated, will no doubt make every effort to promote use of their new money at the market level wherever they can. It is also evident that they will not discourage greater reliance on the euro by nearby governments, particularly in East-Central Europe and the Balkans. But none of this will trigger geopolitical conflict with Washington unless the EU's aspirations begin to spread beyond its immediate neighborhood to regions more traditionally aligned with the United States. The safest bet is that the Europeans will act with restraint to avoid direct confrontation with the United States. Arguably, only in the Middle East is there a significant risk of serious tension.

That is not to say that there are no Europeans with more global ambitions for the euro. Portes and Rey (1998), for example, plainly favor what they call the "big euro" scenario, where the euro would join the dollar as a global currency. The dollar, they declare, "will have to share the number-one position" (Portes and Rey 1998: 308). But this is a minority view. Most informed opinion in Europe accepts that there are limits to what might be regarded as the natural home for a formal euro zone.

An EMU bloc certainly would include most if not all of the countries of Europe itself, including of course all the ten new members that joined in 2004. Beyond EMU's present dozen members, six regional jurisdictions have already adopted the euro as their exclusive legal tender, including the tiny enclaves of Andorra, Monaco, San Marino, and the Vatican, as well as Montenegro and Kosovo, two special cases in the Balkans (Winkler *et al.* 2004). In addition, several regional economies are pegged to the euro via currency boards, including Bosnia and Herzegovina, Bulgaria, Estonia, and Lithuania; and most other nearby currencies are more loosely linked. Some maintain basket pegs that give greatest weight to the euro; others have adopted systems of managed floating, with the euro unofficially used as an anchor. Momentum toward full "euroization" will only grow as EU enlargement proceeds. As Pier Carlo Padoan (2000: 101) suggests: "The case is easily stated. What matters is not 'if' but 'when.'" Every regional government aspiring to join the EU club expects to adopt the euro, too.

Whatever the rate of momentum, however, Washington is unlikely to take offense. The United States has never questioned the EU's privileged interests in what is universally acknowledged as its own backyard. Indeed, for geopolitical reasons Washington might even be inclined to prod the Europeans along. More positive support for the new members promises to bring greater stability to a potentially volatile region. As Randall Henning has observed:

> The consolidation of the monetary union contributes to economic and political stability in Central and Eastern Europe. ... If the monetary union were to fail, Central and Eastern Europe would probably be considerably less stable. ... As a consequence, U.S. manpower and resource commitments would have to be correspondingly greater. This geopolitical consideration is profoundly important for U.S. foreign policy.
>
> (Henning 2000: 18)

Nor is Washington likely to take offense if the growing EMU bloc were extended to encompass as well countries of the Mediterranean littoral and sub-Saharan Africa that have close economic and political linkages with the EU. These too are regarded as part of Europe's backyard. Some of their currencies are already pegged to the euro, including most prominently the CFA franc in central and west Africa, for which Europe's new money has seamlessly taken over the anchor role previously played by the French franc. For most, the euro is already an important reserve currency. Here too Washington might even prod the Europeans along in the interest of regional stability.

Might Europe aspire to go further? There is no evidence that the EU would seriously consider challenging the dollar in Latin America or Asia, where Washington's interests are clearly seen as privileged. These areas, Europeans acknowledge, are America's turf. But what about the Middle East, with its concentration of wealthy oil exporters? If the dollar–euro rivalry is to lead to direct confrontation anywhere, it will be here.

The Middle East

Three factors explain why the Middle East could become a currency battleground. First is the sheer scale of monetary riches in the area controlled directly or indirectly by national governments. Exports of oil generate massive revenues for state authorities in Saudi Arabia, Kuwait, and other countries scattered around the Persian Gulf. Much of this wealth is either stored away in central-bank reserves or invested abroad in publicly held portfolios. What these governments decide to do with their money can have a major impact on the relative fortunes of international currencies.

Second is the instability of great-power alignments in the area. In the euro's immediate neighborhood, the United States may happily defer to the EU; conversely, across Latin America and Asia, Europe may still accept Washington's strategic dominance. But in geopolitical terms the Middle East remains a hotly contested region, as the still-unfinished business of Iraq clearly testifies. For the moment, most governments in the region find it prudent to accept U.S. leadership and even U.S. troops. But with significant and long-standing economic and cultural ties to the area, European governments remain committed to playing an important regional role. Resentment of Washington's displacement of Europe's historical preeminence in the area is rife among Europeans.

And third is the seeming contradiction between the region's commercial ties with the outside world and its financial relations. Foreign trade is dominated by Europe, which is by far the biggest market for the Middle East's oil exports as well as the largest source of its imports. Yet financial relations are dominated by the United States and the almighty dollar. America's currency is not only the standard for invoicing and payments in world energy markets. It also accounts for the vast majority of central-bank reserves and government-held investments in the region and is the anchor, *de jure* or *de facto*, for most local currencies. In the eyes of many, the disjunction seems anomalous, even irrational. Repeatedly, the question is asked: Would it not make more sense to do business with the area's biggest trading partner, Europe, in Europe's own currency rather than the greenback? And if so, would it not then make sense to switch to the euro as a reserve currency and monetary anchor as well?

Together, these three factors add up to an obvious recipe for conflict, should Europe choose to turn up the heat. Certainly, the possibility of a switch to the euro is tempting from a European perspective. Almost immediately, given the large sums involved, the EU's new currency would be vaulted to the "big euro" scenario favored by Portes and Rey (1998) and others, while restoring a measure of Europe's historically privileged position in the Middle East. Arguably, the prospect might be tempting to Middle Eastern governments, too, as a means of diversifying their financial holdings and curbing America's presently overwhelming influence in the region. It is well known that from time to time oil-exporting states have actively explored alternatives to the dollar, only to be discouraged by the lack of a suitable substitute. Now, with the arrival of the euro, they see the possibility of a truly competitive rival for their affections. In the artfully composed words of a high official of the Organization of Petroleum Exporting Countries (OPEC): "It is worthwhile to note that in the long run the euro is not at such a disadvantage versus the dollar. ... I believe that OPEC will not discount entirely the possibility of adopting euro pricing and payments in the future" (Yarjani 2002).[1]

Indeed, some straws are already in the wind. As early as October 2000, in a deliberate snub to the United States, Iraq's now deposed dictator Saddam Hussein began demanding payment in euros for his country's oil exports. He also converted his $10 billion United Nations reserve fund into euros, making a considerable profit once Europe's currency began to appreciate. And more recently Iran is known to have considered a similar strategy. Talk in OPEC of a switch to the euro has only intensified lately as the greenback has weakened. Should Europe seek to take advantage of current market conditions, directly promoting use of its money by regional governments, it might find itself pushing against an open door.

Any effort along these lines, however, would surely provoke determined opposition from the United States, which clearly prefers to keep the region's door as firmly shut to the euro as possible. For Washington today, there is no higher politics than the Great Game being played out in the Middle East. With so much at stake, the level of tolerance for a formal currency challenge from Europe would be correspondingly low, making geopolitical conflict a virtual certainty. Indeed, for some observers the conflict has already begun. America's attack on Iraq, it is said, was motivated above all by the euro's threat to the dollar. In the words of one widely circulated commentary (Clark 2003: 1): "It is an oil currency war. The real reason for [the war] is this administration's goal of preventing further OPEC momentum towards the euro as an oil transaction currency standard."

Such a theory, wholly unsubstantiated by plausible evidence, obviously smacks of conspiratorial thinking.[2] But one does not have to be a sensationalist to recognize the seeds of truth that it contains. A battle of currencies in the Middle East could become serious. Would Europe risk it? In the end, however strongly tempted, the Europeans are more likely to keep their aspirations in check, averting direct confrontation with Washington. Even after the Bush administration's decision to promote "regime change" in Iraq, there is no consensus among Europeans to risk the broader political and security relationship that they have long enjoyed with the United States. Beyond their currency's natural home in Europe's immediate neighborhood, therefore, they will most probably act with restraint. Maneuvering for advantage will undoubtedly persist, particularly in the Middle East. Monetary rivalry, however, is unlikely to be allowed to get out of control.

Conclusion

Overall, therefore, the outlook for the dollar–euro rivalry appears relatively benign. In the global marketplace, competition between the two contenders will continue to be intense, and the authorities on both sides of the Atlantic will do all they can to sustain the competitive appeal of their respective currencies. But at the level of inter-governmental relations, the low politics of market competition is unlikely to be transformed into the high politics of diplomatic confrontation, largely because Europe will not be eager to provoke the United States. Miscalculations are always possible, of course, despite the best of intentions. The Europeans might well go too far in promoting use of the euro in the Middle East. The safest bet, however, is for mutual restraint, limiting geopolitical tensions.

Part II
The euro challenge

3 EMU and the dollar

Who threatens whom?

Much has been written about the implications of Economic and Monetary Union (EMU) for the future of the U.S. dollar. A merger of European currencies, it is said, will quickly challenge the hitherto predominant role of the dollar as an international currency. In the words of two of Europe's most prominent monetary specialists, "The most visible effect of EMU at the global level will be the emergence of a second global currency once the [euro] becomes the common currency" (Gros and Thygesen 1992: 295). The general message is clear. Assuming EMU succeeds, the dollar will be threatened by a new and potentially powerful rival.

In fact, such predictions seem excessively optimistic, if not wholly out of touch with reality. They remind me of the standard definition of second marriages: the triumph of hope over experience. Europeans may wish, even pray, that their new currency will soon assume a global role. In practice, it will not be all that easy for the euro to dislodge the dollar from its historical place of honor. Europe's new money will not become a global currency anytime soon. Indeed, even within the European region itself the euro will not be unchallenged, as the dollar will retain its attractiveness for many cross-border purposes. The real risk is that in trying to promote wider acceptance of the euro at the dollar's expense, the European Union might generate a nasty policy confrontation with the United States. The challenge for officials on both sides of the Atlantic will be to effectively manage future competition between the euro and the dollar in the private marketplace.

The dollar's entrenched advantages

Across the globe, the dollar is still the most widely employed of all moneys for the full range of international purposes—the world's favorite vehicle for foreign trade, its premier investment currency, and the principal intervention and reserve medium for governments. Such popularity is no accident. Quite the contrary, it is the result of a long and quite enduring competitive market struggle that, by today, has taken on much of the character of a self-reinforcing process.

Once, the dollar's preeminence was based on the overwhelming importance of the United States as a trader and capital exporter. But even as America's relative economic position has declined, the dollar has continued to thrive owing to the potent power of economies of scale in currency use. Economic theory teaches that great savings in transactions costs can be gained by concentrating cross-border commercial and investment activities in just one, or at most a few, currencies with wide circulation networks. International currency competition has been described as a kind of Gresham's Law in reverse, where more attractive ("good") money drives out less attractive ("bad") money. And nothing makes a currency more attractive than the prospect of acceptability by others—what analysts refer to as money's "network externalities." The dollar's persistent dominance as an international currency is rooted in the still unrivaled network externalities that accrue from its very widespread use.

Theory also teaches that, once widely adopted, inertial forces set in to perpetuate a currency's attractiveness. Particularly influential is the self-reinforcing impact of "mimesis": the rational impulse of market actors, in conditions of uncertainty, to minimize risk by imitative behavior based on past experience. Once a currency gains a degree of acceptance, its use is apt to be sustained—even after the appearance of powerful new competitors—by regular repetition of previous practice. In effect, a conservative bias is inherent in the dynamics of the marketplace. Such a bias has been evident for centuries, in the prolonged use of such international currencies as the Byzantine solidus, Spanish silver peso, and most recently the pound sterling long after the decline of the imperial powers that first coined them.

In the face of such entrenched advantages, could the new euro really be expected soon to challenge the dollar successfully? Outside the immediate European region, the answer is almost certainly "No." In Latin America or East Asia, where economic ties to the United States are at least as strong as to the EU, the dollar will remain an overwhelming favorite. Barring an unforeseen collapse of the U.S. economy or a new retreat to protectionist isolationism in North America, America's currency seems destined to retain its global predominance for years to come.

The challenge to the euro in Europe

The interesting question is: What is likely to happen within the European region itself: the EU together with its prospective future members and other economic satellites? Presently, even in Europe, the dollar competes effectively with local currencies—even the fabled Deutschmark—because of superior network externalities that are available for many cross-border purposes. Put differently, the dollar is already well established as the most efficient instrument for a range of local market uses. In an uncertain world, such "in-place" network externalities are bound to make the dollar highly attractive as compared with a newly created and largely untested alternative.

Europeans might quite naturally prefer simply to continue using the dollar whenever possible.

The advantage of America's currency for Europeans would presumably be minimal for purely domestic transactions or for mutual trade within the EU—especially if, as is likely, the new euro is supported by restrictive legal-tender legislation. But as a vehicle for exports to the United States or other countries, as well as for import trade, or as a store of value in banking and securities markets, the dollar will undoubtedly enjoy an initial competitive edge, particularly if the euro seems less credible than the local moneys it is meant to supplant. Reputations take time to develop, after all. Can widespread confidence in the new euro's future value be instantly generated? Can a high degree of liquidity and predictability of asset value be immediately assured? In practice, it would not be at all irrational for market agents, at least at the outset, to prefer the tried-and-true to the experimental. Inertias similar to those that prolonged the life of other key currencies in the past, therefore, may well manifest themselves again. The more likely prospect is that it will be the euro that is threatened by a powerful rival, rather than the reverse.

Europe's response: the risk of conflict

In time, of course, things may change. With accumulating experience could come increased credibility and confidence in the usefulness of the new euro. Eventually, its network value to Europeans or others might even come to exceed that of the dollar, particularly if growing use within the EU is reinforced by parallel adoptions elsewhere. A successful challenge by the euro is not impossible.

Getting there, however, may take quite a long time, given the conservative bias introduced by mimesis, and will certainly be resisted initially by private agents unless promoted vigorously by EU governments. The problem is one of collective action: a coordination dilemma. Individual market actors have little incentive to switch from one currency to another, except where compelled to do so by legal-tender requirements, unless they have reason to expect many others to do the same. The EU can increase the probability of widespread acceptance by facilitating expansion of networks for cross-border use—for example by sponsoring development of debt markets denominated in the euro or by subsidizing its use as a vehicle currency for third-country trade. This is one circumstance where public policy can make a real difference.

In doing so, however, the EU would also pose a direct threat to the global role of the dollar—and thus put itself on course for an open confrontation with the United States, which still values the privileges and benefits derived from the dollar's international use. Policy initiatives from Brussels could provoke defensive countermeasures from Washington, as each side strives to defend or promote the competitiveness of its own money. In effect, therefore,

EU members would be forced to make a choice: either tolerate considerable inertia in market practice, which might severely limit the gains of a formal currency union; or else risk increased tensions in relations with the United States. The real challenge for policymakers on both sides of the Atlantic is to find some way to manage the introduction of the euro in a fashion that will not lead to transatlantic monetary conflict.

How serious is the risk? Not surprisingly, empirical estimates of the euro's likely competitive threat to the dollar vary considerably, depending on the source. But even if in quantitative terms the impact turns out to be comparatively small, consequences for political relations could be quite large—at a minimum, one more issue to erode goodwill on both sides of the Atlantic; at a maximum, the final straw to break the camel's back. Prudence suggests that the dangers should not be ignored.

What specifically can be done? Major institutional reforms would seem neither practical nor necessary to prevent a souring of U.S.–European relations. Proposals to "reinvigorate monetary cooperation" or formalize exchange-rate targets appeal more to the academic mind than they do to politicians concerned about the next election. In any event, the issue is not how to promote coordination in decision-making but rather the reverse—how to avoid uncoordinated initiatives that might accidentally trigger a vicious circle of reciprocal tit-for-tat retaliations. For this, the best remedy is the solvent of information. Numerous forums already exist, from the International Monetary Fund to the OECD to the Bank for International Settlements and Group of Seven, to keep channels of communication open between officials in Washington and Brussels. What is needed is a formal commitment to make use of any or all of these contacts to consult regularly on possible policy démarches involving the two currencies. So long as each side is given adequate opportunity to play a role in shaping the thinking of the other, neither should feel impelled to act belligerently or in haste in response to market developments.

Conclusion

In short, monetary integration in Europe, in the presence of widespread international use of the dollar, is almost certain to complicate the future of U.S.–European relations. Though easy to exaggerate, the issue is not inconsequential and needs to be formally addressed. Europeans must acknowledge that U.S. interests are directly involved in the creation of a potential rival to the dollar; Americans must accept the limits of what can be done to preserve all the gains presently accrued from their money's privileged international status. Both sides must explicitly plan for the intense market competition that is likely to follow the birth of the euro.

4   Global currency rivalry

Can the euro ever challenge the dollar?

Europe has a powerful new symbol—the euro. What could better express the desire for an "ever closer union among the peoples of Europe" than a single joint money, replacing diverse francs, lire, and marks? Within a generation, a population will come of age knowing no other currency than the euro. Inevitably, citizens of the European Union (EU) will begin to feel themselves bound together more closely as part of the same social entity. Money, we know, can have a profound effect on how individuals see themselves and, therefore, how they see themselves in relation to others. Much like a flag or an anthem, money contributes to a sense of collective identity—of belonging to a single community. Already Europeans speak of participating nations as a distinct unit, popularly known as "the euro zone" (or "Euroland"; officially the "euro area"). Europe's sense of identity will never be the same.

But can the euro do more? For many, ambitions have been even grander. The aim was never just to help underwrite the integration project inside Europe. At least as importantly, it was to enhance Europe's role on the world stage by creating a potent rival to the U.S. dollar, the dominant international money of the era. Resentment has long simmered among Europeans sensitive to the inordinate power that the greenback's widespread popularity gives to the United States—America's "exorbitant privilege," in Charles de Gaulle's memorable phrase. Europe is the equal of the United States in economic output and trade. Why should it not be America's equal in monetary matters, too? Economic and Monetary Union (EMU) was also meant to challenge the dollar for global currency supremacy. Economist Charles Wyplosz (1999: 76) calls this "the hidden agenda of Europe's long-planned adoption of a single currency."

Can the euro ever truly challenge the dollar? The purpose of this essay is to explore prospects for the euro as an international currency. My assessment, which will disappoint many, is deeply skeptical. The euro will, of course, dominate monetary relations within the European region and may even extend its influence to some neighboring areas, such as the Mediterranean littoral or sub-Saharan Africa—what the European Central Bank, the ECB (2001), calls the "Euro-time zone." As Wyplosz (1999: 89) remarks: "This is the euro's turf." But elsewhere, for the foreseeable future, Europe's new money is fated to remain a distant second to the greenback, however much many Europeans would prefer otherwise.

There are four interrelated reasons for the euro's dim prospects. First is the persistent inertia, characteristic of all monetary behavior, which can be expected to inhibit any rapid market switch from the dollar to the euro. Second is the cost of doing business in euros, which is unlikely to decline to a level significantly below current transactions costs for the greenback. Third is an apparent anti-growth bias built into EMU, which will impact negatively on rates of return on euro-denominated assets. And fourth is the ambiguous governance structure of EMU, which sows doubt and confusion among prospective users of Europe's new currency. Though none of these barriers is insurmountable, there is little sign that they will be overcome in the foreseeable future. Any challenge to the dollar, therefore, will be feeble at best.

A rosy future?

From the very beginning of negotiations for a common currency in the late 1980s, culminating in the Maastricht Treaty of 1992, a rosy future has been predicted for the euro. Typical is the view of Robert Mundell (2000: 57), a Nobel laureate in economics, who expresses no doubt that the euro "will challenge the status of the dollar and alter the power configuration of the system." Similarly, Daniel Gros and Niels Thygesen (1998: 373), two promi-nent European economists, assert that "the most visible effect of EMU at the global level will be the emergence of a second global currency." The conventional wisdom is clear. The dollar will indeed face a potent rival. In the oft-quoted words of Jacques Delors, former head of the European Commis-sion, "le petit euro deviendra grand."

In fact, the only questions seem to be: How great a rival will the euro become, and how soon? For Fred Bergsten (1997), a former U.S. Treasury official, the answer in an early commentary was very great and very soon. Because of the inherent strengths of the European economy, Bergsten declared enthusiastically, the euro would achieve "full parity" with the dollar in as little as five to ten years. And that happy forecast has been echoed by many others, such as economists George Alogoskoufis and Richard Portes (1997: 4), who contend that "the fundamentals point toward a potentially large shift in favor of the euro. ... The dollar would immediately lose its importance as a vehicle currency" (see also Portes and Rey 1998; Walter 2000; Frenkel and Søndergaard 2001). Not everyone agrees, of course. Other ana-lysts have adopted a more cautious tone, stressing factors that might slow the ascent of the euro (see, e.g., McCauley 1997; Wyplosz 1999; Frankel 2000; Rosecrance 2000; Neaime and Paschakis 2002).

But largely these have been quibbles about speed, not trajectory. Few knowledgeable observers doubt that, overall, the markets will ultimately elevate the euro to a top rank alongside the greenback.[1] The mainstream view has been best summarized by political scientist Randall Henning:

> When it is introduced, there will probably be no large, precipitous displacement of the dollar. Nonetheless, much of the increased role of the new European currency can be expected to come at the dollar's expense, and this would reinforce the gradual historical decline in the role of the dollar exhibited over the last several decades.
>
> (Henning 1996: 93)

Top rank, in turn, would be expected to yield considerable benefits for Europe, which of course is precisely what prompted the euro's hidden agenda in the first place. Though minimized by some (e.g., Wyplosz 1999: 97–100), the advantages to be derived from a global currency can in fact be considerable. As I have argued elsewhere (Cohen 1998, 2004), four distinct gains are possible—two economic in nature, two political.

One economic gain is the potential for what economists call seigniorage: the implicit transfer, equivalent to an interest-free loan, that goes to the issuer of a money that is widely used and held abroad. Because it may remain in foreign circulation indefinitely, an international currency is like a claim that might never be exercised. But because it is virtually costless to produce, it enables the issuer to acquire vast amounts of goods, services, and assets from the rest of the world at little or no sacrifice—an exorbitant privilege if there ever was one. The United States is conservatively estimated to earn at least $15–20 billion a year from the circulation of dollar banknotes around the world (Blinder 1996), a phenomenon known as informal dollarization.[2] A second economic gain is the increased flexibility of macroeconomic policy that is afforded by the privilege of being able to rely on one's own money to help finance external deficits. The issuer is less constrained by balance-of-payments concerns in pursuing ambitions on the global stage.

In political terms, one advantage of an international currency is the status and prestige that goes with market dominance. "Great powers have great currencies," Mundell declared (1993: 10). In effect, an international money becomes a potent symbol of primacy, if not hegemony—an example of what political scientist Joseph Nye (1990) has called "soft power," the ability to exercise influence by shaping beliefs and perceptions. Foreign publics cannot help but be impressed when someone else's money successfully penetrates the domestic currency system and gains widespread acceptance. And second is the direct political power that derives from the monetary dependence of others. Not only is the issuer of an international currency better insulated from outside influence or coercion in the domestic policy arena, it is also better positioned to pursue foreign objectives without constraint, or even to exercise a degree of influence or coercion internationally.

In view of all these potential benefits, is it any wonder that many Europeans have hoped to create a rival to the dollar?

Performance

So how well has the euro actually fared since its introduction in 1999? Viewed purely in exchange-rate terms, the currency's record of performance has been mixed—first embarrassing, more recently a point of some pride. From an opening value of $1.17, the euro initially drifted downward, sinking to a low near $0.83 by mid-2000 and subsequently languishing at well below par for nearly two years. In mid-2002, however, the new currency began an impressive recovery, climbing decisively past $1.00 in November 2002 and continuing to rise well into 2003. Today, the euro appears to stand tall in relation to the greenback.

Exchange rates, however, are not the issue. A currency's price is at best an imperfect indicator of its international status. The real issue is not price but use: the extent to which a money is voluntarily chosen by market actors outside the euro area itself for the standard functions of a medium of exchange, unit of account and store of value. Central banks may also adopt the euro, of course, as an intervention medium, currency anchor, or as part of their foreign reserves. But currency use by state actors understandably tends, for the most part, simply to reflect prevailing market practice. The key issue is what happens to the preferences of private actors. If the euro is ever truly to challenge the dollar, it will be by displacing the popular greenback for any or all of the traditional roles of money in the broad global marketplace.

Viewed in these terms, there is little evidence yet of any significant displacement of the dollar, precipitous or otherwise. Accurate analysis demands that we compare the euro not just with its most popular predecessor, Germany's old Deutschmark (DM)—which had already attained a rank among international currencies second only to the dollar—but with all of the euro's other "legacy" currencies as well.[3] A look at data available to date suggests that, in most categories of use, the euro has held its own as compared with the past aggregate shares of EMU's twelve constituent currencies, but that is about all. In its first four years of existence, little more has been achieved.

The clearest indicator of a money's international status is the amplitude of its use as a medium of exchange in the foreign-exchange market, where, according to the latest survey of the Bank for International Settlements (2002), average daily turnover in 2001 approximated some $1.2 trillion worldwide.[4] Top currencies are bought and sold not only for direct use in trade and investment, but also as a low-cost intermediary—a "vehicle"—for the trading of other currencies. A vehicle role is a direct consequence of high market turnover, which yields substantial economies of scale. Typically, it will be less expensive for a market agent to sell a local money for a vehicle currency and then use the vehicle currency to buy the needed foreign money than it would be to exchange one infrequently traded money directly for another. And no currency has more market turnover than the dollar, reflecting the large size of the U.S. economy and its leading role in world exports. The low transactions costs that result from high market volume explain why the greenback has long been the most favored vehicle for global currency exchanges, appearing on one side or the other of some 90 percent of all transactions in 2001 (unchanged from its share in 1989). The euro, by contrast, entered on one side of just 38 percent of all transactions in 2001. That was higher than the share of the Deutschmark, which had appeared in 30 percent of transactions in 1998, but lower than that of all euro's legacy currencies taken together (53 percent).[5] Only in trading in the EU's immediate neighborhood—e.g. in the Nordic countries and East-Central Europe—is the euro clearly the dominant vehicle currency (Detken and Hartmann 2002).

The greenback also remains the most favored vehicle for the invoicing of global trade, which adds the role of unit of account (currency of denomination) to that of medium of exchange (currency of settlement) for international contracts. Overall, the dollar is estimated to account for nearly half of all world exports (Hartmann 1998)—more than double the U.S. share of world exports. The DM's share of trade invoicing in its last years, prior to its replacement by the euro, was 15 percent, roughly equivalent to Germany's proportion of world exports. Preliminary evidence from the European Central Bank (2001: 18) suggests that this share was maintained by the euro after its introduction in 1999 but has not yet shown any sign of increase.

Likewise, the dollar remains the most favored store of value in global capital markets, where the euro has yet to catch on significantly as an investment medium for international portfolio managers. True, there has been some increased use of the euro as a financing currency (a vehicle for borrowing). Non-Europeans have been attracted by the opportunity to tap into the much broader pool of savings created by the consolidation of EMU. In bond and money markets, new foreign issues jumped sharply after the new currency's introduction and have remained significantly higher than the share of EMU legacy currencies prior to 1999. Indeed, for a brief time in 1999, euro-denominated international bond and notes issuance actually exceeded dollar issues for the first time, before leveling off at an average share of some 29 percent in subsequent years (as compared with a dollar share of some 43 percent). The average share of the euro's predecessor currencies in global issuance in the five years prior to 1999 had been just 19 percent (European Central Bank 2001: 7–8; Detken and Hartmann 2002: 566–67). Equity issues have also grown substantially, while the euro share of international bank lending has risen by several percentage points. But these developments represent an increase only in the supply of euro-denominated assets, not demand— and on the demand side foreign managers so far have been slower than anticipated to add to their holdings of euro-denominated assets, despite the greater depth and liquidity on offer. Overall, the euro's share of world portfolios has changed little from the previous aggregate of legacy currencies.

Of course, half a decade is not a very long period in such matters. Given enough time, the euro's rosy future could yet materialize, just as many argue.

But might the mainstream view be mistaken? Could the issue really be trajectory, not just speed? In fact, with each passing year, it becomes increasingly clear that serious obstacles lie in the path of the euro's ascent. Though dominance within the European region seems assured, there are strong reasons to believe that, on the broader world stage, grander ambitions for the euro will be disappointed.

Inertia

One reason is simply inertia, a characteristic that is inherent in all monetary behavior. Two sources of inertia in currency choice can be identified. First is the preexistence of already well-established transactional networks, which generate a well-documented stickiness in user preferences—what specialists call "hysteresis" or "ratchet effects." In effect, prior use confers a certain natural advantage of incumbency. Switching from one money to another is costly, involving an expensive process of financial adaptation, as numerous analysts have emphasized (see, e.g., Dornbusch *et al.* 1990; Guidotti and Rodriguez 1992). Considerable effort must be invested in creating and learning to use new instruments and institutions, with much riding on what other market agents may be expected to do at the same time. Hence, as attractive as a given money may seem, adoption will not prove cost-effective unless others appear likely to make extensive use of it too. In the words of economists Kevin Dowd and David Greenaway:

> Changing currencies is costly—we must learn to reckon in the new currency, we must change the units in which we quote prices, we might have to change our records, and so on. ... [This] explains why agents are often reluctant to switch currencies, even when the currency they are using appears to be manifestly inferior to some other.
>
> (Dowd and Greenaway 1993: 1180)

Inertia is also promoted by the exceptionally high level of uncertainty inherent in any choice between alternative monies. Uncertainty encourages a tendency toward what psychologists call "mimesis": the rational impulse of risk-averse actors, in conditions of contingency, to minimize anxiety by imitative behavior based on past experience. Once a currency gains a degree of acceptance, its use is apt to be perpetuated—even after the appearance of powerful new competitors—simply by regular repetition of previous practice. In effect, a conservative bias is inherent in the dynamics of the marketplace. As one source (Orléan 1989: 81–83) has argued, "imitation leads to the emergence of a convention [wherein] emphasis is placed on a certain 'conformism' or even hermeticism in financial circles."

The salience of inertia in this context is well illustrated by the dollar's own experience when it first began to rival the pound sterling, the dominant currency of the nineteenth century. Even after America's emergence as the world's richest economy, it took literally decades for the greenback to ascend to top rank among currencies. As Paul Krugman (1992: 173) has commented: "The impressive fact here is surely the inertia; sterling remained the first-ranked currency for half a century after Britain had ceased to be the first-ranked economic power."[6] Similar inertia has been evident for millennia in the prolonged use of such international moneys as the Byzantine solidus (otherwise known as the bezant) or the Spanish silver peso (later known as the Mexican silver dollar) long after the decline of the imperial powers that first coined them (Cohen 1998). In fact, such inertias are very much the rule, not the exception, in global monetary relations.

Exceptional or not, even the most stubborn inertias can in time be overcome, as these historical examples also illustrate. But to defeat the conservative bias in market behavior, a new contender like the euro must first offer substantial advantages over the incumbent. The dollar was able to do that, in relation to sterling, once New York overtook London as the world's preeminent source of investment capital. The problem for the euro is that, apart from its appeal as a financing currency, it presently offers no comparable advantages in relation to the dollar.

Transactions costs

Consider, for example, the cost of doing business in euros, which directly affects the currency's attractiveness as a vehicle for foreign-exchange transactions or international trade. Europe's new money does offer many positive features for market agents, including especially a high degree of transactional convenience. It also offers a large and expanding network of constituents. By 2001 twelve of the European Union's fifteen members had already adopted the euro; the reluctant trio of Britain, Denmark, and Sweden may yet do so as well; and so too, eventually, will all the applicant countries that have joined the EU in the years since the currency's birth. But even so, America's greenback will be favored by the natural advantages of incumbency unless euro transactions costs, which historically have been higher than those of the more widely traded dollar, can be lowered to more competitive levels. In turn, the level of euro transactions costs, as measured by bid–offer spreads, will depend directly on what happens to the structural efficiency of Europe's financial markets. Economists Richard Portes and Hélène Rey (1998: 308) put the point most succinctly: "The key determinant of the extent and speed of internationalization of the euro will be transactions costs in foreign exchange and securities markets."

On the face of it, prospects for the efficiency of Europe's financial system would seem good. In purely quantitative terms, introduction of the euro promises to create the largest single-currency capital market in the world. The aggregate value of euro-denominated financial claims (fixed-income securities, equities, and bank loans) is already almost as great as that of the United States, and will undoubtedly keep growing in the future, particularly if Britain ever decides to join the euro area. Beyond that, there are bound to be major qualitative improvements in market depth and liquidity as previously segmented national markets are gradually knitted together into an integrated whole. The elimination of exchange risk inside EMU has already intensified competition among financial institutions, particularly in such hotly contested activities as bond underwriting and syndicated bank lending, encouraging cost-cutting and innovation. Over the longer term, harmonization of laws and conventions and the development of new cross-border payments systems should enhance the marketability of euro assets of all kinds. Empirical studies repeatedly confirm the ample scope for benefits in the future (see, e.g., Giannetti *et al.* 2002; Heinemann and Jopp 2002; London Economics 2002).

Progress to date, however, has been disappointing, and it is not at all clear that the euro's promise in this respect can ever be converted fully into performance. In principle, the EU is firmly committed to financial integration under the financial services action plan first launched in 1999. In practice, however, resistance to many market-opening measures remains stubbornly strong. As a recent EU report on Europe's financial markets—the so-called Lamfalussy Report—firmly insisted: "The European Union has no divine right to the benefits of an integrated financial market. It has to capture those benefits"—and so far, at least, the EU has not done a very good job of doing so (European Union 2001: 8, emphasis added). According to the Lamfalussy Report, market integration continues to be retarded by a plethora of interconnected factors and barriers, including the absence of clear Europe-wide regulation on a wide number of issues, an inefficient regulatory system, inconsistent implementation, and a large number of settlement systems that fragment liquidity and increase costs. Integration has made good progress in money markets and the corporate bond market, where instruments and procedures are already largely standardized (Santillán *et al.* 2000). Primary equity markets have also expanded rapidly and become more closely integrated (Fratzscher 2001), in turn spurring efforts to merge national stock exchanges. Although a projected merger of the Frankfurt and London exchanges failed to materialize, a successful partnership has been created by the bourses of Paris, Amsterdam, and Brussels, under the label Euronext. Overall, however, as the Lamfalussy Report concludes, the system remains "ill-adapted to the pace of global financial market change" (European Union 2001: 7).

A real question exists, therefore, as to whether structural improvements in Europe's financial markets can ever lower euro transactions costs enough to overcome the powerful conservative bias of monetary practice. In key respects the dollar's advantages will persist. Most important, as frequently stressed by knowledgeable observers (Cooper 2000; Henning 2000), is the lack of a universal financial instrument to rival the U.S. Treasury bill for liquidity and convenience—a deficiency that will be difficult, if not impossible, to rectify so long as the EU, with its separate national governments, lacks a counterpart to the Federal government in Washington. Full consolidation of the euro area's markets for public debt is stymied by the persistence of different credit and liquidity risk premiums among participating countries, as well as by variations in legal traditions, procedures, issuance calendars, and primary dealer systems. Market segmentation has also been prolonged by intense competition between governments to establish their own issues as EMU benchmarks (International Monetary Fund 2001: 99–111).

On balance, therefore, it seems quite unlikely that anticipated efficiency gains, though substantial, will soon be enough on their own to displace the greenback from top rank. Early studies (Detken and Hartmann 2000; Danthine *et al.* 2000) found little evidence of reduced transactions costs immediately after the currency's introduction. Indeed, for some types of transactions, bid–offer spreads have actually increased over time relative to the corresponding spreads for the DM, Europe's most widely traded currency prior to EMU (Hau *et al.* 2002a, 2002b; European Central Bank 2001; Goodhart *et al.* 2002). In reality, no one expects that euro transactions costs will ever decline to a level substantially below those presently quoted for the dollar.

To be sure, this has not forestalled widespread use of the new currency in the euro area's immediate neighborhood. For countries whose foreign trade is dominated by the European Union, the euro remains a natural choice even in the absence of a distinct cost advantage. Elsewhere, however, where commercial ties are less heavily concentrated on Europe, high spreads will undoubtedly be far more of a hindrance. Unless the euro can offer competitive transactions costs, it is hard to see what incentive market actors outside the euro-time zone will have to switch away from the greenback on any significant scale when selecting a medium of exchange or unit of account.

Anti-growth bias

The story is much the same with respect to the market's choice of a store of value. Europe's new money also offers many positive features as an investment medium, including in particular the prospect of relatively stable purchasing power. Yet here too it seems doubtful that advantages will be great enough to encourage a sizable switch away from the greenback. For international investors, the store-of-value function involves not only stability of purchasing power, but also future rates of return. The problem in this instance is a serious anti-growth bias that appears to be built into the institutional structure of EMU, which can be expected to impact negatively on yields on euro-denominated assets.[7]

Few doubts were raised about the euro's prospective store-of-value role when the currency was first introduced—quite the contrary, in fact. A merger of the continent's cacophony of national currencies would, by definition, eliminate exchange risk on investments within the region. A massive shift was therefore predicted in the allocation of global savings as compared with holdings of European assets in the past. The world private portfolio of international financial assets, excluding intra-EU claims, was estimated at some $6.1 trillion at the end of 1995 (Henning 1997: 22), of which little more than one-quarter was accounted for by assets denominated in European currencies, compared with a dollar share of more than half. Holdings previously lodged outside the EU, it was assumed, would naturally be attracted by the European market's new depth and liquidity, enhancing the euro's global standing. Knowledgeable sources suggested that foreign demand for euro-denominated assets might soon rise by anything from $400 billion to $800 billion in total, mostly at the dollar's expense (see, e.g., Bergsten 1997: 30; Henning 1997: 22; McCauley 1997: 39; McCauley and White 1997: 358; Frenkel and Søndergaard 2001). Few analysts expected the euro's share of world portfolios, as compared with the previous aggregate of legacy currencies, to change as little as it has done until now. Partly, this may be attributed to the spectacular productivity boom in the U.S. economy in recent years, which helped preserve the appeal of dollar assets. But in good part as well, it plainly reflects a marked lack of appeal of investments in Europe despite the coming of EMU. Foreign investors obviously remain wary about the rates of return that can be expected on euro claims.

What is the reason for investor caution? If portfolio managers are actively discounting the rewards to capital available in Europe, it must be because of doubts about the prospects for longer-term growth of output relative to productive capacity. Arguably, the main cause for such doubts may be said to lie in the core institutional provisions of EMU governing monetary and fiscal policy, the key determinants of macroeconomic performance. In neither policy domain is priority attached to promoting real production. Rather, in each, the main emphasis is on other considerations that can be expected to limit opportunities for future expansion—imparting, as some observers have long feared,[8] a distinct anti-growth bias to the economy of the euro area as a whole.

Consider monetary policy. As is well known, the European Central Bank was created by the Maastricht Treaty with just a single policy mandate—"to maintain price stability" (Article 105). That provision stands in sharp contrast to the charters of central banks elsewhere, such as the Federal Reserve, where comparable emphasis is placed on a responsibility to promote employment and output as well. The Treaty's provision is partially qualified in an additional instruction to "support the general economic policies in the Community," but only if this can be done "without prejudice to the objective of price stability" (Article 105). Moreover, the ECB is endowed with absolute independence, insulating it from political influence of any kind. The ECB cannot "seek or take instructions from Community institutions or bodies, from any government of a Member state or from any other body"; nor may Community institutions or governments "seek to influence the members of the decision-making bodies of the ECB" (Article 107). Legally, the ECB is free to focus exclusively on fighting inflation, even if over time this might be at the cost of stunting real growth.

In practice, of course, the ECB is not wholly insensitive to growth concerns. As students of monetary policy have long understood, a central bank is as much a political actor as any other public institution, keen to preserve its own privileges and prerogatives (see, e.g., Woolley 1984; Goodman 1992). No monetary authority—however independent it may be in formal terms— can afford to be totally impervious to political considerations. In the ECB's case, this has meant tolerating an inflation rate that for most of the period since 1999 has exceeded the Bank's official target of 2 percent per annum. On occasion—most recently in December 2002 when economic activity seemed particularly sluggish—it has even meant lowering interest rates despite possible dangers to the bank's price objective. Nonetheless, the overall orientation of ECB priorities is clear. Since the start of EMU, monetary conditions in the euro area have been among the tightest in the industrial world. The bias of policy has plainly been towards restraint, not expansion.

Likewise, on the side of fiscal policy, the euro-area governments have formally tied their own hands with the controversial Stability and Growth Pact (SGP), signed in 1997. In accordance with the Maastricht Treaty, the SGP mandates a medium-term objective of fiscal balance in all participating economies as well as a strict cap on annual budget deficits of just 3 percent of gross domestic product (GDP). The rationale for these fiscal restraints is clear. It is to prevent potentially profligate policymakers from tapping into the EMU's broader pool of savings to finance large spending programs at the expense of partner countries. But the effective impact of these restraints is equally clear. They make it far more difficult for elected officials to use budgetary policy for contracyclical purposes, to offset the anti-growth bias of monetary policy. Even in the best of times, most governments tend to run deficits of some magnitude. Little room is left, therefore, for participating states to raise public spending or cut taxes when needed to promote production and jobs. Indeed, under a strict reading of the SGP, officials might be obliged to act in a pro-cyclical manner, tightening policy even when the economy slows, in order to maintain momentum toward the goal of budget balance.

Here too, we know, practice has at times diverged from principle. Portugal, for instance, briefly exceeded the 3 percent limit in 2001 in the run-up to a national election before getting its budget back under control once a new government was installed; and more recently, in early 2003, all three of EMU's largest members—France, Germany, and Italy—were publicly chastised by the European Commission for failing to prevent rising deficits. In fact, the Stability and Growth Pact is widely detested across Europe. Typical are the biting words of *The Economist*, which contends that the SGP "serves no positive purpose and risks doing serious harm." Romano Prodi, president of the Commission, simply calls the fiscal restraints "stupid" (*The Economist*, August 25, 2001). Some observers call for the replacement of the SGP with an economic government for Europe (Collignon 2003). Others urge returning authority to national governments, either by scrapping the SGP altogether

(Arestis and Sawyer 2003) or by establishing autonomous fiscal-policy com-mittees comparable to the monetary-policy committees now used by the Bank of England and other central banks (Wyplosz 2002). Yet, until now, appeals for revision or repeal have made little headway. So long as the SGP remains binding on all euro-area governments, an anti-growth bias will be perpetuated in fiscal policy too.

Investor caution may be overdone, of course. Even with the prevailing provisions for EMU monetary and fiscal policy, contraction could be avoided if appropriate structural reforms were to be undertaken to facilitate adjust-ment to unanticipated shocks. Inter alia, this would mean a significant reor-ganization of labor markets, to promote worker mobility and wage flexibility, as well as innovations in competition policy to encourage more efficient adaptation by business. The easier it is for markets to adjust at the micro-economic level, the less need there is for stimulative policy to promote growth at the macroeconomic level. Such reforms have long been sought in Europe's economies, which many have described as sclerotic. Indeed, as a practical matter, some specialists have welcomed the potential anti-growth bias of EMU as precisely the justification needed to get such reforms enacted. In principle, EMU would provide the necessary political leverage for action.

In practice, however, in most EU countries, structural reforms remain a distant dream, owing to the stiff resistance of constituencies whose interests and privileges might be put into jeopardy—thus rendering the tactic moot. In the absence of radical political change, investors do indeed have every reason to anticipate disappointing rates of return on euro-denominated assets; and that in turn will continue to forestall any major shift in the allocation of global savings at the expense of the dollar. Within the euro-time zone, once again, there will undoubtedly be some movement to acquire euro claims as the natural counterpart to growing commercial ties. But elsewhere, Europe's new currency will remain very much at a disadvantage relative to the American greenback.

Governance

Finally, we come to the governance structure of EMU, which for the euro's prospects as an international currency may be the biggest obstacle of all. The basic question is: Who is in charge of the euro area? The answer, regrettably, has never been clear. From the start, much confusion has reigned concerning the delegation of authority among governments and EU institutions. Pro-spective users of the new money, therefore, may be excused for hesitating to commit themselves to what seemingly amounts to a pig in a poke—even if transactions costs could be lowered to competitive levels and rewards to European capital could be significantly improved. For most market agents, particularly beyond the euro area's immediate neighborhood, rationality would appear to dictate sticking to the tried-and-true. Many prefer the devil they know—the good old greenback—to the one they don't.

We tend to forget, after all, just how unique an enterprise EMU is—a group of fully independent states that have made a mutual commitment to replace existing national currencies with one newly created money. True, EMU is not entirely without precedent. Around the world other monetary unions do exist, including most notably the CFA franc zone in Africa and the Eastern Caribbean Currency Union in the Western Hemisphere. But these scattered groupings comprise mostly small developing nations and are based on institutional arrangements whose origins stretch back to colonial days. EMU, by contrast, is the initiative of established states of long standing, including some of the biggest economies in the world, engaged in a gigantic experiment of unparalleled proportions—"a bold step into the unknown," in the words of economist Willem Buiter (1999: 182). Involved here is what one scholar (Litfin 1997) calls a "sovereignty bargain": a voluntary agreement to accept certain limitations on national authority in exchange for anticipated benefits. Because they are the product of negotiations which can often be quite arduous, sovereignty bargains typically embody a variety of artful compromises and deliberate obfuscations; and that is certainly true of EMU, for which there is no obvious prototype in the modern era. Precisely because the undertaking is by way of an experiment, ambiguities abound in the Maastricht Treaty—nowhere more so than in its provisions for the political management of the euro.

Three key provisions are at issue. First is the governance of EMU's core institution, the European Central Bank, itself. Immediate operational control of monetary policy lies in the hands of the ECB's Executive Board, made up of the president, vice-president, and four other members. Ultimate authority, however, is formally lodged in the Governing Council, which in addition to the six-member Executive Board was, according to the Maastricht Treaty, to include the heads of the central banks of all participating states. That has made for a total of eighteen individuals around the table, which is already greater than might seem consistent with efficient collective decision-making. Assuming future participation of Britain, Denmark, and Sweden, as well as of the EU's ten incoming members, the size of the Governing Council would eventually grow to more than thirty—almost certainly too many for serious and productive discussion. As one source commented sarcastically, enlargement of EMU under Maastricht Treaty rules would have left the ECB with "too many [members] to decide on where to go for dinner, let alone agree on how to run monetary policy for more than 400 million people" (Baldwin 2001).[9] As a remedy, the ECB recently obtained approval from the European Council for a new set of rules limiting membership of the Governing Council at any one time to twenty-one members, including fifteen central-bank governors with rotating voting rights. But even this new arrangement would appear to leave the ECB with a serious "number problem."

Sooner or later, therefore, as so often happens in large multinational institutions, real power will have to devolve to a smaller "inner" group formally or informally charged with resolving differences on critical issues.[10] But who will be allowed to join this exclusive club? Would it be the members of the Executive Board, who might be expected to take a broad approach to Euroland's needs and interests? Or would it be a select coterie of central-bank governors, whose views could turn out to be more parochial? For the moment, no one knows.

Second is the critical matter of exchange-rate policy. Under the Maastricht Treaty, the ECB is assigned day-to-day responsibility for the euro's external value (Article 105). Authority over the more general orientation of policy, however, is shared uneasily with both the Council of Ministers, representing national governments, and the Commission, reflecting negotiating compromises that are now firmly embedded in the Treaty (Article 109). On the one hand, to satisfy member countries that wished to retain a role in such matters, it is the Council—not the ECB—that was empowered to "formulate general orientations," albeit only on a recommendation from the Commission or ECB. But, on the other hand, to reassure those who were worried about the possibility of undue political interference in exchange-rate policy, the Treaty also states that "these general orientations shall be without prejudice to the primary objective of the [ECB] to maintain price stability," which would seem to give the ECB, ultimately, something akin to a veto. Plainly, power over exchange rates was meant to be shared in some form of consensual process. But, equally, these provisions could turn out to be a sure recipe for political deadlock and drift. Again, no one knows.

Finally, there is the issue of external representation. Who is to speak for the euro area on broader macroeconomic issues such as policy coordination or the management of financial crises? Here there is no answer at all, leaving a vacuum at the core of EMU. Deeply divided over the question at the time the Maastricht Treaty was negotiated, EU governments—to use American football parlance—in effect chose to punt. No single body was designated to represent EMU at the International Monetary Fund or in other global forums. Instead, the Treaty simply lays down a procedure for resolving the issue at a later date, presumably on a case-by-case basis (Article 109). At a minimum, this cop-out increases confusion about who is in charge. The U.S. Treasury, Henning (2000: 52) writes, has "no coherent counterpart within the euro area when addressing politically sensitive international monetary and financial questions." At worst, the vacuum condemns the euro area to lasting second-class status, since it limits the group's ability to project power in international negotiations. In the words of Kathleen McNamara and Sophie Meunier:

> As long as no "single voice" has the political authority to speak on behalf of the euro area, as the U.S. Secretary of the Treasury does for the American currency, the pre-eminence of the U.S. in international monetary matters, as in other realms, is likely to remain unchallenged.
>
> (McNamara and Meunier 2002: 850)

Given all these ambiguities, can the euro ever hope to rival the dollar? An improvement of EMU's political cohesiveness would certainly seem to be a necessary condition. On its own, institutional reform might not ensure widespread acceptance of the new currency. But without greater clarity about the sovereignty bargain's lines of authority, it is hard to see how the euro can ever attain the level of credibility needed to play a global role. Even Fred Bergsten (2002: 7), the euro enthusiast, concedes that, as it stands, EMU's fissiparous governance structure "dissipates much of the potential for realizing a key international role for the euro." In place of decisive management, market agents see fragmented decision-making and a potential for chronic bickering. In this light, is it really surprising that the currency's ascent has fallen short of expectations?

Conclusion

In short, predictions of a rosy future for the euro are beginning to look increasingly illusory. Even under the best of circumstances it would take years, if not decades, for the new currency to overcome the dollar's natural incumbency advantages. And EMU's circumstances are by no means the best. Europe's markets for public debt remain segmented, inhibiting a substantial reduction of transactions costs. Likewise, an anti-growth bias appears to be built into the institutional structure of EMU, dampening rates of return on euro-denominated assets. And, worst of all, the euro area's governance structure continues to be riddled with ambiguities and obfuscations, perpetuating doubts about the credibility of the whole exercise. The issue really is trajectory, not just speed. A second global currency is not about to emerge.

This does not mean, of course, that EMU was a mistake. The euro will naturally dominate its own region, yielding at least some of the benefits of international use, albeit on a more modest scale than currently available to the greenback. Almost certainly, substantial new seigniorage revenues will be earned from growing circulation of euro banknotes in neighboring countries, a process of "euro-ization" analogous to the informal dollarization that has occurred in many other parts of the world.[11] Moreover, Europe's vulnerability to outside shocks will be significantly reduced by the creation of what Helmut Schmidt once called a "zone of monetary stability." In place of the continent's earlier collection of relatively small and open currency areas, EMU creates one much larger closed unit that is better able to protect the European economy from external disturbances.[12] And possibly most important of all, as indicated at the outset, the new currency will surely enhance Europe's sense of its own identity, greatly reinforcing the historic project of integration that was begun more than a half century ago. Is that not ambition enough for the peoples of Europe?

5 Enlargement and the international role of the euro

How will enlargement of the European Union (EU) affect prospects for the euro as an international currency? Will the addition of a dozen or possibly even more new members to the Economic and Monetary Union (EMU) enhance the euro's ability to challenge the U.S. dollar for global monetary supremacy? Previously, I have argued that Europe's joint currency is fated to remain a distant second to America's greenback long into the foreseeable future (Cohen 2003). In this essay I extend my earlier analysis to consider the impact of enlargement on the euro's international role. My conclusion now is, if anything, even more skeptical than before. Enlargement, I submit, will diminish, not expand, the euro's attractiveness as a rival to the greenback. The dollar will remain the only truly global currency.

To date, progress in building a global role for the euro has been underwhelming. To some extent, this might be due simply to the inertia that is inherent in all monetary behavior—a well-documented stickiness in currency preferences. Since the adoption of a new money is costly, involving an expensive process of adaptation, an already popular currency like the dollar enjoys a certain natural advantage of incumbency. My previous work, however, suggests that there are also more fundamental forces at work. Three factors, all structural in character, have been largely responsible for the euro's slow start as an international currency: relatively high transactions costs, due to inefficiencies in Europe's financial markets; a serious anti-growth bias built into the institutions of EMU; and, most importantly, ambiguities at the heart of the monetary union's governance structure. The analysis offered here suggests that adding new members to EMU will, if anything, simply make matters worse. Larger numbers will aggravate the negative impact of all three factors.

Of particular salience is the impact of enlargement on the governance structure of EMU. I am hardly alone in stressing the degree to which prospects for internationalization of the euro are dimmed by EMU's institutional inadequacies. The theme has featured in the work of economists (e.g. Eichengreen 1998) and political scientists (e.g. Bieling 2006) alike. From the start, it should have been clear that widespread acceptance of Europe's new currency would be retarded by a lack of clarity about the delegation of monetary authority among governments and EU institutions. My argument here is that the addition of a diverse collection of new members, with significantly different interests and priorities, can only make the challenge of governance worse, exacerbating ambiguity at the expense of transparency and accountability.

The organization of the essay is as follows: The first two sections set the stage for analysis. The first section reviews the story of the euro's internationalization to date, while the second outlines prospects for enlargement of EMU and what the addition of new members could mean for the currency's future. The main analysis then follows in three subsequent sections, addressing in turn the impact of enlargement on each of the three structural factors identified in my previous work. The results and implications of the analysis are summarized in a concluding section.

Dream delayed

At its birth, the euro's future as an international currency seemed assured. Yet since the new money's introduction in 1999, acceptance beyond EMU itself has actually been quite slow, limited mainly to the euro's natural hinterland in and around Europe—"the euro's turf," as economist Charles Wyplosz (1999: 89) calls the nearby region. In many respects, Europe's monetary union has been a resounding success. But in terms of its anticipated challenge to the dollar, performance to date can only be described as disappointing. Beyond the European region, in the global marketplace, the greenback remains as dominant as ever.

Grand ambitions

Europe's ambitions for the euro have always been grand. First and foremost, the joint currency was expected to help promote the EU's long-standing goal of an "ever closer union among the peoples of Europe." The benefits would be both practical and psychological. Not only would exchange risk within the group be eliminated, reducing transactions costs that hampered the construction of a single European market. One money for Europe would also provide a powerful new symbol of European identity, enhancing the sense that all Europeans belong to the same emerging community.

But that was never all. For many in the EU, there was an external ambition as well. On the broader world stage, EMU was meant to enhance Europe's role by creating a potent rival to the dollar, the leading international money of our era. Resentment has long simmered among Europeans sensitive to the inordinate power that the greenback's popularity gives to the United States— America's "exorbitant privilege," in Charles de Gaulle's memorable phrase. Europe is the equal of the United States in output and trade. Why should it not be America's equal in monetary matters, too? Though the "old dream of enthusiasts" (Zimmermann 2004: 235) was never formally articulated as such, it was evident from the start. EMU was supposed to challenge the dollar for global supremacy. Wyplosz (1999: 76), an informed insider, calls this "the hidden agenda of Europe's long-planned adoption of a single currency."

The stakes were clear. Four distinct benefits are derived from widespread international circulation of a currency, supplementing internal gains: (1) a potential for seigniorage (the implicit transfer of resources, equivalent to subsidized or interest-free loans, that goes to the issuer of a money that is used and held abroad); (2) an increase of flexibility in macroeconomic policy, afforded by the privilege of being able to rely on one's own currency to help finance foreign deficits; (3) the gain of status and prestige that goes with market dominance, a form of "soft" power; and (4) a gain of influence derived from the monetary dependence of others, a form of "hard" power. America had long enjoyed all four benefits. It is understandable that Europeans might desire a piece of the action, too.

Faith in the euro's potential was widespread. Fundamentally, international currency choice is shaped by three essential attributes. First, at least during the initial stages of a money's cross-border adoption, is widespread confidence in its future value backed by political stability in the economy of origin. No one is apt to be attracted to a currency that does not offer a reasonable promise of stable purchasing power. Second are the qualities of "exchange convenience" and "capital certainty"—a high degree of liquidity and reasonable predictability of asset value—both of which are essential to minimizing transactions costs. The key to each quality is a set of broad and efficient financial markets, exhibiting both depth and resiliency.

Third, a money must promise a broad transactional network, since nothing enhances a currency's acceptability more than the prospect of acceptability by others. Historically, this factor has usually meant an economy that is large in absolute size and well integrated into world markets. The greater the volume of transactions conducted in or with an economy, the greater will be the economies of scale to be derived from use of its currency. Economists describe these gains as a money's "network externalities." Network externalities may be understood as a form of interdependence in which the behavior of one actor depends strategically on the practices adopted by others in the same network of interactions.

Europe's new currency was set to begin life with many of the attributes necessary for competitive success. Together, prospective members would provide an economic base roughly comparable to that of the United States, enjoying extensive trade relations around the world. The potential for network externalities, therefore, was considerable. Likewise, EMU would start with both unquestioned political stability and an enviably low rate of inflation, backed by a joint monetary authority, the European Central Bank (ECB), that was fully committed to preserving confidence in the euro's future value. Much room existed for a successful challenge to the dollar, as frequently predicted. Typical was the view of Robert Mundell (2000: 57), a Nobel laureate in economics, who expressed no doubt that the euro "will challenge the status of the dollar and alter the power configuration of the system." The conventional wisdom was unambiguous. The markets would ultimately elevate the euro to a top rank alongside the greenback. In the oft-quoted words of Jacques Delors, when he was head of the European Commission, "le petit euro deviendra grand."

In fact, the only question seemed to be: How soon? Most analysts understood that the process would take time, owing to the natural advantages of incumbency. It took the dollar, for example, more than half a century to surpass sterling as an international currency, long after America emerged as the world's richest economy. However long it might take, though, the process was expected to start quickly. Not everyone agreed with the optimistic forecast of Fred Bergsten (1997), a former U.S. Treasury official, who predicted that Europe's new currency would achieve "full parity" with the dollar in as little as five to ten years. But few doubted that within such a time frame significant signs of a shift toward the euro would become evident. By the time this essay was written, nearly a decade after the euro's introduction, the displacement of the dollar should clearly have begun.

The story so far

So what is the story so far? Viewed purely in exchange-rate terms, the euro's record of performance has been mixed. From an opening value of $1.17, the currency initially drifted downward, sinking to a low near $0.83 by mid-2000 and subsequently languishing at well below par for upwards of two years. In mid-2002, however, the euro began an impressive recovery, climbing decisively to a high above $1.35 in 2004 before drifting down again in 2005, then up again in 2006. By mid-2007, the euro was once again above $1.35.

Exchange rates, however, are not the issue. A currency's price is at best an imperfect indicator of its international status. What really matters is not price but use: the extent to which a money is voluntarily chosen by market actors outside EMU for the standard functions of medium of exchange, unit of account, and store of value. Central banks, of course, may also adopt the euro, as an intervention medium, currency anchor, or as part of their foreign reserves. But currency use by state actors understandably tends, for efficiency reasons, to reflect prevailing market practice. In the absence of political pressures, central banks prefer to use a currency that will be most helpful to them in managing their exchange rates and monetary policy. The key issue, therefore, is what happens to the preferences of private actors. If the euro is ever truly to challenge the dollar, it will be by displacing the popular greenback for any or all of the traditional roles of money in the broad global marketplace.

Viewed in these terms, there is little evidence yet of any significant progress. The expected fast start has not occurred. As of January 2008 the euro zone, as it is commonly known, comprised fifteen EU members. A look at the available data suggests that in most categories of international use (adjusting for the elimination of intra-EMU transactions) the euro has managed to hold its own as compared with the past aggregate shares of EMU's "legacy" currencies. Hence, Europe's new money has easily taken its place as successor to Germany's old Deutschmark (DM), which among international currencies had already attained a rank second only to the dollar. But that is about all. As economist Hélène Rey (2005: 114) concludes, the euro "has established itself immediately as the second most important currency in the world. ... It has not, however, displaced in any significant way the dollar as the currency of choice for most international transactions." Indeed, after an initial spurt of enthusiasm, use in most market segments has actually leveled off or even declined in recent years (European Central Bank 2007c). Worse, the only significant gains to date have been in the European Union's immediate neighborhood, including the EU's newest members before they joined, as well as other actual or potential candidate countries. In the words of the European Central Bank (2007c: 7), a "strong institutional and regional pattern continues to characterise the internationalisation of the euro." Globally, Europe's new currency remains in the dollar's shadow.

The clearest indicator of a money's international status is the amplitude of its use as a medium of exchange in the foreign-exchange market, where average daily turnover now exceeds some \$2 trillion worldwide. Top currencies are bought and sold not only for direct use in trade and investment but also as a low-cost intermediary—a "vehicle"—for the trading of other currencies. A vehicle role is a direct consequence of high market turnover, which yields substantial economies of scale. Typically, it will be less expensive for a market agent to sell a local money for a vehicle currency and then use the vehicle currency to buy the needed foreign money than it would be to exchange one infrequently traded money directly for another.

No currency has more market turnover than the dollar, reflecting the large size of the U.S. economy and its leading role in world trade. The low transactions costs that result from high market volume explain why the greenback has long been the most favored vehicle for global currency exchanges, appearing on one side or the other of some 93 percent of all transactions in 2005–06 (European Central Bank 2007c). The euro, by contrast, entered on one side of just 39 percent of all transactions. That was higher than the share of the Deutschmark, which had appeared in 30 percent of transactions in 1998 (its last year of existence) but lower than that of all euro's legacy currencies taken together (53 percent) and actually down from a high of 41 percent in 2004–05 (European Central Bank 2007c). Only in trading in the Nordic countries and East-Central Europe, where commercial ties are largely concentrated on the EU, is the euro clearly the favored vehicle.

The greenback also remains the most favored vehicle for the invoicing of global trade, which adds the role of unit of account (currency of denomination) to that of medium of exchange (currency of settlement) for international contracts. Overall, the dollar is estimated to account for nearly half of all world exports—more than double the U.S. share of world exports. The DM's share of trade invoicing in its last years, prior to its replacement by the euro, was 15 percent, roughly equivalent to Germany's proportion of world exports. Evidence from the International Monetary Fund (IMF) (Bertuch-Samuels and Ramlogan 2007) suggests that this share was maintained by the euro after its introduction in 1999 but has not yet shown any sign of increase except in neighboring European countries.

Likewise, the dollar remains the most favored store of value in global capital markets, where the euro has yet to catch on significantly as an investment medium for international portfolio managers. There has been some increased use of the euro as a financing currency (a vehicle for borrowing). Non-European borrowers have been attracted by the opportunity to tap into the much broader pool of savings created by the consolidation of EMU. Overall, the share of the euro in the stock of international debt securities rose strongly, from roughly one-fifth in 1999 to nearly one-half by the end of 2005, before falling back by a few percentage points in 2006 (European Central Bank 2007c). But again, most of the increase came from immediate neighbors (mainly recent or prospective EU members). Borrowers in Asia and Latin America continue primarily to use the dollar. Moreover, these developments represent an increase only in the supply of euro-denominated assets. On the demand side, foreign investors so far have been slower than anticipated to add to their holdings of euro-denominated assets, despite the greater depth and liquidity on offer. Most issues have been taken up by European investors, making them in effect "domestic." Outside EMU, the euro's overall share of portfolios has changed little from the previous aggregate of legacy currencies. Similar patterns have also prevailed in international banking markets (European Central Bank 2007c).

So far, therefore, the story is unencouraging—certainly not the happy outcome that so many had predicted. The old dream has been delayed. Other than within the European region itself, use of Europe's new currency has shown little sign of growth and may indeed have already begun to settle down. All this is a far cry from attaining full parity with the dollar in as little as five to ten years.

Dream revived?

Yet despite the euro's disappointing performance to date, hope lives on, now buoyed by the prospect of a significant increase in membership. Enlargement of the EU will mean, in time, an expanded EMU, too. Bigger, it is said, will also be better. Greater numbers will enhance the currency's power and prestige, increasing its attractiveness as a rival to the dollar. Europe's grand dream has been revived.

Enlargement

The European Union's enlargement in May 2004 added ten new "accession countries," bringing total membership of the EU to twenty-five. Two more neighbors, Bulgaria and Romania, joined in January, 2007; and yet others, including more successor states of the former Yugoslavia and even Turkey, hope to follow in the more or less distant future. All are legally obligated, sooner or later, to adopt the euro. The only question is when.

Upon entering the EU, each accession country is automatically enrolled in EMU with a "derogation." Simply put, derogation means that adoption of the euro is mandatory but only when the country is deemed ready. Several critical conditions must be satisfied first—the same so-called convergence criteria that were demanded of present participants before they could join EMU. The convergence criteria were first spelled out in the 1992 Maastricht Treaty (Article 109j), which brought the euro into existence. The four familiar conditions are:

1   Relative price stability—in practical terms, an average rate of consumer price inflation, observed over a one-year period, that does not exceed by more than one-and-a-half percentage points the average rate of inflation in the "three best performing member states in terms of price stability."
2   Interest-rate stability—in practical terms, a year-average nominal interest rate on a ten-year benchmark government bond no more than two percentage points above the average in the three best performing members.
3   Fiscal stability—specifically, a fiscal deficit below 3 percent of gross domestic product (GDP) and public debt totaling less than 60 percent of GDP.
4   Exchange-rate stability—specifically, participation in the pegging arrangement known as the Exchange Rate Mechanism (ERM) for at least two years while the country's currency trades against the euro without severe tensions, within "normal fluctuation margins." Because the present Exchange Rate Mechanism is a successor to an earlier arrangement that existed before 1999, it is usually referred to as ERM2 to distinguish it from its predecessor.

It is not expected that all accession countries will manage to satisfy the necessary conditions at the same pace. Key is the exchange-rate criterion. Only eight of the twelve new members admitted in 2004 and 2007 have even tried to commit formally to ERM2. These are Bulgaria, Estonia, and Lithuania, which carried over their long-standing currency boards anchored on the euro; Cyprus, which already had a firm euro peg; Latvia and Malta, which converted basket pegs to the euro; and Slovakia and Slovenia, which moved from managed flexibility to stable euro pegs. The largest accession countries—the Czech Republic, Hungary, Poland, and Romania—so far have opted to preserve a higher degree of exchange-rate flexibility.

Accordingly, target dates for adoption of the euro vary considerably. The first to make the move were Slovenia, which joined the zone in January 2007, and Cyprus and Malta, which entered in January 2008. Estonia, Latvia, and Lithuania had all hoped to join in 2007 or 2008 but were forced to postpone because of excessively high inflation rates. Slovakia tentatively penciled in January 2009, while Bulgaria and the Czech Republic had in mind 2010 at the earliest. Hungary abandoned its target of 2010 without rescheduling. Poland and Romania have not even tried to set a timetable for joining.

Goals have slipped because disillusionment with the euro is on the rise, especially in the larger accession countries. Adoption of the euro was once viewed as a badge of honor. But policymakers have come to understand, as one recent study puts it, that while "membership has its benefits ... these benefits are not free. Being part of a currency union requires discipline, and the loss of the exchange rate as an instrument for coping with economic shocks can be costly (Ahearne and Pisani-Ferry 2006: 1). The convergence criteria are proving a very tough hurdle. Moreover, resistance is spurred by concerns over the prospective loss of monetary autonomy. In some instances, adoption could be delayed for years.

Much, obviously, remains uncertain. All we know for sure is that, sooner or later, the number of economies in the euro zone is supposed to be a lot bigger than it is now.

Size matters, but ...

But will bigger really be better? The case for such a presumption seems clear. Larger numbers will mean an even broader transactional network, increasing exponentially the potential for network externalities. Hence, conclude many, the euro is bound to grow even more attractive as a rival to America's greenback. That is the logic of Mundell (2000: 60), for example, who has argued that "the outlook for the euro is very favorable [because] as the EU expands into the rest of Central Europe, the euro will have a substantially larger transactional domain than the dollar." Likewise, it is the logic of Jacques de Larosiere, former managing director of the IMF. "The euro's position as a reserve currency will progress in the future," de Larosiere (2002: 15–16) asserts, because "with the monetary integration of candidate countries to the European Union, we see the geographic reach of the euro is likely to expand considerably." Prospects for Europe's money as an international currency are assumed to depend directly on the absolute size of its economic base.

Nowhere is the logic clearer than in the writing of Fred Bergsten, long one of the euro's biggest boosters. What qualifies a currency for international status? "There is good reason," Bergsten (1997: 25, 27) contends, "to believe that the relative size of key currency countries' economies and trade flows is of central salience. ... The sharp increase in the size of the economy and trading unit underlying the European key currency could produce a quantum leap in the international role of that asset." The old DM had first gained widespread acceptance when Germany accounted for no more than 9 percent of world output and 12 percent of world trade. The twelve original members of EMU would more than double both ratios; enlargement is adding even more. A dramatic rise in euro use, therefore, should be expected as well. In Bergsten's (1997: 27) words: "In the eventual steady state, a rise of 65–250 per cent in the size of the relevant economic base could be expected, which would expand the potential size of the currency's role by 30–335 per cent."

Arguments like these, however, are far too simplistic to be taken seriously. As economist Barry Eichengreen (1997: 50) has noted in a comment on Bergsten: "This argument allows no role for other determinants. ... One cannot forecast the international role of the euro simply by replacing a Germany that accounts for 9 per cent of world output with an EU that accounts for 31 per cent." Size no doubt matters. Economies as small as, say, Norway or Sweden could never realistically hope to see their currency compete for global status. Patently, the network externalities would be too limited. But while a large economic base may be necessary, it is hardly sufficient. For a period in the 1980s, Italy's GDP surpassed that of Britain. No one, however, rushed to substitute lire for sterling as a vehicle for trade or investment. Clearly other factors matter, too.

Transaction costs

What are these factors? As indicated, my previous work suggests that three factors, in particular, have played a crucial role in the euro's story so far—transactions costs, an anti-growth bias and issues of governance. The question is: How will enlargement affect each of the three? In each instance, my answer is unequivocal: Large numbers will simply make matters worse. Enlargement will delay even more Europe's grand dream for the euro.

Market segmentation ...

Begin first with transactions costs—the cost of doing business in euros. Transactions costs directly affect a currency's attractiveness as a vehicle for exchange transactions or international trade. At its birth, Europe's new money obviously offered a large and expanding transactional network, thus promising substantial network externalities. But even so, it was clear that the dollar would be favored by the natural advantages of incumbency unless euro transactions costs, which began high relative to the widely traded greenback, could be lowered to a more competitive level. The same scale economies that encourage use of a currency in the first place are also responsible for what specialists call "hysteresis" or "ratchet effects." Adoption of a new currency tends to be resisted unless the money can be expected to be truly cost-effective.

From the start it was understood that the cost of doing business in euros would depend directly on what could be done to improve the structural efficiency of Europe's financial markets. The point was put most cogently by economists Richard Portes and Hélène Rey (1998: 308): "The key determinant of the extent and speed of internationalization of the euro will be transactions costs in foreign exchange and securities markets."

On the face of it, prospects for euro transactions costs looked good. In purely quantitative terms, introduction of the new currency promised to create the largest single-currency capital market in the world. That expansion, in turn, was expected to trigger major qualitative improvements in depth and liquidity, knitting previously segmented national markets together into an integrated whole. As matters have turned out, however, Europe's reach has fallen considerably short of its grasp.

In practical terms, admittedly, much has been accomplished despite some foot-dragging by member governments. Integration at the retail level—the realm of bank accounts, mortgages, insurance policies, and the like—continues to be impeded by a plethora of interconnected barriers, including a diversity of settlement systems that fragment liquidity and reduce transactional convenience (Berglöf *et al.* 2005). But change clearly has been significant at the wholesale level where, in the words of the *The Economist* (2005b: 10), "financial markets in Europe became much more integrated and more interesting." The elimination of exchange risk inside the euro zone has intensified competition among financial institutions, encouraging cost-cutting, innovation, and consolidation. Progress has been particularly impressive in short-term money markets, syndicated bank lending, credit derivatives, and the corporate bond sector.

Nevertheless, it is evident that the dollar's cost advantage will persist so long as the EU is unable to offer a universal financial instrument to match the U.S. Treasury bill for international investor liquidity and convenience. This is a deficiency that will be difficult, if not impossible, to rectify so long as Europe, with its separate national governments, lacks a counterpart to the Federal government in Washington. Under the circumstances, the best the Europeans could do was to encourage establishment of selected benchmark securities for the public debt market. Gradually three euro benchmarks have emerged: the German Bund at ten years, the French bond at five years, and the Italian bond at two years (Rey 2005: 112). But such a piecemeal approach falls far short of creating a single market as large and liquid as that for U.S. government securities. Full consolidation of the public debt market remains stymied by variations in legal traditions, procedures, issuance calendars, and primary dealer systems.

Notably, yield differentials in the public debt market have shrunk significantly since the euro was born, suggesting that interchangeability among national issues has increased somewhat. But the convergence of yields is far from complete. Investors continue to treat the debts of EMU governments as imperfect substitutes, mostly owing to differences in perceived default risk (Codogno *et al.* 2003). And these differences of perception could now be compounded as a result of a decision by the ECB in November 2005 to limit the collateral it will accept in refinancing ("repo") operations with European

commercial banks. Previously, the ECB had accepted all euro-zone government bonds indiscriminately, as if the debts of EMU member states were all
equally creditworthy. Now, however, the Bank intends to be more selective.
Bonds must have a single A-rating or better from at least one of the three
main rating agencies (Moody's, Standard and Poor's, or Fitch). Observers
expect that this decision will lead commercial banks, over time, to be much
more selective in their choice of issues, accentuating yield spreads (*Financial
Times*, November 9, 2005).

On balance, therefore, segmentation of the public debt market has proved
difficult to overcome; and that, in turn, means that the cost of doing business
in euros remains a drag on the currency's attractiveness. Though efficiency
gains in financial markets have been substantial, they clearly are insufficient
on their own to significantly improve the euro's cost-effectiveness relative
to the dollar. Owing to the greater liquidity and convenience of the U.S.
Treasury bill, America's greenback continues to benefit from the advantages
of incumbency.

... Prolonged

None of this will be improved by enlargement. Indeed, the reverse is more
likely to be true. Larger numbers, obviously, will make it even more difficult
to overcome the segmentation of Europe's public debt market. The variety of
securities, procedures, and dealer systems will become even more pronounced.
Likewise, spreads are likely to diverge even more as compared with yields on
the issues of present EMU members. The euro zone will be even further from
creation of a universal instrument comparable to the U.S. Treasury bill.

Indeed, larger numbers could even slow the pace of financial-market integration generally. The main reason is the more primitive level of development
of institutions and regulatory arrangements in accession countries, as compared with EMU's original members. Banking systems, exceptionally, are
relatively advanced due to widespread foreign ownership. In the 1990s, banks
in the Baltic states and East-Central Europe were largely privatized. Most
ended up in foreign hands, bringing immediate benefits in terms of fresh
capital and innovation. Other sectors, however, have lagged behind, especially
markets for equities and derivatives. Regulatory and supervisory systems,
despite efforts at modernization, are still largely deficient in such key
areas as the assessment of credit risk (Schadler *et al.* 2005: 41–42). Weaknesses like these are likely to encourage foot-dragging by new members even
more pronounced than that of existing EMU members, for two reasons.

First is the sheer cost of the adjustments that will be required to knit the
new entrants into the euro zone's nascent capital market. Since they start
from a lower level of development, they will need even more extensive
reforms at both the retail and wholesale levels in order to get up to speed. But
since these are by no means rich economies, governments could prove to be
even more stubborn in their resistance to further market-opening measures.

Second is the higher risk of financial crisis in the accession countries as they move into the euro zone. Most of these economies offer relatively high rates of return on capital, making them attractive targets for investment. Analysts generally expect that with the elimination of exchange risk there will be even greater incentives for capital inflows, which eventually could generate over-heating, asset price bubbles, and unsustainable increases in indebtedness. The risk is concisely summarized by a recent IMF study:

> Rapid credit growth looms on the horizon for each [accession country] ... A critical concern with rapid credit expansion is the risk of banking distress or even a banking crisis ... Adjustment in the aftermath of overheating or asset price bubbles may well be difficult without an exchange-rate instrument to effect needed changes of relative prices.
>
> (Schadler *et al.* 2005: 56, 65–66)

Worries about such vulnerabilities could make governments even less willing to rush into the process of financial integration.

For both reasons, the path to efficiency gains in financial markets could be even more obstructed than in the present EMU. If anything, enlargement will prolong the segmentation of most financial markets in the euro zone, not just the public debt market. Significant reductions in the cost of doing business in euros will long remain beyond Europe's grasp.

Anti-growth bias

A second critical factor inhibiting the internationalization of the euro is a serious anti-growth bias that appears to be built into the institutional struc-ture of EMU. By impacting negatively on yields on euro-denominated assets, this bias directly affects the currency's attractiveness as a long-term invest-ment medium.

When EMU first came into existence, eliminating exchange risk within the European region, a massive shift was predicted in the allocation of global savings as compared with holdings of European assets in the past. Yet as the ECB (2007c) has ruefully noted, international portfolio managers have been slow to move into the euro. Liquid funds have been attracted when there was prospect of short-term appreciation. But underlying investor preferences have barely budged, in good part because of doubts about prospects for longer-term economic growth in the euro zone. In turn, one of the main causes for such doubts seems to lie in the core institutional provisions of EMU govern-ing monetary and fiscal policy, the key determinants of macroeconomic performance. In neither policy domain is priority attached to promoting real output. Rather, in each, the main emphasis is on other considerations that tend to tilt policy toward restraint, imparting a distinct anti-growth bias to the euro zone as a whole. As *The Economist* (April 29, 2006) laments, the euro "has provided currency stability but has done little to promote growth."

Opportunities for future investment returns are therefore more limited than they might be otherwise.

Here too there is reason to believe that enlargement will simply make matters worse. Overall, the economies of the accession countries may be small as compared with older members. Together, the EU's newest members have added no more than 10 percent to the GDP of the economic union as a whole. Nonetheless, the entrance of new members into the euro zone can be expected to tilt monetary and fiscal policy even more toward restraint, further dampening investment returns.

Monetary policy

On the monetary policy side, the European Central Bank, unlike many other monetary authorities, was created with just one policy mandate—to maintain price stability. Moreover, the ECB is formally endowed with absolute independence, largely insulating it from political influence. Legally, the ECB is free to focus exclusively on fighting inflation, even if over time this might be at the cost of stunting real growth. In practice, naturally, the ECB is not wholly insensitive to growth concerns. Nonetheless, the overall orientation of ECB priorities is clear. Summarizes Hannes Androsch (2007: 48), formerly finance minister of Austria: "The ECB is obliged to focus on fighting inflation, not promoting general economic development, and they are overdoing it. ... We are not fully using the growth potential I think Europe has."

With enlargement, the ECB's restrictive bias may be expected to become even more pronounced owing to an inherent tendency toward higher inflation in the EU's new member economies. All of the accession countries are relatively poor as compared with the older partners. All will be seeking to catch up to the income levels of the more advanced economies by promoting productivity gains in key sectors. Generally, in such situations, productivity gains tend to be more rapid for tradable goods (exports and import-competing production) than for nontradables, since tradables face the most competition and tend to attract the largest share of technology-intensive foreign direct investment. However, as wages in the tradables sectors rise with productivity, they also bid up wages in nontradables production, which in turn forces up the prices of nontradables relative to those of tradables. The result is an increase of aggregate inflation even though tradables prices are held down by competition from abroad—a process known as the Balassa–Samuelson effect (Schadler *et al.* 2005: 5).

The pressures of the Balassa–Samuelson effect are already evident in many of the accession countries, including, most notably, the three Baltic states, all of which have been forced to postpone entry into the euro zone because of high inflation. Only a few, such as the Czech Republic and Lithuania, have come even close to matching the low inflation experience of the euro zone's best performing economies. True, all the new members are making a determined effort to keep prices under control. With luck, most may even be able to compress their inflation rates long enough to meet the first of the Maastricht Treaty's four convergence criteria (relative price stability). Once inside EMU, however, they almost certainly will find it difficult to suppress sustained price increases for long.

Over time, higher inflation in the accession countries could be avoided only by allowing an appreciation of their nominal exchange rate. But once they become part of the euro zone, that option is ruled out *ex hypothesi*. Hence the average inflation rate for the EMU as a whole will be subject to systematic upward pressure, inducing an even more restrictive monetary policy than has prevailed until now. The ECB can be expected to get even tougher in fighting inflation. That in turn will lower even more the prospects for growth of returns on euro-denominated assets.

Fiscal policy

The story is much the same on the fiscal policy side, where euro-zone governments have formally tied their hands with their controversial Stability and Growth Pact (SGP). The SGP, first set up in 1997, was intended to implement the "excessive deficit procedure" called for by the Maastricht Treaty (Article 104c). In effect, it extrapolates from the third of the Treaty's four convergence criteria (fiscal stability) to the period after countries join the euro zone. The key provision is a strict cap on national budget deficits at 3 percent of GDP. The tight restraint makes it difficult for elected officials to use budgetary policy for countercyclical purposes, to offset the anti-growth bias of monetary policy.

Here also, we know, practice has increasingly diverged from principle, with a number of EMU's present members—including, most notably, France and Germany—repeatedly missing the SGP's 3 percent target. We also know that little has been accomplished to make the Pact more effective, apart from some limited reforms in 2005. To some, these facts mean that the SGP has no "bite." Empirical evidence, however, suggests that for most of EMU's smaller members the Pact has in fact exercised a significant discipline (Annett 2006). Moreover, can anyone doubt that deficits might be even larger yet in the absence of the SGP? Historically, many EMU governments routinely ran deficits in excess of 3 percent; most had to struggle to qualify for membership in the first place. De facto, therefore, if not *de jure*, the SGP straitjacket remains a constraint on euro-zone countries, perpetuating an anti-growth bias in fiscal policy, too. And here also the restrictive impact is likely to become even more pronounced as EMU grows in size.

The reason is simple. EU membership imposes a heavy burden on government budgets. Once they join the club, new members must begin contributing to the central EU budget. They must also conform to all of the requirements of EU legislation, the *acquis communautaire*, which will compel them to increase spending on such vital needs as infrastructure, social services, and environmental quality. Though most will find some of the pressure alleviated by financial assistance from EU institutions, net benefits will be limited by cofinancing requirements. Overall, therefore, there is no doubt that fiscal policy in the accession countries will be severely tested. Membership could raise budget deficits by amounts as large as 3 or 4 percent of GDP unless offset by higher taxes or parallel expenditure cuts (Kenen and Meade 2003: 5–7)

Accordingly, most new members can be expected to be persistently pre-occupied with deficit reduction, leaving little leeway for the use of budgetary policy to counterbalance a restrictive monetary policy. Apart from the first three accession countries that were admitted to the euro zone (Cyprus, Malta, and Slovenia), only the Baltic states today seem able to live comfortably under the SGP's 3 percent cap. Elsewhere, substantial deficit problems are the rule, particularly in the largest accession countries. Almost certainly, austerity measures will be called for that could have the effect of retarding real growth.

The net impact will be considerable. It may be an exaggeration to claim, as has the president of the Czech Republic, that the rigidities of the SGP will create weak and dependent "transfer economies" like East Germany after reunification (Klaus 2004: 176). The outlook need not be that dismal. But for many of the accession countries, budget constraints clearly will be tight. It does not seem unreasonable, therefore, to expect that for entering countries budgetary policy will on balance be tilted even more toward restraint. Overall, the extra fiscal pressures will add substantially to EMU's anti-growth bias, again lowering prospects for improvement of returns on euro-denominated assets.

Governance

Finally, there is the governance structure of EMU, which for the euro's prospects as an international currency may be the biggest obstacle of all. The basic question is: Who is in charge? The answer, regrettably, has never been easy. From the start, uncertainty has reigned concerning the delegation of monetary authority among governments and EU institutions. In principle, the distribution of responsibilities is clear. In practice, however, the Maastricht Treaty—being the product of a complex political negotiation—naturally embodies a variety of artful compromises and deliberate obfuscations, resulting in a strikingly high degree of ambiguity about just how the euro zone is actually to be managed. Jurisdictional lines are anything but transparent; the details of accountability are equivocal and obscure. None of this is apt to cultivate an easy confidence in the euro. Indeed, market actors outside EMU may be excused for hesitating to commit themselves to what looks rather like a pig in a poke—even if transactions costs could be lowered to competitive levels and even if returns on European assets could be significantly improved.

Three key provisions may be cited. First is the governance of EMU's core institution, the European Central Bank. Second is the delegation of responsibility for ensuring financial stability across the euro zone as a whole. And third is the issue of external representation: Who speaks for the euro on the broader world stage?

The European Central Bank

Practical operational control of monetary policy lies in the hands of the ECB's Executive Board, made up of the president, vice-president, and four other members. Overall managerial authority, however, is formally lodged in the Governing Council, which in addition to the six-member Executive Board include the heads of the central banks of all participating states, each with the same voting rights. From the start, it was understood that the large size and mixed representation of the Governing Council might be inconsistent with efficient or transparent governance.

The issue was obvious. Even before enlargement, the Governing Council—with the six Executive Board members and twelve national governors—was already bigger than the top managerial unit in any other central bank in the world. Observers were quick to question how decisions would be made with so many bodies around the table. Discussions would undoubtedly be time consuming and complicated. In the words of one informed observer (Meade 2003: 129): "The mere thought of a *tour-de-table* is exhausting." Organization theory teaches that the costs of preparing and making policy rise not just in proportion but exponentially with the number of people involved. Hence the conventional advice is to keep executive units small in order to maximize decision-making efficiency. The prescribed size of the Governing Council was almost certainly too great for serious and productive dialogue. The ECB had a "numbers problem."

Sooner or later, it seemed, real power would have to devolve to a smaller "inner" group formally or informally charged with resolving differences on critical issues, as so often happens in large organizations. But who would be included in this exclusive club? Would it be the Executive Board, which might be expected to take a broad approach to the euro zone's needs and interests? Or would it be a select coterie of central-bank governors, whose views could turn out to be more parochial? No one could be sure.

Enlargement simply makes the numbers problem worse. Upon joining the EU, all ten accession countries immediately gained observer status on the Governing Council, with voting rights to follow once they adopt the euro. Now that Bulgaria and Romania have become EU members, that puts the number at thirty, with even more governors to be added down the road as other candidate governments successfully negotiate their way into the club (or if Britain, Denmark, or Sweden ever decide to join). A gaggle of three dozen or more strong-willed individuals could hardly be considered conducive to efficient decision-making. As one source (Baldwin 2001) commented sarcastically, enlargement would leave the Governing Council with "too many to decide on where to go to dinner, let alone agree on how to run monetary policy for more than 400 million people." Of particular concern, once EMU was up and running, was the risk that equal voting rights for all Council members would give excessive weight to smaller countries in setting policy parameters (Berger *et al.* 2004; de Grauwe 2004; de Haan *et al.* 2004).

To their credit, Europe's leaders recognized the problem early on and sought to provide a remedy. In March 2003, following a proposal from the ECB, the European Council (comprising the heads of state or government of all EU members) approved a reform of the Governing Council restricting votes to a smaller total on a rotating basis (European Central Bank 2003a). Membership of the Governing Council will continue to include the Executive Board and all national central-bank governors; moreover, all six members of the Executive Board will retain their individual votes. But voting rights of national governors are now to be limited to no more than fifteen and will rotate among governors according to a specified formula, taking explicit account of the diversity among member states. The rotation was to start in 2008, once total membership of the zone was brought up to fifteen with the addition of Cyprus and Malta, and will be implemented in two stages, as follows:

1　With participation of between fifteen and twenty-two member states, euro-zone countries will be divided into two groups, using size as a criterion. Size will be measured by a weighted average of an economy's share in total EU GDP and total assets of monetary financial institutions. A first group of governors originating from the five largest states will receive four votes. The second group of up to seventeen governors will receive up to eleven votes.
2　Once participation on the Governing Council moves beyond twenty-two member states, a third group of up to five governors from the smallest countries will be formed, with up to three votes. Correspondingly, the number of voting rights of the middle group will be reduced from eleven to eight. The four votes of the five biggest countries will remain unchanged.

The remedy, however, may be worse than the disease, creating more problems than it solves. On the one hand, the reform leaves intact the large number of bodies at the table. Every national governor, as well as the six Executive Board members, will continue to participate in all policy discussions, with full speaking rights. The approach has been defended on the grounds that it is vital to promoting the legitimacy of the euro enterprise. No other EU institution denies representation to any member state. In addition, it is argued, full participation may be expected to facilitate consensus building and contribute to a better flow of information (Cukierman 2004: 70). But the approach may also be criticized for perpetuating all the gross inefficiencies of the ECB's numbers problem. As one astute observer (Gros 2003: 124) puts it, the Governing Council will remain "more like a mini-parliament than a decision-making body."

On the other hand, the reform introduces several new ambiguities that add even more uncertainty to decision-making at the ECB. How, for instance, will votes rotate within each of the two (eventually three) groups? Will the rules for rotation be the same in all groups? How often will the membership of groups be adjusted as economies change in size? And could the formula for measuring size itself be changed at any time? Transparency is hardly served by such a complex arrangement.

Worse, the reform may well deepen rifts within the Governing Council, since the rotation model is so unabashedly state-based. Votes are allocated strictly along lines of national identity. In principle, governors are supposed to be fully independent professionals operating in a personal capacity, making monetary policy objectively for the euro zone as a whole. In practice, they may now be forgiven for thinking first of their own countries rather than in terms of collective interests. In the words of a prominent German economist (Belke 2003: 122): "The reform proposal does not meet the rationale of an integrative monetary policy. ... It re-nationalizes European monetary policy." The current president of the ECB, Jean-Claude Trichet, has already more than once been forced to reprimand individual governors for publicly opposing established policies that seemed inconsistent with the needs of their home economies (*New York Times*, February 3, 2006).

Of course, the danger can be exaggerated. In the Federal Reserve's key decision-making body, the Federal Open Market Committee (FOMC), participation of district-bank presidents is also based on a rotation model that allocates voting rights along geographic lines. Yet few observers worry that individual FOMC members will promote the interests of their regions at the expense of national objectives. The difference, however, is that Federal Reserve districts have nothing like the same sense of identity as do the sovereign states that comprise EMU. National allegiance remains a potent force in Europe that could, consciously or unconsciously, have a major influence on the deliberations of the Governing Council.

The danger would not be so serious if all EMU economies were largely convergent in real terms. The reality, however, is just the reverse. Econometric analysis shows little correlation of output shocks between accession countries, on the one hand, and the older members of the euro zone, on the other (Berger *et al.* 2004; Hall and Hondroyiannis 2006; Pramor and Tamirisa 2006). Except for Slovenia and, to a lesser extent, Cyprus, synchronization of business-cycle activity between the two groups appears actually to have weakened since the euro was born. National policy preferences, therefore, appear likely to diverge sharply as well.

The shame is that an alternative model was at hand that might have avoided many of these problems. Reacting to the ECB's initial proposal, the European Parliament recommended a radically different approach based on a redistribution of authority between the Executive Board and Governing Council. A broader range of practical powers over interest rates and intermediate policy objectives would be delegated to the Executive Board, converting it into a full-fledged monetary committee. Responsibilities of the Governing Council, by contrast, would be limited to questions of general strategy and guidelines for the monetary regime. The Governing Council, which presently meets twice a month, would instead convene no more than once or twice a year.

With this alternative, no changes would have been required in either the size or the voting rules of the Governing Council. Lines of accountability, however, would have been far clearer. In its operations, the Executive Board would have been directly answerable to the Governing Council; the Governing Council, in turn, would have stood as the institutional embodiment of European monetary sovereignty. But member states, clearly, were reluctant to give up direct representation in the decision-making process. Hence the European Council never even seriously considered the Parliament's alternative model. Instead, the unwieldy proposal of the ECB was swiftly approved and ratified, storing up the risk of serious problems in the future.

Financial stability

Serious problems could also arise from EMU's provisions for maintenance of financial stability. No monetary regime is invulnerable to the risk of occasional crisis. At any time, asset prices could become excessively volatile, adversely affecting real economic conditions; or there might be a spreading contagion of illiquidity or insolvency among monetary institutions. Financial systems are inherently fragile. Unfortunately, the prevailing rules of the euro zone are not at all clear about who, ultimately, is responsible either for crisis prevention or for the management of crises should they occur. Transparency is not served in these circumstances, either.

According to the Maastricht Treaty, the European Central Bank is expected to "contribute to the smooth conduct of policies pursued by the competent authorities relating to the prudential supervision of credit institutions and the stability of the financial system" (Article 105.5). But no specific tasks are assigned to the ECB to help forestall crisis, and none may be assumed by the ECB unless expressly delegated by the Council of Ministers (Article 105.6). Though linkages have grown among national financial markets since the euro's birth, the ruling principle remains decentralization, otherwise known as subsidiarity—the notion that the lowest level of government that can efficiently carry out a function should do so. Formal authority for prudential supervision and regulation continues to reside at the national level, as it did before EMU. Each central bank is charged with responsibility for the financial institutions based within its own national borders.

Nor does the ECB have specific powers to deal with any crises that might occur. General language in the Maastricht Treaty does appear to empower the Bank to backstop TARGET, the large intra-European clearing system, in the event of a payments gridlock or other difficulties. One of the basic tasks of the ECB, declares the Treaty, shall be "to promote the smooth operation of payment systems" (Article 105.2). But for any other contingency, such as a sudden wave of illiquidity in the banking sector, the Treaty is as uncommunicative as the Oracle of Delphi. Nothing is said about any authority for the ECB to act as a lender of last resort. Economist Garry Schinasi (2003: 3) says that this silence makes the ECB the "ultimate 'narrow' central bank." The ECB has a mandate for price stability but not for financial stability.

The Treaty's silence has been a source of much debate. Some specialists interpret it as a form of "constructive ambiguity"—an indication that, in practice, the ECB's crisis-management powers could be enhanced if and when needed. As one legal commentator puts it: "The wording of the subsidiarity principle leaves the door open for a possible Community competence" (Lastra 2003: 57). But others disagree, arguing that because the responsibility has not been specifically transferred, it must remain at the national level. The Treaty's language is seen as restrictive rather than permissive.

In practice decentralization rules here, too. As in pre-EMU Europe, the lender-of-last-resort function is left to the individual central banks. And again, each central bank remains responsible only for financial institutions within its own national borders. Beyond that, all is opaque. No one, it appears, is directly accountable for the stability of the euro zone as a whole.

Can such a decentralized arrangement be counted on to assure smooth operation of the overall system? There is certainly room for doubt. What would happen, for instance, if in a given country a large financial institution with extensive cross-border business were to find itself in trouble? Would the national authorities be evenhanded in their response, fully recognizing the interests of claimants elsewhere in the euro zone? Or would they act protectively, even at the risk of conflict with the regulatory authorities of partner countries? We have no way of knowing. The scheme "may work well," observes Schinasi (2005: 119–20), "but this still remains to be seen. ... It is [not] obvious that national supervision in Europe would tend, as a first priority, to focus on European priorities. ... It is difficult to imagine the national supervisor pursuing European interests first and national interests second." Echoes the IMF in a recent review of euro-zone policies:

> Progress on the ground is being held back by the governance framework. The core problem is the tension between the impulse toward integration, on the one hand, and the preference for a decentralized approach, on the other. ... This setting rules out efficient and effective crisis management and resolution.
>
> (International Monetary Fund 2007a: para. 12)

In short, the possibility that central banks might work at cross-purposes, provoking or aggravating a crisis, is certainly not outside the realm of possibility. There is no Invisible Hand for public agencies. Decentralized decision-making among governments without some form of coordination is potentially a recipe for disaster.

Here, too, enlargement just makes the situation worse, for two reasons. First, once again, is the numbers problem. If uncoordinated decision-making is risky with fifteen central banks in the game, how much more vulnerable would be an EMU of double that number? Recall organization theory's suggestion that, with expansion, decision-making problems increase not just proportionally but exponentially. This does not mean that as the euro zone grows, financial instability becomes unavoidable. There is no certainty about such matters. But it does mean that with each new member the probability of some kind of crisis keeps rising.

Second, compounding the numbers problem is the relative poverty of the accession countries as compared with the present membership of EMU. On the one hand, this means that their supervisory institutions, on average, are apt to be more rudimentary—less practiced at the essential tasks of monitoring markets and assessing risk. On the other hand, it means that in their eagerness to catch up with the EU's more advanced economies they are apt to do all they can to promote lending for productive investment. The combination is deadly. The result, as previously noted, could be an excessively rapid expansion of credit, testing the limits of financial prudence and risking overheating and asset-price bubbles. The ice under the feet of the euro zone will grow increasingly thin.

External representation

Finally, there is the issue of external representation. Who is to speak for the euro zone on broader macroeconomic issues such as policy coordination, crisis management, or reform of the international financial architecture? Here there is no answer at all, leaving a vacuum at the heart of EMU.

No single body is designated to represent EMU at the IMF or in other global forums. Instead, the Maastricht Treaty simply laid down a procedure for resolving the issue at a later date, presumably on a case-by-case basis (Article 109). Some sources excuse this on the grounds that it achieved a balance between the need to convey a common position and the prerogatives of member states. But that seems far too kind. In fact, it was a cop-out, a diplomatic formula to mask failure to reach agreement.

At a minimum, the text compounds confusion about who is in charge. At worst, it condemns the euro zone to lasting second-class status, since it limits the group's ability to project power on monetary matters. As booster Fred Bergsten laments:

> Europe still speaks with a multiplicity, even a cacophony, of voices. … Organizational reforms that enable the countries making up Euroland to act together and speak with a single voice will probably be an essential prerequisite of full European equivalence with the United States.

> (Bergsten 2005: 33)

The point has been best put by political scientists Kathleen McNamara and Sophie Meunier (2002: 850): "As long as no 'single voice' has the political authority to speak on behalf of the euro area, as the U.S. Secretary of the Treasury does for the American currency, the pre-eminence of the United States in international monetary matters, as in other realms, is likely to remain unchallenged." Washington has no single phone number to call when negotiations are required.

Clearly, the phone number cannot be in Frankfurt, where the European Central Bank is headquartered. In international monetary forums, countries are normally represented not by central banks but by finance ministers or equivalent—public officials with the political clout to speak for their respective governments. The ECB obviously cannot claim that kind of authority. Indeed, it is difficult to imagine the elected governments of Europe ever delegating such a fundamental power to an institution that has been deliberately designed to be as free from political influence as possible.

Alternatively, some have suggested the appointment of a single individual with sufficient credentials and legitimacy to act as interlocutor for the euro zone (Henning 1997; McNamara and Meunier 2002; Zimmermann 2004)—a Mr. (or Ms.) Euro, as it were. Precedent exists in the realm of foreign and security affairs, where EU members already agreed a decade ago to name a single high representative to stand for them all—a Mr. Europe (presently Javier Solana of Spain). But experience has shown that Mr. Europe's ability to speak authoritatively for the entire EU is persistently hamstrung by policy differences among individual governments. A single appointed official cannot ignore or overrule the preferences of diverse sovereign states.

The most practical solution would be a collective one, centered on the informal committee of EMU finance ministers that has emerged since the birth of the euro—what has come to be known as the Eurogroup. Like comparable EU institutions, such as the Council of Ministers or European Council, the Eurogroup could be represented at any given time by its chair; the chairmanship itself, as with those other institutions, rotates periodically among members. In 2005 the Eurogroup chair began attending meetings of the Group of Seven, but with no specified responsibilities. A more effective approach might be to explicitly delegate authority to the chair to speak on behalf of the euro zone.

Some criticize the idea, fearing that it could lead to a politicization of monetary policy in the euro zone and might even compromise the independence of the ECB. But such apprehensions seem overblown. Participation in international forums by America's treasury secretary, for instance, has by no means compromised the independence of the Federal Reserve. In fact, this kind of division of labor between central bank and finance ministries is the rule around the world, not the exception. For EMU, the advantage of the Eurogroup is that it does embody the necessary degree of political authority. At last, there would be not only a single number to call but also someone empowered to pick up the phone.

So what is stopping EMU? Romano Prodi (2004: 14), a former Commission president (and more recently prime minister of Italy) says that it is "a lack of will." But that is surely an oversimplification. The question is: Why is there a lack of will? The answer, plainly, has to do with the lingering influence of national allegiance. Though EMU members may share a joint money, their interests are hardly identical. Divergent circumstances and preferences make them reluctant to give up the right to speak for themselves. Even after more than half a decade of living with the euro, national identity trumps collective interest.

Once again, enlargement just makes the situation worse. Adding the accession countries will not only amplify the numbers problem, complicating decision-making. Entrance of such a diverse group of relatively poor economies will also multiply and deepen internal cleavages, making it increasingly difficult to hammer out common positions on external issues. The fundamental rationale for developing a single voice for EMU, McNamara and Meunier (2002: 851) remind us, "lies in the potential ... to project the image of a unified, strong Europe to key international political and financial actors." Enlargement will leave the Europeans further from that goal than ever.

Conclusion

The bottom line, therefore, seems clear. Bigger will not be better, despite the broader economic base and the increased potential for network externalities that come with enlargement. On the contrary, bringing accession countries into EMU will only exacerbate the impact of factors impeding the euro's emergence as an international currency. By prolonging the segmentation of Europe's financial markets, larger numbers will delay any significant reduction of the cost of doing business in euros. By adding to inflationary and budgetary pressures, enlargement will reinforce the anti-growth bias built into the institutional structure of EMU. And by further complicating an already complex governance structure, the new entrants will cloud even more the fundamental question of who is in charge. None of this is calculated to make the euro more attractive to outside users.

Could the risks be even worse? Could EMU founder under the weight of enlargement? Though unlikely, the possibility cannot be lightly dismissed. The euro zone's problems, writes the respected economist Anna Schwartz (2004: 25), "will only worsen with the inclusion of new members. Is this a recipe for political disintegration? Would the euro survive political disintegration?" Others warn of "EMU's coming stress test" (Gros *et al.* 2005), which could lead to unilateral secessions. Italy is considered a prime candidate, owing to its deteriorating public finances, sluggish growth, and eroding competitiveness. In 2005 several prominent Italian legislators publicly called for reintroduction of the lira; one, a government minister, even tried to collect enough signatures for a referendum on the matter. They are unlikely to be the last European politicians to use the euro as a scapegoat for disappointing economic performance.

Given Europe's historical commitment to the integration process, however, breakdown seems improbable. EMU will not be allowed to fail. As *The Economist* (June 11, 2005) writes: "A break-up of the euro area is still in the realm of small probability rather than likelihood." The real question is whether EMU can succeed. Can the euro ever rise above its defects to become a genuine rival to the dollar? Will the "old dream of enthusiasts," at long last, be realized?

The answer, regrettably, is also in the realm of small probability rather than likelihood. Nothing is impossible, of course—particularly if the United States continues to mismanage its own currency as badly as it has in recent years. America's payments deficit widened to over $800 billion in 2006 (more than 7 percent of GDP) and could soon top a trillion dollars. The more the U.S. deficit grows, threatening a crisis for the greenback, the more attractive the euro could begin to appear, whatever its defects. But that is hardly a case of leading from strength. The analysis offered here focuses on the case for the euro on its own merits, independent of what might happen to the dollar. That case, I conclude, is weak at best and likely to be made weaker by enlargement.

The fundamental problem for EMU is the mismatch between the domain of its currency and the jurisdictions of its member governments. The euro is a currency without a country—the product of an international agreement, not the expression of a single sovereign power. Its success, therefore, is critically dependent on the continued cooperation of EMU's member states, which can hardly be guaranteed for all time. Should it be any wonder, then, that outsiders might hesitate to commit themselves to the currency's future?

Monetary unions among sovereign states have existed before, of course, without major disruption. In the contemporary era one thinks of the East Caribbean Currency Area or the CFA franc zone in Africa. But these have all involved relatively small developing countries with no aspiration to major currency status. EMU, by contrast, encompasses some of the largest economies on the face of the earth and has never hidden its grand global ambitions. Unfortunately, Europe's divisions have never been hidden, either. For that reason, prospects for the euro's international role were poor even before enlargement. Enlargement of the euro zone's membership will simply make them even poorer.

6 The euro in a global context
Challenges and capacities

The birth of the euro in 1999 was expected to create a new power in international monetary relations. Even without the participation of Britain and some other European Union (EU) members, the euro area would constitute one of the largest economic units in the world, rivaling even the United States in terms of output and share of foreign trade. Consequences for the geopolitics of finance promised to be momentous. Europe's Economic and Monetary Union (EMU) would become a major player on the monetary stage. Europe's new money, building on the widespread popularity of Germany's old Deutschmark (DM), would pose a serious threat to the predominance of America's greenback as an international currency.

A decade later, how have matters turned out? The purpose of this essay is to evaluate the experience of the euro area to date in a broad global context. The central question is: How has the creation of the euro affected the power of participating states to cope with external challenges?

International monetary power, as I have suggested elsewhere (Cohen 2006b), may be understood to have two dimensions, internal and external. The internal dimension has to do with the ability to exercise policy independence—to act freely, insulated from outside pressure. A useful synonym for this meaning of power is autonomy. The external dimension has to do with the ability to shape the actions of others—to exercise leverage or enforce compliance. A common synonym for this meaning of power is influence. Challenges for the euro area encompass both dimensions.

With regard to the dimension of autonomy, two key issues are involved. One is the global macroeconomic environment, including especially the evolution of exchange rates and regional payments imbalances. Though Europe itself has remained relatively close to payments equilibrium in relation to the rest of the world, EMU cannot help but be affected by any stresses created by broader global imbalances or the risk of contagious debt defaults. How well equipped is the euro area to deal with any threat of financial instability? The other issue is the potential competition with the greenback for use as an international currency. Perhaps the greatest benefit of an international currency is the ability to finance external deficits with one's own money, thus enhancing internal policy flexibility (Cohen 2004). Can the euro compete

effectively with America's dollar in global markets? With regard to the dimension of influence, the key issue has to do with institutional participation. Does membership in the euro area enable EU governments to play a more authoritative role in the International Monetary Fund (IMF) or other financial forums?

Overall, this essay concludes, EMU has failed to live up to expectations. Though exposure to exchange-rate disturbances has obviously been reduced inside Europe, member states remain vulnerable to fluctuations of the euro's exchange rate vis-à-vis outside currencies. The euro area is largely a passive participant in global payments developments and, if anything, has become even more exposed to threats of financial instability. Likewise, the euro has failed to mount a significant challenge to the dollar and the bloc continues to punch below its weight in monetary diplomacy. The fundamental problem lies in the mismatch between the domain of EMU and the jurisdictions of its member governments. The euro is a currency without a country—the product of an interstate agreement, not the expression of a single sovereign power. Hence EMU's power to cope with external challenges is structurally constrained. It is difficult to become a major player when speaking with many voices.

Financial stability

In one key respect, EMU has clearly enhanced the autonomy of its members. With a single joint money replacing a plethora of national currencies, participants no longer have to fear the risk of exchange-rate disturbances inside Europe. For a continent long plagued by currency instability, that is no small accomplishment. But in other respects vulnerability remains considerable, particularly in relation to the world outside Europe. The euro area is largely a passive participant in global payment developments, leaving members critically exposed to fluctuations of the euro's exchange rate vis-à-vis the U.S. dollar and other major currencies. Moreover, even though European states could hardly expect to be unaffected should a crisis hit the broader financial system, the euro area remains remarkably unprepared to cope with any major disruption in banking or credit markets.

A bystander

To date, the euro area has been something of a bystander in global monetary affairs, more reactive than active. For the newly created European Central Bank (ECB), the highest priority was to establish its own anti-inflationary credentials, consistent with its narrowly drawn mandate under the Maastricht Treaty, EMU's founding document. Policy was targeted almost exclusively at the domestic price level. The balance of payments and exchange rate were left largely to their own devices.

As measured by the current account (the balance on trade in goods and services plus unilateral transfers), EMU's external position has been very near balance throughout the period since 1999, varying from mild deficits in 1991–2001 to small surpluses in most succeeding years. Imbalances in either direction have never exceeded 1 percent of the euro area's gross domestic product (GDP) and in most years have amounted to a mere fraction of 1 percent, adding little to global disequilibrium.

Variations in the euro exchange rate have been greater but have largely reflected the fluctuating fortunes of the U.S. dollar. Born at a time of substantial dollar strength, Europe's fledgling currency first depreciated sharply, dropping from an initial value just above $1.18 to a low near $0.82 in October 2000, before settling around 90 cents for the remainder of 2000 and 2001. Then, when a weakening trend began to afflict the greenback, the euro came roaring back, passing $1.00 in mid-2002 and peaking in late 2004 at above $1.36. In 2005, the euro again declined modestly as U.S. interest rates rose, languishing around $1.20 until mid-2006. In the latter half of 2006, a new ascent began, surpassing $1.35 by mid-2007. Rates in relation to other major currencies have largely mirrored the euro's movements in relation to the greenback. Overall, the trade-weighted ("effective") exchange rate of the euro has differed little from its bilateral dollar rate (Zestos 2006: ch. 5).

An appreciation of some 40–60 percent from the euro's lows in 2000–01 was a source of some satisfaction to the ECB, which had been worried about the effect of the currency's initial depreciation on the credibility of Europe's grand monetary experiment. "I welcome the recent appreciation of the euro," declared the Bank's first president, Wim Duisenberg (quoted in the New York Times, January 10, 2003). Many Europeans experienced a surge of pride when their new currency left the greenback in its wake. But there was also an obvious downside—the dampening effect that a more expensive euro might have on economic growth. In the words of one commentary: "A stronger euro may give Europeans bragging rights, but it has also hobbled their exports" (Landler 2004). By one common rule of thumb, a 5 percent rise in the euro's trade-weighted exchange rate would be expected to have the same negative impact on growth as an increase of 1 percent in interest rates (Economist, May 10, 2003). Predictably, appreciation brought an anguished chorus of complaints from European exporters. Jean-Claude Trichet, the ECB's second president, called the rise "brutal."

Particularly distressing to many Europeans was the knowledge that the appreciation had more to do with dollar weakness than with euro strength. Confidence in the greenback, already undermined by America's persistent payments deficits, had been shaken by the Wall Street slump and consequent recession of 2001–02, as well as by war fears prior to the invasion of Iraq in 2003. Later came the bursting of America's real-estate bubble and the subprime mortgage crisis in 2007. And compounding it all was a distinct change of tone by the U.S. government, especially once John Snow took over as treasury secretary two years into the administration of George W. Bush. Gone was the "strong dollar" rhetoric of the previous Clinton administration. Instead, Snow now spoke of the benefits of a "modest realignment of currencies," suggesting that some depreciation of the greenback would not be at all unwelcome in Washington as a means to improve U.S. trade competitiveness. In effect, America seemed to be "talking the dollar down" at Europe's expense, rankling many Europeans. Declared the chief economist of Germany's Deutsche Bank: "The U.S. has always had the philosophy, 'the dollar is our currency, and your problem.' We have to come to grips with that" (quoted in the *New York Times*, May 25, 2003).

But Europe could not come to grips with that. Except for one brief episode in the fall of 2000, the ECB has studiously avoided any manner of direct intervention in the foreign-exchange market. Partly, this is because the anti-inflationary impact of a rising currency is welcome to the Bank's management. But mainly it reflects an understanding that any attempt to reverse the rise abroad, via sales of newly issued euros, would simply undermine the battle against inflation at home. In practice, the euro area can do little but remain passive witness to its currency's appreciation.

As a group, therefore, members remain critically exposed to damaging fluctuations in the euro's exchange rate—though, individually, effects are likely to vary considerably. For the bigger participants, such as Germany and France, the negative consequences of a prolonged appreciation are regrettable but manageable. For some smaller members, by contrast, impacts could be much more painful, possibly more than offsetting the evident benefits of the new currency stability within Europe. Countries like Finland or Ireland, with their more open economies and greater dependence on trade outside the euro area, appear to be at particular risk.

Coping with instability

Worse, European states seem remarkably unprepared to cope with any wider instability that might erupt in international finance. The euro area's prevailing rules are not at all clear about who, ultimately, is responsible for management of a monetary crisis, should one occur.

Two central issues have dominated the global macroeconomic environment over the last decade. One is the huge gap in America's balance of payments, matched by corresponding surpluses in East Asia and among energy-exporting nations. The world has never seen such a massive monetary disequilibrium. The other is the continuing vulnerability of emerging or transition economies to the kind of financial disruptions that struck Asia in 1997–98 or Argentina in 2001. Though market conditions have been relatively benign in more recent years, the risk of instability remains an ever-present threat. At any moment, global imbalances or a debt default could explode into a full-fledged crisis, destabilizing asset prices and possibly spreading illiquidity or insolvency among financial institutions. EMU, however, does not seem well equipped to maintain stability in the event of such rude shocks.

According to the Maastricht Treaty, the ECB has no specific powers to deal with any disruptions that might occur. Financial integration among EMU members has bourgeoned since the euro's birth; as a result, the risk of contagion within the bloc, should troubles hit, has clearly grown. In the words of the European Central Bank (2007b: 74): EMU has "led to broader and deeper systemic inter-linkages between Member States, increasing the likelihood of potential financial market disturbances in one Member State spreading across borders." Yet the ruling principle of the euro area remains decentralization, otherwise known as subsidiarity—the notion that the lowest level of government that can efficiently carry out a function should do so. Formal authority for crisis management continues to reside at the national level, as it did before EMU. Each central bank is charged with responsibility for the financial institutions and markets based within its own borders.

There is only one exception. General language in the Maastricht Treaty does appear to empower the ECB to backstop TARGET, the large intra-European clearing system, in the event of a payments gridlock or other difficulties. One of the basic tasks of the ECB (Article 105: 2), declares the Treaty, shall be "to promote the smooth operation of payment systems." But for any other contingency, such as a sudden wave of illiquidity in the banking sector, the Treaty is as uncommunicative as the Oracle of Delphi. Nothing is said about any authority for the ECB to act as a lender of last resort. Economist Garry Schinasi (2003: 3) says that this silence makes the ECB the "ultimate 'narrow' central bank." The ECB has a mandate for price stability but not for financial stability.

The Treaty's silence in this regard has been a source of much debate. Some specialists interpret it as a form of "constructive ambiguity"—an indication that, in practice, the ECB's crisis-management powers could be enhanced if and when needed. As one legal commentator puts it: "The wording of the subsidiarity principle leaves the door open for a possible Community competence" (Lastra 2003: 57). But others disagree, arguing that, because the responsibility has not been specifically delegated, it must remain at the national level. The Treaty's language is seen as restrictive rather than permissive. In practice, as in pre-EMU Europe, the lender-of-last-resort function has been left to the individual central banks. In September 2007, EU officials again declined to fix rules in advance on how to bail out banks that have cross-border operations within the union. No one, it appears, is directly accountable for the stability of the euro area as a whole.

Can such a decentralized arrangement be counted on to ensure smooth operation of the overall system? The European Central Bank (2007b: 84) remains optimistic, emphasizing the extent to which member states, by a variety of measures, have sought to provide "a comprehensive, multi-layered and flexible framework ... with the potential to adapt to the specific challenges that a crisis situation may pose." But there is certainly room for doubt.

What would happen, for instance, if in a given country a large financial institution with extensive cross-border business were to find itself in trouble? Would the national authorities be evenhanded in their response, fully recognizing the interests of claimants elsewhere in the euro area? Or would they act protectively, even at the risk of conflict with the regulatory authorities of partner countries? We have no way of knowing. The scheme "may work well," observes Schinasi (2005: 119–20), "but this still remains to be seen. ... It is [not] obvious that national supervision in Europe would tend, as a first priority, to focus on European priorities. ... It is difficult to imagine the national supervisor pursuing European interests first and national interests second." The International Monetary Fund echoes this concern in a recent review of euro area policies:

> Progress on the ground is being held back by the governance framework. The core problem is the tension between the impulse toward integration, on the one hand, and the preference for a decentralized approach, on the other. ... This setting rules out efficient and effective crisis management and resolution.
>
> (International Monetary Fund 2007a: para. 12)

In short, the possibility that central banks might work at cross-purposes, aggravating a crisis, is certainly not outside the realm of possibility. There is no Invisible Hand for public agencies. Decentralized decision-making among sovereign governments without some form of coordination is potentially a recipe for disaster.

Competition with the U.S. dollar

At the time of EMU's birth, many predicted a bright future for the euro as an international currency. Though the dollar had long reigned supreme in monetary affairs, Europe's new currency was expected to quickly assert itself as a major competitor. If the euro area could be the equal of the United States in output and trade, why should it not be America's equal in monetary matters, too? Typical was the view of Robert Mundell (2000: 57), a Nobel laureate in economics, who expressed no doubt that the euro "will challenge the status of the dollar and alter the power configuration of the system." In the oft-quoted words of Jacques Delors, when he was president of the European Commission, "le petit euro deviendra grand."

In reality, however, Europe's little euro has not become big—and for good reason. The currency clearly did start with many of the attributes necessary for competitive success, including a large economic base, unquestioned political stability, and an enviably low rate of inflation, all backed by a joint monetary authority, the ECB, that was fully committed to preserving confidence in the money's future value. But, as I have argued previously (Cohen 2003), the euro is also hampered by several critical deficiencies, all structural in character, that dull its attractiveness as a rival to the greenback. These include limited cost-effectiveness, a serious anti-growth bias, and, most importantly, ambiguities at the heart of the monetary union's governance structure. Only in the EU's immediate neighborhood, where trade and financial ties are especially close, does the euro enjoy any special advantages. That is EMU's natural hinterland—"the euro's turf," as Charles Wyplosz (1999: 89) calls it. Elsewhere, Europe's money is at a distinct disadvantage.

Cost-effectiveness

The first problem is the cost of doing business in euros. Transaction costs directly affect a currency's attractiveness as a vehicle for exchange transactions or foreign trade. From the start, it was clear that the dollar would continue to be favored unless euro transaction costs, which began high relative to the widely traded greenback, could be lowered to a more competitive level. The same scale economies and network externalities that encourage use of a money such as the dollar in the first place are also responsible for what economists call "hysteresis" or "ratchet" effects. Switching costs can be steep. Hence, international adoption of a new currency like the euro tends to be resisted unless the money can be expected to be truly cost-effective.

Could the euro become sufficiently cost-effective? That, in turn, depended directly on what might be done to improve the structural efficiency of Europe's financial markets. In practical terms, much has indeed been accomplished to knit together previously segmented national markets, particularly in short-term money-market instruments, syndicated bank lending, credit derivatives, and the corporate bond sector. Though numerous obstacles remain—including significant differences in clearing and settlement systems, tax structures, and accounting and business conventions—the EU seems well on its way to creating the largest single-currency capital market in the world. In turn, costs have shrunk considerably as measured by spreads in bond markets or the market for foreign exchange. Costs have not shrunk enough, however, to overcome the greenback's natural advantages of incumbency.

The core problem is evident. The euro is condemned to remain at a disadvantage vis-à-vis the dollar so long as EMU is unable to offer a universal financial instrument that can match the U.S. Treasury bill for international investor liquidity and convenience. This is a deficiency that will be impossible to rectify so long as the euro area, with its separate national governments, lacks a counterpart to the Federal government in Washington. As Ben Bernanke, chair of the Federal Reserve Board of Governors, has observed:

> The European government bond market ... has not attained the liquidity of the US Treasury market (and may never do so). ... The fundamental difference [is] that euro zone debt is the debt of 12 sovereign entities rather than one, as in the United States.
>
> (Bernanke 2005: 187)

The best the Europeans could do was encourage establishment of selected benchmark securities for investors. Gradually, three euro benchmarks have emerged: the German Bund at ten years, the French bond at five years, and the Italian bond at two years. But such a piecemeal approach falls far short of creating a single market as large and liquid as that for U.S. government securities.

Admittedly, yield differentials in the public debt market have shrunk since the euro was born, suggesting that interchangeability among national issues has increased considerably. But the convergence of yields is hardly complete. Investors continue to treat the obligations of EMU governments as imperfect substitutes, mostly owing to differences in perceived default risk. And these differences of perception could eventually be compounded as a result of a decision by the ECB in November 2005 to limit the collateral it will accept in refinancing ("repo") operations with European commercial banks. Previously, the ECB had accepted all euro-area government bonds indiscriminately, as if the debts of EMU member states were all of equal creditworthiness. Now, however, the Bank is more selective. Bonds must have a single A-rating or better from at least one of the three main rating agencies (Moody's, Standard and Poor's, and Fitch). Observers predict that this decision will lead commercial banks, in turn, to be rather more selective in their choice of issues, accentuating yield spreads.

On balance, therefore, segmentation of the public debt market is proving difficult to overcome; and that, in turn, means that the cost of doing business in euros is likely to remain a drag on the currency's appeal for years to come. Though, to date, efficiency gains in financial markets have been substantial, they clearly have not, on their own, been enough to make the euro more cost-effective than the dollar. The greater liquidity and convenience of the U.S. Treasury bill market continues to give an advantage to the greenback.

Anti-growth bias

A second critical factor inhibiting the internationalization of the euro is a serious anti-growth bias that appears to be built into the institutional structure of EMU. By impacting negatively on yields on euro-denominated assets, this bias directly affects the currency's attractiveness as a long-term investment medium.

When EMU first came into existence, eliminating exchange risk within the European region, a massive shift was predicted in the allocation of global savings as compared with holdings of European assets in the past. Yet, as the European Central Bank (2007a) has ruefully noted, international portfolio managers have actually been quite slow to commit to the euro. Liquid funds have been attracted when there was a prospect of short-term appreciation, as in 2002–04. But underlying investor preferences have barely budged, in good part because of doubts about prospects for longer-term economic growth in the euro area. Many factors contribute to these doubts—aging populations, which limit manpower increases and stress old-age pension systems; rigid labor markets, which hinder economic adaptability; and extensive government regulation, which can constrain innovation and entrepreneurship. Europe's monetary union, regrettably, adds yet one more brake on growth.

The core problem here lies in EMU's institutional provisions governing monetary and fiscal policy, two key determinants of macroeconomic performance. In neither policy domain is priority attached to promoting output expansion. Rather, in each, the main emphasis is on other considerations that tend to tilt policy towards restraint, producing a distinct anti-growth bias to the euro area as a whole. As *The Economist* (April 29, 2006) laments, the euro "has provided currency stability but has done little to promote growth." Opportunities for future investment returns thus are even more limited than they might be otherwise.

On the monetary policy side, the ECB, unlike many other monetary authorities, was created with just one policy mandate—to maintain price stability. Moreover, the ECB is formally endowed with absolute independence, largely insulating it from political influence. Legally, the ECB is free to focus exclusively on fighting inflation, even if over time this might be at the cost of stunting growth. In practice, naturally, the ECB is not wholly insensitive to growth concerns. Nonetheless, the overall orientation of ECB priorities is clear. Since EMU's start, the bias of monetary policy has mainly been towards restraint, not expansion. Summarizes Hannes Androsch (2007: 48), formerly finance minister of Austria: "The ECB is obliged to focus on fighting inflation, not promoting general economic development, and they are overdoing it. ... We are not fully using the growth potential I think Europe has."

Similarly, on the fiscal policy side, euro-area governments have formally tied their hands with their controversial Stability and Growth Pact (SGP). The SGP, first set up in 1997, was intended to implement the "excessive deficit procedure" called for by the Maastricht Treaty (Article 104c). The Pact's key provision is a strict cap on national budget deficits at 3 percent of GDP. That tight restraint makes it difficult for elected officials to use budgetary policy for contracyclical purposes, to offset the anti-growth bias of monetary policy.

The Pact is not airtight, of course. In reality, we know, practice has increasingly diverged from principle, with a number of EMU's original members—including, most notably, France and Germany—repeatedly missing the 3 percent target. We also know that little has been accomplished to make the Pact more effective, apart from some limited reforms in 2005. To many, these facts mean that the SGP has no "bite." But empirical evidence clearly demonstrates that overall the Pact has in fact exercised a significant discipline, with an especially strong impact on most of EMU's smaller members (Annett 2006). Moreover, can anyone doubt that in most cases deficits might be even larger in the absence of the SGP? Historically, many EMU governments routinely ran deficits in excess of 3 percent; most had to struggle to qualify for membership in the first place. De facto, if not *de jure*, the SGP straitjacket remains a constraint on euro-area states, perpetuating an anti-growth bias in fiscal policy, too.

Is it any wonder, then, that the anticipated shift of global savings has turned out to be largely illusory? Is it any wonder that many politicians, including France's president Nicolas Sarkozy, have been calling for improvements of EMU's "economic governance?" EMU's built-in tilt towards restraint exacerbates an already serious growth problem in Europe. Dim prospects for returns on euro-denominated assets inevitably discourage use of the currency for investment purposes.

Governance

Finally, there is the governance structure of EMU, which for the euro's prospects as an international currency may be the biggest handicap of all. The basic question is: Who is in charge of monetary policy? From the start, uncertainty has reigned over how decisions are to be made in EMU's core agency, the ECB.

The problem goes back, once again, to the institutional provisions of the Maastricht Treaty. Practical operational control of monetary policy was to lie in the hands of the ECB's Executive Board, made up of the president, vice-president, and four other members. Overall managerial authority, however, was formally lodged in the Governing Council which, in addition to the six-member Executive Board, would include the heads of the central banks of all participating states, each with the same voting rights. Evidently, the drafters of the Treaty were not overly concerned that the large size and mixed representation of the Governing Council might be inconsistent with efficient governance.

The flaw is obvious. Even before the EU's enlargements in 2004 and 2007, the Governing Council—with the six Executive Board members and twelve (now fifteen) national governors—was already significantly larger than the top managerial unit of any other central bank in the world. With the entrance of a dozen new countries into the EU, bringing total membership to twenty-seven, the size of the Council threatened to become utterly unwieldy as the euro area enlarged. Upon joining the EU, all new members immediately gain observer status on the Council, with voting rights to follow once they adopt the euro. Cyprus, Malta, and Slovenia have already made the jump to full participation. The number could thus grow to as many as thirty, with even more governors to be added down the road as other candidate governments successfully negotiate their way into the club (or if Britain, Denmark, or Sweden ever decide to adopt the euro). A gaggle of three dozen or more strong willed individuals could hardly be considered conducive to efficient decision-making. With so many bodies around the table, discussions would undoubtedly be time consuming and complicated. As one source commented sarcastically, enlargement would leave the Council with "too many to decide on where to go to dinner, let alone agree on how to run monetary policy for more than 400 million people" (Baldwin 2001). In short, the ECB had a "numbers problem."

To their credit, Europe's leaders did come soon to recognize the problem and sought to provide a remedy. In March 2003, a reform was approved, restricting votes on the Council to a smaller total on a rotating basis. Membership of the Council will continue to include the Executive Board and all national central-bank governors; moreover, all six members of the Executive Board will retain their individual votes. But voting rights of national governors are now to be limited to no more than fifteen and will rotate among governors according to a specified formula, taking explicit account of the diversity among member states.

The remedy, however, may be worse than the disease. On the one hand, the reform leaves intact the large number of bodies at the table. Every national governor, as well as the six Executive Board members, will continue to participate in all policy discussions, with full speaking rights. The approach has been defended on the grounds that it is vital to promoting the legitimacy of the euro enterprise. No other EU institution denies representation to any member state. In addition, it is argued, full participation may be expected to facilitate consensus building and contribute to a better flow of information. But the approach can also be criticized for perpetuating all the inefficiencies of the ECB's numbers problem. As one astute observer puts it, the Governing Council will remain "more like a mini-parliament than a decision-making body" (Gros 2003: 124).

On the other hand, the reform may well deepen rifts within the Governing Council, since the rotation model is so unabashedly state-based. Votes are allocated strictly along lines of national identity. In principle, governors are supposed to be fully independent professionals operating in a personal capacity, making monetary policy objectively for the euro area as a whole. In practice, however, they may now be forgiven for thinking first of their own countries rather than in terms of collective interests. In the words of a prominent German economist (Belke 2003: 122): "The reform proposal does not meet the rationale of an integrative monetary policy. ... It re-nationalises European monetary policy." The dollar's advantage in this regard is obvious.

A regional destiny

For all these reasons, it should be no surprise that the euro's experience as an international currency to date has been underwhelming, even allowing for the characteristic stickiness of monetary preferences. In most categories of cross-border use, adjusting for the elimination of intra-EMU transactions, the euro has managed roughly to hold its own as compared with the past aggregate shares of EMU's "legacy" currencies. This means that Europe's joint money has smoothly taken its place as successor to Germany's old Deutschmark, which among international currencies had already attained a rank second only to the dollar. But that is about all. After an initial spurt of enthusiasm for the new currency, use in most market segments has leveled off or even declined in recent years. Moreover, since its birth, the euro's only enduring gains have been among neighboring states with strong regional or political ties to the EU—what might be described as EMU's natural hinterland. In the European Central Bank's words (2007c: 7), a "strong institutional and regional pattern continues to characterise the internationalisation of the euro." Beyond the European region, the euro remains very much in the dollar's shadow.

For example, in the foreign-exchange market, according to the European Central Bank (2007c), the euro entered on one side of just 39 percent of all transactions in the period from mid-2005 to end-2006—less than half the dollar's share (93 percent). That was higher than the share of the DM, which had appeared in 30 percent of transactions in 1998 (its last year of existence), but lower than that of all euro's legacy currencies taken together (53 percent) and actually down from a high of 41 percent in the preceding twelve-month period from mid-2004 to mid-2005. Only in the Nordic states and East-Central Europe, where commercial ties are largely concentrated on the EU, is the euro the favored vehicle. Likewise, evidence from the IMF on trade invoicing (Bertuch-Samuels and Ramlogan 2007) suggests that at best the euro has been able to maintain the DM's share of world exports— roughly 15 percent, less than one-third of the dollar's share. It has yet to show any sign of increase except, again, in neighboring European states.

There has been some new use of the euro as a vehicle for lending. Once the new currency was born, outside borrowers were attracted by the oppor- tunity to tap into the much broader pool of savings created by the con- solidation of EMU financial markets. Overall, the euro's share in the stock of international bonds and notes rose strongly, from roughly one-fifth in 1999 to nearly half by the end of 2005, before falling back by a few percentage points in 2006. But again, most of the increase came from immediate neighbors (mainly recent or prospective EU members). Borrowers in Asia and Latin America continue primarily to use the dollar. Moreover, these developments represent growth only in the supply of euro-denominated assets. On the demand side, as indicated, foreign portfolio managers have been slower than anticipated to add to their holdings of euro-denominated claims, despite the greater depth and liquidity on offer. Most issues have been taken up by investors inside Europe itself, making them in effect "domestic." Outside EMU, the euro's overall share of portfolios has changed little from the previous aggregate of legacy currencies. Similar patterns have also pre- vailed in international banking markets (European Central Bank 2007c).

Only in official reserves has there been a sustained increase of use as com- pared with the DM and other legacy currencies. From its birth in 1999 to end-2006, the euro's share of currency reserves advanced from 18 percent to nearly 26 percent. It is noteworthy, though, that as much as half the growth came at the expense of Japan's yen and miscellaneous "other" currencies rather than the dollar. Moreover, much of the increase vis-à-vis the greenback has been the result of exchange-rate shifts rather than deliberate dollar sales.

Direct conversions from the greenback to the euro have been cautious and slow. As economists Edwin Truman and Anna Wong (2006: 36) conclude: "The available evidence suggests that the amount of *active* diversification of countries' foreign exchange reserves has been limited to date" (emphasis in the original). The dollar's share of reserves is still two-and-a-half times that of the euro.

None of this, therefore, adds up to a serious challenge to the greenback. The dollar's appeal may be eroded by America's persistent payment deficits. But that by itself does not ensure success for the euro so long as the new currency's own deficiencies remain uncorrected. The euro clearly does have a future as an international currency. But its allure is not unqualified and, worse, seems limited mainly to the EU's own backyard. The currency's destiny appears to be regional, not global.

Institutional participation

Finally, there is the issue of institutional participation. With a population presently exceeding 300 million and a GDP rivaling that of the United States, the euro area was expected to start playing a major role in international monetary diplomacy. Joined together in EMU, it was widely thought, members would surely have more bargaining leverage than if each acted on its own. Europe's voice would be amplified on a broad range of macroeconomic issues; from policy coordination or crisis management to reform of the international financial architecture. Yet here, too, experience to date has been underwhelming. In practice, membership in EMU has not enabled EU governments to play a more influential role in the IMF or other global forums. Europe's voice has been muted at best.

The problem

The problem is that no one knows who, precisely, speaks for the euro area. Here too the Maastricht Treaty is regrettably uncommunicative. No single body is formally designated to represent EMU in international discussions. Instead, the text simply lays down a procedure for resolving the issue of external representation at a later date, presumably on a case-by-case basis (Article 109). Some sources excuse this on the grounds that it achieves a balance between the need to convey a common position and the prerogatives of member states. But that seems too kind. In fact, it was a cop-out, a diplomatic formula to mask failure to reach consensus.

At a minimum, therefore, the Treaty compounds confusion about who is in charge. At worst, it condemns the euro area to lasting second-class status, since it limits its ability to project power on monetary matters. EMU, laments Fred Bergsten (2005: 33), a euro enthusiast, "still speaks with a multiplicity, even a cacophony, of voices. ... Hence it dissipates much of the potential for realizing a key international role."

At the IMF, for example, the euro area's thirteen members in 2007 were split up among no fewer than eight different constituencies. France and Germany each have a single chair on the Fund's twenty-four-member Executive Board. The other eleven are all part of diverse constituencies that include non-EMU states as well as EMU members and in some cases are led by non-EMU governments. Belgium, for instance, provides the elected executive director for a constituency that includes four EMU countries, three non-EMU members of the EU, and three non-EU states. Italy, similarly, leads a constituency with three EMU countries, one non-EMU member of the EU, and three non-EU states. The Netherlands heads a group that includes not a single other EMU country, while Finland, Ireland, and Spain all are minority members of constituencies led by non-EMU governments. Collectively, EMU's membership accounts for some 23 percent of total voting power at the Fund. But, because representation is so fragmented, it is difficult for the euro area to exercise a commensurate influence on decision-making or even to develop common policy positions.

Likewise, in the influential Group of Seven (G-7), which with nearly half of all IMF voting power plays a decisive role in Fund decision-making, only the three biggest EMU states—Germany, France, and Italy—are formally included. Each speaks for itself alone. Other EMU governments have no direct voice at all.

The result is a lack of coherence that saps much of the authority that the euro area might otherwise be expected to exercise. Informally, efforts have been made to address the problem through tactical cooperation among the euro area's members on an *ad hoc* basis (Bini Smaghi 2004). At the IMF, for example, EMU's representatives all stand together on issues related directly to the euro area and its single monetary and exchange-rate policies. But, in the absence of a strategic commitment to achieve and defend common positions, backed by genuine political agreement, such actions are bound to lack impact. The point has been best put by political scientists Kathleen McNamara and Sophie Meunier (2002: 850):

> As long as no "single voice" has the political authority to speak on behalf of the euro area, as the U.S. Secretary of the Treasury does for the American currency, the preeminence of the US in international monetary matters, as in other realms, is likely to remain unchallenged.
>
> (McNamara and Meunier 2002: 850)

EMU will continue to punch below its weight.

A single voice?

Is there any way to provide that single voice? In principle, any of several bodies might be designated to represent the euro area internationally. In practice, however, none is fully up to solving the problem.

One possibility, for example, might be the ECB. As the euro area's only truly collective institution, the ECB would in fact seem to be the most natural candidate to speak for EMU on global monetary issues. But this choice runs up against the tradition that in most such settings states are normally represented not by central banks but by finance ministers—officials with the political clout to speak for their respective governments. The ECB obviously cannot claim that kind of authority. Indeed, it is difficult to imagine the elected governments of Europe ever delegating such a fundamental power to an institution that has been deliberately designed to be as free from political influence as possible.

Alternatively, some have suggested the appointment of a single individual with sufficient credentials and legitimacy to act as the equivalent of a finance minister for the euro area (McNamara and Meunier 2002)—a Mr. (or Ms.) Euro, as it were. Precedent exists in the realm of foreign and security affairs, where EU members already agreed a decade ago to name a single high representative to stand for them all—a Mr. Europe. But experience has shown that Mr. Europe's ability to speak authoritatively for the entire EU can be easily hamstrung by policy differences among individual governments. A single appointed official cannot ignore or overrule the preferences of diverse sovereign states.

A third possibility would be a collective one, centered on the informal committee of EMU finance ministers that has emerged since the birth of the euro—what has come to be known as the Eurogroup. Like comparable EU institutions, such as the Council of Ministers or European Council, the Eurogroup can be represented at any given time by its chair; the chairmanship itself, as with those other institutions, rotates periodically among members. This appears to be the euro area's preferred route to date. Already, in 2005, the Eurogroup chair began attending meetings of the G-7, albeit with no specified responsibilities. Likewise, when issues related to the euro are discussed at the IMF, the chair is invited to make a statement on behalf of all EMU members. But here too the authority of EMU's voice can be easily constrained by underlying policy differences. In no venue is the Eurogroup chair permitted to negotiate on behalf of EMU as a whole.

The underlying obstacle is of course the lingering influence of national allegiance. Though EMU members share a joint money, their interests are hardly identical. Thus, however advantageous a single voice might be for the group, any effort to consolidate the euro area's institutional participation is bound to run into resistance from at least some individual participants. As Jeffry Frieden (2004: 262) observed, any such reform "requires that member states weigh the potential benefits of a common policy against the potential costs of a policy that is not to their liking. ... There is a clear trade-off between the advantages of scale and the disadvantages of overriding heterogeneous preferences." Divergent preferences make members reluctant to give up the right to speak for themselves. Even after a decade of living with the euro, national identity still trumps collective interest.

Conclusion

Overall, the conclusion seems clear. For all its undoubted success in other respects, EMU has failed to improve the power of participating states to cope with external challenges. Neither the autonomy nor the influence of the bloc has been significantly enhanced. The reason seems equally clear. Based as it is on an agreement among sovereign states—what one scholar calls a "sovereignty bargain" (Litfin 1997)—the euro area lacks the clean lines of authority traditionally associated with the management of money by individual states. Its founding document, the Maastricht Treaty, is full of artful compromises and deliberate obfuscations, reflecting unresolved disagreements among governments at the time of negotiation (Dyson and Featherstone 1999). In the decade since the euro's birth, the Treaty's ambiguities have persistently clouded understandings about decision-making and the distribution of competences and responsibilities. As long as it remains a sovereignty bargain rather than a genuine federal union, EMU will always be at a structural disadvantage in the geopolitics of finance.

7 Dollar dominance, euro aspirations
Recipe for discord?

After nearly a century of dominance of the international monetary system, has the U.S. dollar finally met its match in the euro? For many observers, the prospect has long been self-evident. Even before Europe's Economic and Monetary Union (EMU) came into existence in 1999, prominent economists such as George Alogoskoufis (later to become finance minister of Greece) and Richard Portes were predicting that "the fundamentals point toward a potentially large shift in favor of the euro" (Alogoskoufis and Portes 1997: 63). The joint currency of the European Union (EU) could legitimately aspire to join America's greenback at the peak of global finance. Over the decade since the euro's debut, Europe has seemed well on its way to becoming a new monetary power. The fate of the dollar appeared to be sealed following the collapse of America's housing market in mid-2007, which triggered the greatest crisis in U.S. financial markets since the Great Depression.

Appearances, however, can be misleading. In fact, the euro's achievements as an international currency have fallen disappointingly short of aspiration. Admittedly, the money has done well in exchange-rate terms. Market value soared from a low near $0.83 in mid-2002 to as high as $1.60 in mid-2008, before dropping back. But exchange rates are at best an imperfect indicator of a currency's global standing. The real issue is not price but use: the extent to which the euro is being adopted by actors outside EMU for the standard functions of a medium of exchange, unit of account, or store of value. When it comes to international use, the shift in favor of Europe's money has, for the most part, been anything but large. After an initial spurt of enthusiasm, interest in the euro actually appears now to have leveled off, even stalled, and so far seems confined largely to a limited range of markets and regions. Not even the present troubles of the U.S. financial sector, which have required massive government interventions and in some cases de facto nationalization, have sufficed to tip preferences away from the dollar. If anything, the crisis has ironically served to reinforce the greenback's global dominance.

In short, power configurations in currency relations have changed much less than expected. The euro has successfully attained a rank second only to the greenback—but it remains, and is likely to remain, a quite distant second.

Without a determined effort by EMU authorities to promote their money's role, any challenge to the dollar will remain modest at best.

Would Europe dare to mount a direct challenge? No one really knows, but the temptation will surely be great—particularly at a time when America's financial stresses would seem to have heightened the greenback's vulnerability. European policymakers understand the material benefits that would result from wider use of their currency. These include a sizable gain of seigniorage, which would accrue from increased foreign holdings of euros or euro-denominated assets, as well as a higher degree of macroeconomic flexibility that would derive from the ability to finance external deficits with Europe's own money. In practical terms, it is difficult to imagine that EMU authorities will refrain entirely from trying to encourage a greater role for the euro. But that, in turn, could turn out to be a recipe for discord with the United States, which has never made any secret of its commitment to preserving the greenback's worldwide dominance. An overt struggle for monetary leadership could become a source of sustained tensions in U.S.–European relations.

The purpose of this essay is twofold: first, to review the euro's global performance to date; and, second, to explore the implications of a possible leadership struggle for monetary dominance in years to come. A careful look at a broad array of available data, spelled out in the first two sections of the essay, confirms the euro's limited achievements in most international uses, falling far short of enthusiasts' aspirations. A glimpse at future prospects for the dollar–euro rivalry, in the essay's final section, confirms the possibility of U.S.–European tensions but, happily, suggests little risk of a destabilizing escalation into outright geopolitical conflict.

The broad picture

Early forecasts for the euro's future were strikingly optimistic. A decade ago U.S. economist Fred Bergsten (1997) proclaimed emphatically that in terms of international use, the euro would achieve "full parity" with the greenback in as little as five to ten years. Alogoskoufis and Portes (1997) thought that it might even happen "immediately." In fact, however, nothing like that has yet come to pass. It is perhaps not surprising, therefore, that as the years have gone by enthusiasts have grown more hesitant to set a date for the euro's ascendance. The most notable exceptions are Menzie Chinn and Jeffrey Frankel, who in successive econometric studies have daringly suggested that Europe's currency might overtake the dollar by 2022 (Chinn and Frankel 2007) or possibly even as early as 2015 (Chinn and Frankel 2008). But even that is much further off than many were forecasting back when the euro was born. Enthusiasts still firmly believe that the euro is the currency of the future. But, frustratingly, the future keeps receding.

Even now, in the midst of the greatest economic crisis since the 1930s, the dollar has retained its historical dominance. If ever there was an opportunity to tip preferences in favor of the euro, it should have been during the past two years, following the sub-prime mortgage collapse in the United States. Very soon the soundness of America's entire financial structure was thrown into question. One after another, venerable banking institutions fell into insolvency; whole classes of "toxic" securities become unsalable at any price; the Treasury and Federal Reserve were forced into ever-deeper interventions to keep the system afloat; and the broader American economy sank rapidly into recession. Yet even at moments of greatest panic, market actors looked to the greenback, not the euro, for safety. As the crisis intensified, spreading to the EU and elsewhere, the dollar actually rose sharply against Europe's money. Global demand for U.S. Treasury bills was so great that yields fell nearly to zero, while euro-denominated assets have been abandoned. The future of Europe's money, it seems, still lies out of reach.

A structural disadvantage

Will the future ever arrive? Of course it will, say the currency's fans. "The euro has the capacity to catch up," firmly asserts one source (Walter and Becker 2008: 10). Declares another: "To keep the euro down forever, you would need to rely on some rather far-fetched conspiracy theories" (Munchau 2008). Conspiracy theories, however, are hardly necessary to warrant a healthy dose of skepticism. A decade after the monetary union's birth, it is becoming increasingly clear that the obstacles in the euro's path are by no means trivial, as I have long argued (Cohen 2003, 2008). In fact, there are serious deficiencies inherent in the institutional design of EMU that are bound to limit the currency's appeal (Cohen and Subacchi 2008). The euro's handicaps include troubling ambiguities in EMU's governance structure—difficult to avoid when a single currency is jointly managed by more than one sovereign state—as well as a strong anti-growth bias built into the bloc's provisions for monetary and fiscal policy. As a rival to the dollar, Europe's money is at a distinct structural disadvantage. The greenback may have deficiencies of its own, but Europe has failed to provide an attractive alternative.

The core problem is that the euro area—also referred to as the euro zone or the eurosystem—is an artificial construct, lacking the clear lines of authority traditionally associated with the management of money by a single national government. Though the bloc does have a central monetary agency, the European Central Bank (ECB), there is neither a common regulatory regime nor a unified fiscal authority to provide overall direction. As Jean-Claude Trichet, the ECB's president, has lamented: "We are not a political federation. ... We do not have a federal budget" (*New York Times*, October 6, 2008). Effectively the euro is a currency without a country, the product of an international treaty rather than the expression of one sovereign power. For actors outside EMU, Europe's money can be considered only as good as the political agreement underlying it.

The dilemma has long been apparent (Cohen 2008). The underlying political agreement might remain solid in "normal" times. But would it hold up in the midst of a crisis? Under the Maastricht Treaty, EMU's founding document, few specific tasks were assigned to the ECB to maintain financial stability. For most supervisory or regulatory powers the ruling principle was to be decentralization, otherwise known as subsidiarity—the notion that the lowest level of government that can efficiently carry out a function should do so. Formal authority for crisis management was to remain at the national level, just as it did before EMU. Watchful observers had repeatedly warned about the risks of such a fragmented governance structure, which left EMU remarkably unprepared to cope with any major disruption. In the words of the International Monetary Fund (IMF 2007a: para. 12): "The core problem is the tension between the impulse toward integration, on the one hand, and the preference for a decentralized approach, on the other. ... This setting rules out efficient and effective crisis management and resolution." No one, it seemed, was directly accountable for the stability of the euro area as a whole.

Now, with the spread of the current crisis, EMU's chickens have come home to roost. The necessary political agreement has proved lacking. While the U.S. Treasury and Federal Reserve have been able to react to developments decisively and with alacrity (if not always with great efficacy), European governments remain divided and uncertain. The ECB has been active in injecting liquidity into the system—but under the Maastricht Treaty that is all it can do. National policymakers, in the meantime, have clung to a piecemeal, patchwork approach—an "every-country-for-itself" response that certainly has done little to bolster confidence in Europe's joint currency. Even when an agreement was announced a year ago to recapitalize financial institutions and guarantee inter-bank lending, the details of implementation were left to individual governments. Policymakers resisted setting up a Europe-wide fund for fear that their own taxpayers might end up bailing out other countries' banks or depositors. Similarly, responsibility for fiscal stimulus has been left to the separate members, with predictably poor results. An emergency summit last March, called in hopes of crafting a joint European response to the crisis, ended in total disarray. The EU, said a prominent German journalist, had proved that it is "just a fair-weather union" (*New York Times*, March 2, 2009). The absence of effective coordination no doubt helps explain why, despite America's considerable travails, global preferences have still failed to tip towards the euro. Market actors recognize that, in the end, Europe's governments simply do not seem to trust each other enough to act decisively in their common interest. As the *Wall Street Journal* wryly commented: "This is a poor record for the EU 51 years after its founding" (*Wall Street Journal*, October 7, 2008).

To a large extent, the hopes of euro enthusiasts have always been a reflection of their ambitions for the broader EU project. The appeal of the currency would grow naturally with the construction of a united Europe.

But market forces alone cannot guarantee success. Given EMU's structural handicaps, it seems clear that a determined public effort will be required if the currency is ever to live up to its fans' aspirations. Promotion of the international role of the euro would have to be made an explicit goal of policy. Otherwise, Europe's money in a sense could turn out always to be the "currency of the future"—forever aspiring to catch up with the dollar but, like an asymptote, destined never to quite get there.

Vague vision

The vision of euro enthusiasts was always a bit vague. What does it mean to "catch up with" or "overtake" the dollar? At issue is the degree or extent of use of a money for various international purposes—what is commonly referred to as currency "internationalization." Cross-border usage of Europe's currency was expected to grow. Without further explication, however, the notion of currency internationalization is ambiguous at best. In practical terms, at least three separate dimensions are involved: trajectory, scope, and domain. To assess the euro's achievements and prospects, all three dimensions must be considered.

By trajectory I mean the path traced by the euro as its use increases. Can the growth of usage be expected to continue ever upwards until parity with the dollar (or more) is attained, or is some ceiling likely to be hit short of that goal? By scope I mean the range of functional categories of use. Can euro usage be expected to grow for all international purposes, or just a select few? By domain I mean the geographic scale of use. Can euro usage be expected to expand across most parts of the globe, or in just a more limited number of countries or regions?

Euro enthusiasts anticipated that Europe's currency would do well in all three dimensions. Cross-border usage would not bump up against a low ceiling and would be extensive in terms of both function and geography. In short the euro's reach would in time span the globe, fully matching if not surpassing the dollar in both scope and domain. Reality, however, has turned out to be much more mundane. The vision of the currency's fans has proved faulty.

For a broad picture of what is really happening, there is no more authoritative source than the *Review of the International Role of the Euro*, published annually by the European Central Bank (2008b). Data are provided on all three dimensions involved. With respect to all three, the ECB's conclusions are unambiguous—and damning. The euro's reach, it turns out, has greatly exceeded its grasp.

Concerning trajectory, the ECB observes that international use of the euro has decelerated noticeably and appears to have stabilized. A fast early start was certainly to be expected, once market actors were persuaded that the euro was here to stay. From the moment of its birth, Europe's new money clearly enjoyed many of the attributes necessary for competitive success.

These included a large economic base in the membership of the euro area, initially numbering some eleven countries—including some of the richest economies in the world—and at time of writing now up to sixteen partners. They also included unquestioned political stability and an enviably low rate of inflation, all backed by a joint monetary authority, the ECB, that was fully committed to preserving confidence in the currency's future value. Moreover, there was every reason to believe that sooner or later the global position of the dollar would weaken, owing to America's persistent payments deficits and looming foreign debt. Hence it was no surprise that in the euro's early days use seemed to be expanding exponentially. "Momentum has led to an increase in the international role of the euro," proclaimed the ECB in 2002 (European Central Bank 2002: 11). But subsequently, it is plain, that momentum has slowed considerably. After its fast start, the ECB now ruefully concedes, the international role of the euro "has been broadly stable for around five years" (European Central Bank 2008b: 11).

In effect, the euro has done little more than hold its own as compared with the past aggregate market shares of EMU's "legacy" currencies. Given the fact that Germany's old Deutschmark (DM) had already attained a number two ranking in the monetary system, second to the greenback, anything less would have been a real shock. But beyond that, a ceiling does indeed appear to exist. Straight-line extrapolation of the euro's early acceleration far into the future does not seem warranted.

Likewise, with respect to scope, it is evident that growth of euro usage has been uneven across functional categories. The expansion of international use has been especially dramatic in the issuance of debt securities, reflecting the growing integration of EMU financial markets. There has also been some modest increase in the euro's share of trade invoicing and central-bank reserves. But in other categories, such as foreign-exchange trading or banking, the dominance of the dollar remains as great as ever. The ECB's (2008b: 7) polite way of putting this is that use of the euro has been "heterogeneous across market segments."

The picture is also clear with respect to domain, which is sharply bifurcated. For the most part, internationalization of the euro has been confined to countries with close geographical and/or institutional links to the euro area— what might be considered EMU's natural hinterland. "The euro's turf," economist Charles Wyplosz (1999: 89) calls it. These countries include the newest members of the EU, all destined eventually to join the EMU, as well as other candidate states (for example Croatia or Montenegro) and non-member neighbors like Norway and Switzerland. They also include most of the nations around the Mediterranean littoral as well as a good portion of sub-Saharan Africa. In these countries, where trade and financial ties are deep, the euro obviously enjoys a special advantage. Elsewhere, in stark contrast, scale of use drops off abruptly, and Europe's currency remains very much in the greenback's shadow. The ECB (2008b: 7) concludes: "The *Review* confirms the largely regional character of the euro."

Details

The ECB's broad picture is corroborated by a more detailed look at the various categories of euro usage. The conventional framework for analysis of international currencies separates out the three standard functions of money—medium of exchange, unit of account, store of value—at two levels of analysis: the private market and public policy. Following that lead, we can speak of the role of the euro at the private level in foreign-exchange trading (medium of exchange), trade invoicing and settlement (medium of exchange and unit of account), financial markets (store of value), and currency substitution (all three functions). At the level of public policy, we can speak of the role of the euro as an anchor (unit of account) and reserve currency (medium of exchange and store of value). Because the available data on most of these roles are not nearly as complete as we would like, a considerable amount of subjective judgment about their meaning ultimately is required. Nonetheless, the overall impression seems clear. In the face of the evidence, it is hard to sustain the view that Europe's currency is well on track to overtake the dollar. The data plainly suggest otherwise.

Foreign-exchange trading

Consider, for example, the foreign-exchange market, where the dollar has long dominated wholesale trading in its role as a vehicle currency (the intermediary for trades between other less widely used monies). The main source of information on the currency distribution of foreign-exchange trading is the Bank for International Settlements (BIS), which since 1989 has published a triennial survey of foreign-exchange market activity. A summary of market shares since 1989 for the dollar, euro (since its birth), and the euro's legacy currencies (prior to its birth) is provided in Table 7.1. Market shares are measured by the percentage of transactions in which each currency appeared. (Since every transaction involves two currencies, percentages add up to 200 percent.) The survey is always taken at the same time of year, in the month of April.

Table 7.1 Currency distribution of foreign-exchange market turnover (% share of daily transactions in April)

	1989	1992	1995	1998	2001	2004	2007
Dollar	90.0	82.0	83.3	87.3	90.3	88.7	86.3
Euro					37.6	36.9	37.0
Deutschmark	27.0	39.6	36.1	30.1			
French franc	n/a	3.8	7.9	5.1			
Other EMU currencies	n/a	11.8	15.7	17.3			
All other currencies	n/a	62.8	57.0	60.2	72.1	74.4	76.7

Source: Bank for International Settlements (2007).

Note: Since every transaction involves two currencies, percentages add up to 200 percent.

Two facts stand out. The first is the overwhelming dominance of the dollar, which at the time of the most recent survey in 2007 appeared on one side or the other of some 86 percent of all market transactions, down only slightly from its level in 1989 and up substantially from the early 1990s. The second is the relatively poor showing of the euro, whose share, at 37 percent, has been essentially flat since the start of EMU. There certainly has been no challenge to the greenback in this category of use.

A similar picture also emerges from the data reported by the Continuous Linked Settlement (CLS) system, which was launched in 2002. The CLS system is managed by CLS Bank International, a single-purpose institution operating under the supervision of the U.S. Federal Reserve. According to CLS data as reported by the ECB (2008b: 36), the average shares of the dollar and euro in 2007 were, respectively, 90.5 percent and 37.8 percent—not significantly different from the BIS numbers. Preliminary evidence suggests that these shares did not change significantly in 2008.

Superficially, it might even appear from the BIS numbers that the euro's role in foreign-exchange trading has actually fallen over time, since its share is clearly smaller now than it was for the combination of the DM and EMU's other legacy currencies prior to 1999. But that would be a misinterpretation. The apparent decline of the euro's share is really an artifact of the statistics, due entirely to the elimination of trading among legacy currencies once the monetary union began. After netting out, the euro's share overall is in fact marginally greater than before.

On the other hand, it is also evident from the BIS surveys that most transactions involving the euro are concentrated in the EU and neighboring countries—evidence of the currency's bifurcated domain. Beyond the European hinterland, euro turnover is strikingly low, at 20 percent or less. The share of the dollar, by contrast, is much more equally distributed across regions. The greenback even dominates activity within Europe's markets, at close to 90 percent of turnover as compared with less than 50 percent for the euro. The greenback functions as a vehicle currency globally; the euro does not.

Why has the dollar remained so popular as a foreign-exchange vehicle? Low transaction costs combined with inertia would appear to provide much of the explanation. Trading costs for the euro have come down sharply since the currency was launched and are now roughly commensurate with those for the greenback (Papaioannou *et al.* 2006). But since no significant price advantage is offered, ingrained habit and institutional rigidities have favored continued use of the dollar. Switching from one money to another can be costly, involving an expensive process of financial adaptation. The same scale economies and network externalities that make a currency attractive in the first place also promote a pronounced stickiness of user preferences—what economists call "hysteresis" or "ratchet effects." In the words of one commentary (Lim 2006: 28): "These findings are consistent with the stylized facts that network externalities/path dependence will tend to 'lock in' the dominance of the network good, here, the dollar." The greenback is the beneficiary of a natural advantage of incumbency.

Trade invoicing and settlement

Once the euro was created, it was natural to expect growth in its role as a settlement or invoicing currency for trade in goods and services. The large size of the EMU economy was bound to encourage adoption of the new money in import and export markets, for reasons of transactional convenience. Data from the ECB's annual reviews and other sources (Kamps 2006) show a significant increase in the euro's share of trade between EMU countries and the rest of the world, from an estimated 40 percent or so in 2000 to as much as 60 percent by 2006. Concludes one recent analysis (Papaioannou and Portes 2008: 37): "The euro has clearly more than replaced the legacy currencies in European imports and exports."

Here too, however, there has been a leveling off after a fast start. As the ECB (2007c: 34) puts it, "the role of the euro as a settlement currency for euro area [trade] appears to have stabilized." Little overall change has occurred in recent years. Moreover, here too the geographic pattern is sharply bifurcated. The increase in usage has been concentrated mainly in Euroland's trade with neighbors—particularly non-euro EU members and candidate states, where the euro now dominates in invoicing and settlement. Outside the European region, use of the currency for trade with EMU economies remains limited; in transactions between third countries, where neither counterparty is an EMU member, it is practically non-existent. According to the ECB (2008b: 42), this plainly indicates that "close proximity to or institutional links with the euro area or the EU ... remain the determining factors for the use of the euro in international trade transactions."

Once again, the contrast with the dollar is striking. The greenback dominates in U.S. trade with all parts of the world and is also widely used for trade between third countries. Overall, America's currency is thought to account for roughly half of global exports—close to three times as much as the euro.

Could the euro yet catch up? Much depends on what happens in the world's markets for primary products of various kinds: foodstuffs, agricultural raw materials, minerals, and fuels. At present, virtually all transactions in reference-priced and organized-exchange traded commodities are invoiced and settled in dollars. Most notably, this includes the global market for oil, the world's most widely traded commodity. In commodities markets, as in the foreign-exchange market, the dollar enjoys an incumbency advantage that will be difficult to overcome. As one authoritative study concludes (Goldberg and Tille 2005: 29), "The role of the dollar as a transaction currency in international trade has elements of industry herding and hysteresis" that militate against rapid change.

The point is conceded even by euro enthusiasts. Acknowledges one source (Papaioannou and Portes 2008: 38): "Theories of network externalities suggest that it is unlikely that these markets will switch to another currency, unless transactions costs (broadly defined to include exchange rate volatility, inflation, and other risk considerations) in the dollar increase significantly." A weak hope is held out that "the euro might still play some role in newly established markets" (Papaioannou and Portes 2008: 38), but such prospects do not look bright. Concludes another recent study (Kamps 2006: 22), "it is evident that the dollar is still the dominant currency in world trade and that the euro is not likely to challenge the leading role of the US dollar in the foreseeable future."

Financial markets

With the birth of EMU, it was also natural to expect growth in the euro's role in global financial markets. Introduction of the euro promised to create the largest single-currency capital market in the world, with a huge pool of savings and increasingly attractive transactions costs. Data show that the consolidation of EMU financial markets has shrunk euro trading costs significantly. Just as in the foreign-exchange market, costs for euro-denominated corporate and government securities, as measured by bid–ask spreads, are now commensurate with those for the dollar (Biais *et al.* 2006; Dunne *et al.* 2006). The result, not surprisingly, has been a dramatic increase in use of the euro for international bonds and notes.

Indeed, by mid-decade, the euro had actually surpassed the dollar as the world's most important currency of issue, with net new issues in euros rising faster than for any other currency. At the end of 2007, according to the ECB (2008b), euro issues accounted for roughly one-third of the outstanding stock of international debt instruments (defined as issues in a currency other than that of the borrower's home country), up from just 19 percent in 1999. Over the same period, the greenback's share fell from around 50 percent to 43 percent. The securities markets have proved to be, by far, the area of greatest success in the internationalization of the euro.

Yet even here success has been qualified. In this role too there has been a leveling off after a fast start. A peak was reached in 2005, when the euro share in the stock of international issues reached 33.8 percent (European Central Bank 2008b). Since then, the currency's share has actually dropped marginally, to 32.2 percent at the end of 2007 (European Central Bank 2008b) and even lower in 2008 (Bank for International Settlements 2008), while the dollar's share has risen correspondingly. Moreover, here too it is clear that the geographic pattern is sharply bifurcated, in terms of both borrowers and investors. On the supply side, where the euro performs a financing function (a medium for borrowing), most new issues come from neighboring countries like Britain, Denmark, and Sweden. Issuers farther afield, in Latin America or Asia, continue to borrow mainly in dollars. Likewise, on the demand side, where the euro performs a store-of-value function (an investment medium), the largest part of new euro-denominated issues is taken up by investors within the EMU itself, making them effectively "domestic," while most of the rest go to the nearby European region. Elsewhere, available data indicate that the dollar still dominates in holdings of debt instruments as foreign assets. Once again, the ECB (2008b: 23) concludes: "These figures confirm the geographical pattern of the international role of the euro."

Finally, it should be noted that the euro's success in securities markets, however qualified, has not been matched by comparable gains in international banking, despite a sharp fall in euro-area banking costs at the wholesale level. At the end of 2007, the euro's share of international bank loans (excluding inter-bank activity) stood at some 22 percent, close to its level at the time of the currency's birth, while its share of international deposits, at 21 percent, was actually lower than in 1999 (European Central Bank 2008b). On both sides, the dollar's share was more than twice as great. Preliminary data from the Bank for International Settlements (2008) suggest that the euro's role fell even further in 2008. Here too a distinctively regional pattern has prevailed, showing a modest increase of cross-border banking business with the European hinterland offset by a decline in other parts of the world, mainly to the benefit of the greenback. Very few loans by banks outside the euro area to non-EMU borrowers or deposits in non-EMU banks from savers outside the euro area are denominated in euros (Lane and Walti 2007: 225). The ECB (2008b: 33) suggests that these patterns probably reflect the fact that the use of the euro in international banking is strongly linked to the proximity of counterparts.

Currency substitution

Another traditional indicator of the internationalization of a national money is the extent to which banknotes come to be held and used beyond the borders of the issuing country or countries—a process that economists call currency substitution. As the popular synonym "dollarization" implies, the most prominent example of currency substitution in the modern era involves the greenback, which is known to circulate extensively in many parts of the world, from Latin America to the Middle East and southeast Asia. The United States Treasury (2006) estimates that something in the order of 60 percent of Federal Reserve notes by value are presently located outside the United States, amounting to perhaps $450 billion. But now with EMU, the dollar is no longer alone. Foreign holdings of euro banknotes are known to be rising at a fast pace, amounting at the end of 2007 to some 10–20 percent of euro banknotes by value (European Central Bank 2008b). With roughly €700 billion overall then in circulation, that amounted to something between €70 billion and €140 billion in total. This too may be regarded as an area of success in the internationalization of Europe's money.

But here also success has been mainly regional in nature, rather than global. The greatest gains have been concentrated in the euro area's immediate neighbors, particularly to the east and south-east. In some other parts of the world, use of euro banknotes has also increased, but at much more moderate rates (European Central Bank 2008b).

To some degree, the apparent spread of "euroization" is misleading, insofar as it reflects the expectation in newer EU members or candidate countries that the euro will one day become legal tender. Once these economies formally become part of the euro area, the banknotes within their borders will no longer be "abroad." Nonetheless, a good part must be considered genuine currency substitution, reflecting real economic motivation. One impetus is proximity, which makes it convenient to have euro banknotes on hand to buy goods or to travel in EMU countries. Another is the availability of high-denomination notes—up to €250 and €500—that are attractive for large transactions or as a store of value. These denominations are much larger than anything available in U.S. dollar banknotes, the largest of which is $100. The phenomenon of euroization, at least in the European region, would appear to be here to stay.

Anchor currency

At the level of public policy, an international currency can play a prominent role as an anchor for exchange rates. Euro enthusiasts point proudly to the fact that in the short time since 1999 as many as 40 countries have formally aligned their exchange-rate policy with the euro, as compared with no more than 60 for the dollar (Walter and Becker 2008). These 40 countries include some 29 single-currency pegs and 11 arrangements that include the euro as part of a currency basket. Surely this is evidence that Europe's money is catching up with the greenback.

In fact, however, there is far less here than meets the eye. Of the 40, 4 are European mini-states (Andorra, Monaco, San Marino, and Vatican); 7 are EU members (Bulgaria, Czech Republic, Denmark, Estonia, Latvia, Lithuania, and Romania), and 4 are actual or potential candidates for EU membership (Bosnia, Croatia, Macedonia, and Serbia). None of these governments have much choice in the matter. The mini-states are literally embedded in the euro area; apart from Denmark, all the others are obligated to adopt the currency sooner or later as part of their terms of EU membership. Another 16 include the 14 members of the CFA franc zone in Africa together with two affiliated economies (Cape Verde and Comoros), all of which were long pegged to the French franc, a euro legacy currency, even before Europe's money was born. And the few others are either in the European hinterland or have well-established institutional ties with the EU or EU member states. Once more, what is really demonstrated is the strictly regional character of the euro.

Looking beyond formal (*de jure*) exchange-rate policies to actual (de facto) behavior, as indicated by the co-movement of currencies, Gabriele Galati and Philip Wooldridge (2006: 11–12) claim to find evidence of an "increasingly important gravitational pull" towards the euro, though they concede that "it is unclear whether [this] reflects a structural change or cyclical developments." However, in a more refined study David Cobham (2008) constructs a hierarchy of indicators for de facto anchoring to the euro and dollar. Three degrees of pegging are identified: (1) a "very narrow" margin of fluctuation; (2) a "narrow" margin; and (3) "relatively more aligned" with one anchor currency or the other. Cobham's analysis shows that over the period from 1999 to 2007, some 23 countries anchored "narrowly" or "very narrowly" to the euro, as contrasted with just 16 to the dollar—seeming to confirm Galati and Wooldridge's interpretation. However, Cobham also shows that the number of countries "narrowly" or "very narrowly" pegged to the dollar actually rose over the period, while that for the euro remained unchanged. Moreover, far more countries are "relatively more aligned" with the dollar (30) than with Europe's currency (16). And, perhaps most critically, it is clear that most of the economies that follow the euro are quite small as compared with some of the much larger financial powers aligned with the greenback (including China, Hong Kong, Saudi Arabia, and the United Arab Emirates). The countries that are "narrowly" or "very narrowly" pegged to the dollar are far more important when weighted by income or share of world trade. If any currency is exerting increasing gravitational force, it would appear to be the greenback, not the euro.

The reality is that almost all of the currencies "narrowly" or "very narrowly" aligned with the euro come from Europe's natural hinterland and have been linked to EMU from the start. It is obvious that Europe's money plays an important role as an anchor currency. But the data clearly do not justify the assertion, as one source (Papaioannou and Portes 2008: 32) put it recently, that in this respect "the importance of the euro is steadily increasing." On the contrary, what we see again is a distinct regional focus and a quick takeoff followed by relative stability.

Reserve currency

Finally, we come to the role of the euro as a reserve currency—a money that central banks hold in their reserves and use for intervention purposes to manage their exchange rates. The best source of information available on reserve-currency preferences is the IMF, which since 2005 has maintained a public database on the Currency Composition of Official Foreign Exchange Reserves (COFER). The COFER data are regrettably incomplete, since not all countries report the distribution of their holdings. Most importantly, many Asian central banks (including China's) are absent. But with about two-thirds of global reserves included, the data are considered sufficiently comprehensive to be useful for analytical purposes. A summary of market shares for the euro and dollar since 1999 is provided in Table 7.2. Most noticeable is what looks like a considerable shift in favor of the euro over time. While the dollar's share of allocated reserves declined from 71.5 percent

Table 7.2 Dollar and euro shares of official foreign-exchange reserves (% end of year)

	1999	2000	2001	2002	2003	2004	2005	2006	2007	2008[a]
Dollar	71.5	71.1	71.5	67.1	65.9	65.9	66.9	65.5	64.3	64.6
Euro	17.9	18.2	19.2	23.8	25.2	24.8	24.0	25.1	26.1	25.5

Source: International Monetary Fund (2007a).
Note: [a]End of third quarter, preliminary.

at the end of 1999 to under 65 percent in 2008, the euro's share rose from 17.9 percent to 25.5 percent.

Here too, however, there is far less than meets the eye. In the first place, the decline in the dollar's share is more apparent than real. In 1999 the greenback was at an artificial peak, reflecting the success of the Clinton administration's determined "strong-dollar" policy in preceding years. The 64.6 percent figure reached in 2008 is no lower than the dollar's share in the mid-1990s and is significantly above its nadir in 1990, when the percentage sank to as low as 45 percent. Over the course of the 1980s reserve managers around the globe had diversified actively into the DM and yen, before switching back again to the greenback in the 1990s. Second, it is evident that almost all of the euro's gain came in its first four years of existence. Since 2002 the relative positions of the dollar and euro have barely changed. Even now the euro's percentage of global reserves is less than the 39 percent share attained by EMU's legacy currencies in 1990, though it is higher than the legacy currencies' share of around 20 percent in 1998 (Wooldridge 2006: 35).

Furthermore, as a variety of studies have demonstrated, little of the apparent shift since 1999 has resulted from direct conversions out of the greenback into Europe's currency (Lim 2006; Truman and Wong 2006; Wooldridge 2006). As much as half of the euro's net gain has come at the expense of Japan's faltering yen and miscellaneous other currencies rather than the dollar. The rest resulted from the sharp appreciation of the euro's nominal exchange rate after its low early in the decade (a price effect) rather than deliberate dollar sales (a quantity effect). Indeed, when measured at constant exchange rates, the euro's share of global reserves has actually declined modestly in recent years rather than risen (European Central Bank 2008b). As Edwin Truman and Anna Wong (2006: 36) conclude: "The available evidence suggests that the amount of *active* diversification of countries' foreign exchange reserves has been limited" (emphasis in the original). In reality, the trajectory of Europe's currency has been essentially flat after its fast start. The greenback's share of reserves is still almost two-and-a-half times greater.

But what of the future? Little encouragement is provided by a formal study by Papaioannou *et al.* (2006) intended to quantify the potential monetary gains for central banks from reserve diversification, employing a finance-based approach. A "dynamic mean-variance currency portfolio optimizer with rebalancing costs" is developed to obtain what might be considered an optimal composition of global reserves since the euro's birth. Included are the five most widely used international currencies—the dollar, euro, yen, pound sterling, and Swiss franc. Interestingly, the optimizer calls for roughly equal allocations of about 10 percent for each of the four non-dollar currencies, including the euro. Since the actual share of Europe's currency in global reserves is already well above 10 percent, that would seem to leave little reason to expect much further growth.

Euro enthusiasts, however, remain undaunted. Some, like Papaioannou and Portes (2008), pin their hopes on the possibility of a sudden tipping point, when the floodgates will open and central banks worldwide will rush to trade in their dollars for euros. In their words: "Theories of network externalities usually feature multiple equilibria ... suggesting that there might be an abrupt switch between equilibria if expectations change. ... There are some noteworthy dynamic patterns" (Papaioannou and Portes 2008: 23, 25). But if the current worldwide economic crisis has not been "dynamic" enough to shift preferences, it is hard to see what might suffice to do the trick.

Others simply recycle old predictions. Typical is bank economist Werner Becker (2008: 19), who firmly declares that "the euro's share is likely to increase by 30 per cent to 40 per cent by 2010," albeit without any supporting explanation or evidence. Bravest are Chinn and Frankel (2007, 2008), who have been prepared to back their forecast of a euro takeover with hard data, formal modeling and a variety of detailed scenarios. Their focus is on the reserve-currency preferences of central banks. Their latest projections suggest that Europe's currency could surpass the greenback in official holdings as early as 2015. Should we be persuaded?

It is obvious that central-bank preferences may be influenced by an abundance of factors. Economists like Chinn and Frankel, naturally enough, find it convenient to focus on purely economic determinants, emphasizing considerations that make a currency attractive to private market actors. A typical list would include confidence in a money's future value, backed by macro-economic stability in the country of origin; well-developed financial markets that give assurance of a high degree of transactional liquidity ("exchange convenience") and reasonable predictability of asset value ("capital certainty"); and a broad transactional network based on an economy that is large in absolute size and well integrated into world markets. The logic is unexceptionable. It is not unreasonable to assume that central-bank choices are related in some way to prevailing market practice. It is simply not efficient for a public authority to rely on a currency that is not already extensively used at the private level.

But there is also a political side, as even mainstream economists are now beginning to acknowledge (Posen 2008). Political considerations include both the quality of governance in the reserve center and the nature of its diplomatic and security relations. Is the issuer of a reserve currency capable of effective policy management at home? Can it project power abroad? Does it enjoy strong foreign-policy ties with other countries—perhaps a traditional patron–client linkage or a formal military alliance? Though it is by no means easy to operationalize many of these factors for empirical purposes, it is hard to deny their importance.

Yet, conveniently, Chinn and Frankel set all such considerations aside in order to build a parsimonious model that they feel they can use for forecasting purposes. Only three independent variables are highlighted in their regressions, all chosen presumably because the numbers are readily available: country size (relative income), foreign-exchange turnover (representing the depth of competing financial markets), and trend exchange-rate changes (representing the rate of return on currency balances). The result is a series of scenarios that are simplistic at best and at worst seriously misleading. For example, why should we believe that the attractiveness of the euro will be increased by adding more countries to the euro area's economic base? Analysis suggests, to the contrary, that enlargement of EMU, by adding a diverse collection of new members with significantly different interests and priorities, could actually diminish the currency's appeal, not enhance it (Cohen 2007). Why should we assume that foreign-exchange turnover is an accurate proxy for the depth and breadth of financial markets? A high volume of currency trading may reinforce a currency's exchange convenience, but it does little to augment capital certainty.

Most importantly, why should we assume that politics, either at home or abroad, will play no part in the outcome? To ignore the political side in a context like this is like trying to put on a production of Hamlet without the prince. With the conspicuous exception of China, most of the biggest dollar holders around the world are all formal or informal allies of the United States, who are unlikely to risk seriously alienating their most powerful patron for the sake of a few points of return on their reserves. This is certainly true of the fragile regimes in Saudi Arabia and other Gulf states, which under a series of unwritten understandings dating back decades are highly dependent on security assurances from Washington for protection against enemies, both within and without. Middle Eastern governments, as one knowledgeable source (Momani 2008: 297) puts it, "are unwilling to purposefully undermine the dollar because they are ultimately mindful of their precarious security situation." The same is manifestly also true of Japan, which has long relied on its defense alliance with the United States as a shield against external threats.

The EMU, by contrast, is no more than a club—a gaggle of states with limited military capabilities and with foreign policy interests that only partly overlap or coincide. In practical terms, it is virtually impossible for Europe to substitute for the political influence of the United States. As Adam Posen (2008: 80) comments: "The European Union, let alone the euro area itself, is unable or unwilling to offer these systemic or security benefits beyond a very limited area." Echoes Bessma Momani (2008: 309): "While there are viable currency alternatives to the US dollar, there are no alternatives to the US military security umbrella." Chinn and Frankel are to be applauded for the courage of their dramatic forecasts, which have attracted headlines. But they are almost certainly wrong.

Discord?

In sum, the conclusion seems undeniable. As an international currency, the euro's prospects are limited. There is no doubt of the money's dominance in its own neighborhood; nor can one deny the considerable success it has attained in selected activities such as bond issuance and currency substitution. But overall, after a fast start, its trajectory has clearly bumped up against a ceiling, falling short of enthusiasts' aspirations. Left on its own, Europe's money appears destined to remain in the dollar's shadow far into the foreseeable future.

But what will happen if EMU authorities choose not to leave the euro on its own? Officially, European aspirations remain modest. According to authoritative statements by the ECB, the euro's development as an international currency—to the extent it happens—will mainly be a market-driven process, simply one of many possible by-products of monetary unification. From the very beginning, the ECB has insisted that euro internationalization "is not a policy objective [and] will be neither fostered nor hindered by the Eurosystem. ... The Eurosystem therefore adopts a neutral stance" (European Central Bank 1999: 31, 45). Behind the scenes, however, there are known to be considerable differences of opinion, with the eventual direction of policy still unsettled. While many in Europe are indeed inclined to leave the future of the euro to the logic of market competition, many others—aware of the dollar's strong incumbency advantages—favor a more proactive stance to reinforce their currency's potential. The temptation is bound to be especially great so long as America's economy and financial markets remain weakened by today's ongoing crisis.

In short, the chance of a leadership struggle with the United States cannot be ruled out. The risk of discord is real. The question is: Should we be worried?

Leadership struggle

Much depends on how aggressive policymakers on each side might choose to be in promoting their respective monies. As I have noted elsewhere (Cohen 2004), a critical distinction must be drawn between two different kinds of leadership aspirations in monetary affairs: informal and formal. Much rides on the difference.

Informal leadership refers to dominance among market actors—the scope of a money's use for private market purposes. At this level, a competitive struggle already exists. In EMU, policy is already actively engaged in trying to improve the appeal of the euro, particularly via financial-market reform; in defensive reaction, the United States will do what it can to sustain the attractiveness of the greenback. The consequences of an informal leadership struggle, however, are apt to be largely benign, since governments take this sort of contestation very much in their stride. Rivalry to promote or sustain each currency's competitiveness can be regarded as a natural feature of a decentralized monetary system based largely on market principles. The global community might even benefit if the result is lower transaction costs and more efficient capital markets.

But what if the players elect to go a step further, to seek to alter the behavior of state actors—what I term formal leadership? The aim in this case is to alter currency choices at the level of public policy: to induce governments to switch to a different reserve currency or perhaps even to adopt the foreign currency domestically in place of their own national money. The result, ultimately, would be the formation of organized currency blocs, not unlike the old sterling area that coalesced around Britain's pound in the interwar period.

As in interstate relations generally, tactics in a formal leadership struggle in monetary affairs may involve varieties of either coercion or persuasion, depending on circumstances. Currencies might be directly imposed on client states in a manner similar to what Susan Strange (1971b) meant by a "Master Currency." In the language of Jonathan Kirshner (1995), countries could be threatened with enforcement or expulsion if they do not align themselves monetarily—a threat of sanctions, say, or a withdrawal of past commercial or financial privileges. Alternatively, attractive inducements of an economic or political nature might be offered to reshape policy preferences in a manner analogous to Strange's notion of a "Negotiated Currency"—what Kirshner (1995) describes as entrapment.

Whatever the tactics used, the consequences for the global monetary system could be dangerous. In a formal leadership struggle, by definition, competition becomes more overtly politicized and hence less easy to contain. Economically, increasingly antagonistic relations could develop between mutually exclusive groupings, reversing decades of multilateral liberalization in trade and financial markets. Politically, currency rivalry could become transformed into serious geopolitical conflict.

Many observers discount the probability of a formal leadership struggle, pointing to the evident perils involved. Any efforts to alter prevailing currency choices at the state level would imply a cutback of dollar accumulations, which in turn could lead to a sharp depreciation of the greenback, causing massive losses on existing reserve holdings. Would governments truly risk such self-inflicted wounds? To avert a doomsday scenario, it makes more sense for state actors to support the greenback—or, at least, not undermine it— whether they like it or not. Optimists see this as nothing more than enlightened self-interest.

Others, however, see it as more like the notorious balance of terror that existed between the nuclear powers during the Cold War—a "balance of financial terror," as former treasury secretary Larry Summers (2004) has described it. A fear of mutually assured destruction is surely a powerful deterrent to overtly destabilizing behavior. But fear cannot rule out the possibility of miscalculation or even mischief by critical players. In fact, the balance of financial terror is inherently unstable and could conceivably break down at any time.

Breakdown?

Will the balance break down? Prediction is hazardous, of course; a doomsday scenario can hardly be excluded. But I am less persuaded than some observers, such as Kirshner (2008), that the wolf is actually at the door, ready to wreak systemic havoc. Certainly the foundations for a confrontation over formal leadership are in place, suggesting that a threat somewhere, sometime, is possible. There seems little reason for concern in the Western Hemisphere, where a dollar bloc has effectively existed for some time; there, the greenback remains largely unchallenged. Conversely, few question the euro's increasing dominance in EMU's nearby hinterland, including much of Africa. But elsewhere room does indeed exist for serious clashes. The greatest danger is to be found in the Middle East, where the greenback has long reigned supreme. Here, as I have previously suggested (Cohen 2006a), Europe could understandably be tempted to seek a greater role for the euro.

With its concentration of wealthy oil exporters, the Middle East would seem a prize well worth fighting for. At the moment, America's dollar is not only the standard for invoicing and payments in world energy markets. It also accounts for the vast majority of central-bank reserves and government-held investments in Middle Eastern countries and, except for Kuwait, is the sole anchor for their exchange rates. Yet, overall, the region's commercial ties are far more oriented toward Europe—a disjunction that many Europeans find anomalous, even irrational. Repeatedly, the question is asked: Would it not make more sense for the area to do business with its largest trading partner, Europe, in Europe's own currency rather than the greenback? And if so, would it not then make sense to switch to the euro as an anchor and reserve currency as well? Europe is well placed to make the Middle East a currency battleground.

Certainly, the possibility of a switch to the euro is tempting from a European perspective. Displacement of the dollar might go far toward restoring a measure of Europe's historically privileged position in the region. Arguably, the prospect might be tempting for Middle Eastern governments too from a purely economic point of view. It is well known that from time to time oil-exporting states have explored alternatives to the dollar, only to be discouraged by the lack of a suitable substitute. Now, with the arrival of the euro, many see the possibility of a truly competitive rival to the greenback. Talk of a switch to the euro (or to a currency basket heavily weighted toward the euro) has been particularly intense in recent years as a result of the dollar's most recent bouts of weakness.

Any effort to capitalize on the greenback's travails, however, would surely provoke determined resistance from the United States, which has long linked the region's use of the dollar to broader security concerns. For Washington, there is no higher politics than the Great Game being played out today in the energy-rich Middle East. America needs both the region's oil and continued support for the greenback; the security assurances provided to local governments are the price paid for both. With so much at stake, the level of U.S. tolerance for a formal currency challenge from Europe would be correspondingly low, making geopolitical conflict a virtual certainty.

Indeed, for some observers, the conflict has already begun. Theories abound that America's 2003 attack on Iraq, following as it did shortly after Saddam Hussein's decision to demand payment in euros for Iraqi oil exports, was motivated above all by a desire to sustain the dollar's role in the region. Though the idea is wholly unsubstantiated by hard evidence, one need not be a sensationalist to recognize the seeds of truth that it contains. A battle of currencies in the Middle East could get nasty.

Would Europe risk it? In the end, however strongly tempted, the Europeans are more likely to keep their aspirations in check, averting direct confrontation with Washington. Even after the Bush administration's decision to promote "regime change" in Iraq, there is no consensus among Europeans to risk the broader political and security relationship that they have long enjoyed with the United States. Beyond their currency's natural home in Europe's immediate neighborhood, therefore, they will most probably act with restraint. Maneuvering for advantage in the Middle Eastern region will undoubtedly persist, but the euro's challenge to the dollar is unlikely to be allowed to get out of control.

Conclusion

The bottom line, therefore, is clear. Despite the aspirations of euro enthusiasts, the dollar has not in fact met its match. The greenback's margin of dominance may have narrowed somewhat, but not even the stubborn crisis in U.S. financial markets has served to tip market preferences. Whether the new administration of President Barack Obama can succeed in restoring the vitality of America's economy remains an open question. But with its vigorous policy initiatives Washington has at least succeeded in stemming past erosion of confidence in U.S. financial leadership. The euro, meanwhile, remains at a distinct structural disadvantage, with little natural appeal beyond the European hinterland. In the absence of a determined effort to overcome the obstacles in the euro's path, Europe's money seems destined to dominate nowhere beyond its own backyard.

Can Europe's leaders undertake the reforms needed to improve EMU's governance structure? Can they frame the policies needed to promote the euro's role without provoking a serious conflict with the United States? The global economic crisis that erupted two years ago offered a golden opportunity for Europe to wrest financial leadership from the United States, either on its own or in coordination with Japan, China, and others. To date, however, European governments have not proved equal to the challenge, seemingly unable to coordinate initiatives even within their own institutions. The EU remains a "fair-weather union," hampering euro aspirations.

Both data and political analysis, therefore, point to the same conclusion. Europe's money is unlikely to catch up with, let alone overtake, the dollar. America's greenback, long preeminent in monetary affairs, will remain the only truly global currency.

Part III

Glimpses of the future

8   A one-and-a-half currency system

With Paola Subacchi

Even before Europe's Economic and Monetary Union (EMU) came into existence nearly a decade ago, a brilliant future was predicted for the euro as an international currency. At last, many argued, the European Union (EU) would have a monetary unit that could challenge the global dominance of the U.S. dollar. Typical was the confident assertion of two prominent European economists that "the most visible effect of EMU at the global level will be the emergence of a second global currency" (Gros and Thygesen 1998: 373). The conventional wisdom was clear. Leadership in monetary affairs would no longer be the privilege of the United States alone. The currency system would now rest on two pillars, not one.

Reality, however, has turned out to be quite different. There is no doubt that the system has changed. The euro has firmly established itself as an international currency, smoothly taking its place as successor to Germany's old Deutschmark (DM), which had already attained a rank second only to the dollar. The euro zone has grown from eleven members to, at time of writing, sixteen, with as many as a dozen or more set to join in the future. Yet the degree of change has been considerably smaller than expected. Euro enthusiasts assumed that once the tilt began a new two-currency system would naturally emerge. But this was based on a fundamental misunderstanding of the nature of monetary power. In fact, the euro's success has been limited by structural constraints on Europe's ability to project power in monetary affairs. The euro zone is largely a passive participant in global payments developments and remains a weak force in monetary diplomacy.

In this essay we argue that the euro is not yet ready for prime time and, at present, can play only a subordinate role in the global system as compared to the dollar. This can be described as a one-and-a-half currency system—certainly not a two-pillar world. We address two critical questions. First, how has the global system been changed by the arrival of the euro? We elaborate on what is meant by a one-and-a-half currency system and discuss why the euro is still not ready for prime time. Second, what can Europe do to overcome the euro's disadvantages and thus enhance the euro's role as the second pillar of the international monetary system? We argue that the main imperative is to improve the bloc's ability to project power effectively. Dual leadership at the global level is not out of reach, but will require determined reform of the EMU's governance structure.

One-and-a-half currencies

Predictions about the euro's brilliant future were not misguided. From the start, the euro clearly enjoyed many of the attributes necessary for competitive success as an international currency. These include a large economic base, unquestioned political stability, and an enviably low rate of inflation, all backed by a joint monetary authority—the European Central Bank (ECB)—that was fully committed to preserving confidence in the currency's future value. Moreover, there was every reason to believe that sooner or later the global position of the dollar would weaken, owing to the United States' persistent payments deficits. Surely it was only a matter of time before the balance of monetary power across the Atlantic would tilt significantly in Europe's direction, naturally giving rise to a new two-currency system. But that belief was based on a fundamental misunderstanding of the nature of power in monetary affairs. In fact, capabilities in the broader currency system have changed much less than anticipated.

Monetary power

Briefly summarizing an argument that has been developed at greater length elsewhere (Cohen 2006b), we suggest that international monetary power is comprised of two critical dimensions: autonomy and influence. More familiar is the dimension of influence, defined as the ability to shape events or outcomes. An actor, in this sense, is powerful to the extent that it can effectively pressure or coerce others—in short, to the extent that it can exercise leverage. As a dimension of power, influence is the sine qua non of systemic leadership. A clear example of the power influence dynamic can be found in the United States' ability to get its way in global monetary matters during the first decades after World War II.

The second dimension, autonomy, corresponds to the dictionary definition of power as a capacity for action. An actor is also powerful to the extent that it is able to exercise operational independence or to act freely, insulated from outside pressure. In this sense, power does not mean influencing others; rather, it means not allowing others to influence you. An example of this is provided by modern-day China, which successfully continues to resist foreign appeals for a major appreciation of its currency.

The distinction between the two dimensions of power is critical. Logically power begins with autonomy. Influence is best understood as functionally derivative, inconceivable in practical terms without first attaining and sustaining a relatively high degree of operational independence. First and foremost, actors must be free to pursue their goals without outside constraint. Only then will an actor be in a position to exercise authority elsewhere.

But influence does not automatically flow from autonomy. The actor must also be in a position to actualize its potential leverage—in practical terms, to translate passive autonomy into effective control. To aspire to a leadership role, an actor must have both the will and the ability to project its power onto others. Herein lies the problem for the euro: The EMU may have succeeded in augmenting Europe's autonomy in currency affairs, but it has yet to endow its members with enough direct influence to match the degree of leverage traditionally exercised by the United States.

Greater autonomy ...

That there has been an increase in autonomy is without question. With one joint money replacing a plethora of national currencies, the EMU's members need no longer fear the risk of exchange-rate disturbances inside Europe. In the words of the European Commission (2008: 4), "The exchange rate realignments that periodically traumatized the European economies have become a thing of the past." For a continent long plagued by currency instability, this is no small accomplishment. Moreover, with the now widespread acceptability of the euro, EMU countries have come to enjoy a much improved international liquidity position. Deficits that previously had required foreign exchange may now be financed with Europe's own money. Operational independence is now greater.

However, the gain should not be exaggerated. In some respects, considerable vulnerability remains, particularly in relation to the world outside Europe. The euro zone is largely a passive participant in global payments developments, leaving members critically exposed to fluctuations of the euro's exchange rate vis-à-vis the dollar and other major currencies. Indeed, to date, the bloc has been something of a bystander, more reactive than active. For the ECB, the highest priority has been to establish its own credentials as a champion of monetary stability consistent with its narrowly drawn mandate under the Maastricht Treaty, the EMU's founding document. Policy has been targeted almost exclusively on the domestic price level. The balance of payments and exchange rates have been left largely to their own devices.

A near doubling of the euro's value since its lows in 2000 and 2001 has been a source of satisfaction to some, including the ECB, which initially had worried about the effect of the currency's early depreciation on the credibility of Europe's grand monetary experiment. Many Europeans have experienced a surge of pride as their currency has left the greenback in its wake. But there is also an obvious downside: the dampening effect that an increasingly expensive euro could have on economic growth. Particularly distressing to many Europeans is the knowledge that the euro's appreciation has more to do with dollar weakness than with euro strength. The euro has been favored by currency traders because of policy failures on the U.S. side, not because of relative productivity improvements or brighter growth prospects in Europe.

Yet, except for one brief episode in the fall of 2000, the ECB has studiously avoided any manner of direct intervention in the foreign exchange market. The bank's management knows that any attempt to reverse the rise abroad, via sales of newly issued euros, would simply undermine the battle against inflation at home. In practice, the euro zone can do little but remain a passive witness to its currency's appreciation. Overall, the bloc's gain of autonomy, while undeniable, remains less substantial than many had hoped.

... But not greater influence

However, this is not the heart of the problem. The issue is not the scale of the gains in autonomy, but what the governments of Europe have been able to do with it. In fact, they have been able to do little. Slight or not, greater autonomy has not translated into more effective influence. Though freer now to pursue internal objectives without outside constraint, the euro zone has yet to realize its potential for overt leverage over others.

In principle, currency unification should have been expected to enable Europe's governments to play a much larger role in monetary affairs. Joined together in the EMU, European states would surely have more bargaining power than if each had continued to act on its own. Europe's voice would be amplified on a wide range of issues from policy coordination or crisis management to reforming the international financial architecture. Power would be more effectively exercised in a purposeful manner.

In practice, however, Europe's voice has remained muted. A comparison with the United States is telling. Even without the participation of Britain and some other EU countries, the euro constitutes one of the largest economic units in the world—rivaling the United States in terms of output, population, and share of foreign trade. Yet despite the dollar's recent tribulations, Washington still speaks with a much louder voice in global forums such as the International Monetary Fund (IMF) or Group of Seven (G-7). As the European Commission (2008: 11) unhappily acknowledges, Europe "still punches below its economic weight in international fora." Europe has proved no match for the American heavyweight.

The reason for this lies in the governance structure of EMU, the constellation of rules and institutions that constitute the framework for euro-zone economic policy. Under the terms established by the Maastricht Treaty, no one knows who, precisely, speaks for the EMU. No single body is formally designated to represent the bloc in international discussions. As a result, Europe is at a permanent disadvantage in any effort to exert influence. The euro zone, laments euro enthusiast Fred Bergsten (2005: 33), "still speaks with a multiplicity, even a cacophony of voices. ... Hence it dissipates much of the potential for realizing a key international role."

For example, at the IMF the bloc's present members are split up among no fewer than eight different constituencies. France and Germany each have a single chair on the Fund's twenty-four-member Executive Board. The other thirteen are all part of diverse constituencies that include non-EMU states as well as EMU members and in some cases are led by non-EMU governments. Collectively, the EMU's membership accounts for some 23 percent of total voting power at the IMF. But, because representation is so fragmented, it is difficult for Europe to exercise a commensurate influence on decision-making or even to develop common policy positions.

Likewise, only the three biggest EMU countries—Germany, France, and Italy—are formally included in the influential G-7, which, with nearly half of all IMF voting power, plays a decisive role in IMF decision-making. Each speaks only for itself. Other EMU governments have no direct voice at all.

The result is a lack of coherence that saps much of the authority that the euro zone might otherwise be expected to exercise. Informally, efforts have been made to address the problem through tactical cooperation among the bloc's members on an *ad hoc* basis. However, in the absence of a strategic commitment to achieve and defend common positions backed by genuine political agreement, such actions are bound to lack impact. As one senior official of the European Commission, speaking anonymously, concedes, "We're a political dwarf and an economic giant." Without significant change, the euro zone will remain condemned to lasting second-class status.

What can Europe do?

The problem for Europe lies in the fundamental mismatch between the domain of the EMU and the jurisdictions of its member governments. The euro is a currency without a country, the product of an interstate agreement. It is not, like the dollar, an expression of a single sovereign power. Hence the bloc's capacity to project power is structurally constrained. It is difficult to become a major player when speaking with many voices. The solution, therefore, lies in reform of the EMU's governance structure.

Building a credible currency

Addressing the structure of governance in this context is critical because of the institutional complexity of a monetary union established by a group of states that retain their sovereignty in most economic matters other than monetary policy. In the EMU, governance broadly covers four policy areas: monetary policy, fiscal policy, market structure, and exchange rates. All of these aspire to the same goals of promoting economic growth and employment. However, not all policy areas are addressed at all levels of policy-making. Monetary policy is a matter for the ECB, while fiscal policy and strategic exchange-rate policy remain in the hands of EMU member states—the latter through the EU's Economic and Financial Affairs Council (Ecofin). The locus of responsibility for the external value of the euro is divided ambiguously.

The EMU's governance structure, not surprisingly, reflects issues that were embedded in the circumstances of the 1990s. In the process of building the EMU's institutional framework, the establishment of an independent central bank with a mandate over monetary policy for the currency union as a whole took priority. Using the DM as a template, the main concern was to ensure a smooth functioning of the single-monetary area in order to create a strong and credible currency. It was correctly thought that confidence in the euro could only be established with the backing of a central bank firmly committed to price stability, on the model of the Deutsche Bundesbank, together with a set of rather stringent criteria to smooth the convergence process and ease adjustments to asymmetric shocks. The goal was to give credibility to the new currency by ensuring lasting macroeconomic stability across Europe's internal market. Besides appeasing German concerns about scrapping the DM, macroeconomic stability promised to protect the EMU's members from unnecessary volatility to lower the cost of capital and to encourage investment across Europe as a whole.

In short, the focus was placed single-mindedly on the EMU's internal conditions. The development of the euro as an international currency was not identified as an explicit policy goal. In the words of the ECB:

> From a policy perspective, the Eurosystem has adopted a neutral stance on the international use of its currency. It does not pursue the internationalisation of the euro as a policy goal. ... The currency's use outside the euro area's borders is and should remain the outcome of economic and financial developments. ... In any case, in a globalised world with deeply integrated and market-based financial systems, policymakers have limited scope to influence the internationalisation of a currency, even if they want to do so.
>
> (European Central Bank 2008a: 96)

Over the last ten years, the ECB has managed to build a solid reputation for independence by firmly sticking to its mandate of price stability. Even during the recent credit crisis, Jean-Claude Trichet, the ECB's president, maintained that price stability was the ECB's sole priority, reinforcing the bank's inflation-fighting credentials. The ECB, he declared, would not bow to political pressures to ease monetary policy in order to promote economic growth (Trichet 2008). In other words, the ECB has played the "confidence game" well (Krugman 1998). It has successfully established a track record of preserving market confidence in the value and usability of Europe's money.

After ten years, however, it is becoming clear that a single-minded focus on internal conditions is no longer enough if Europe is to be able to project power in monetary affairs to an extent commensurate with the growing international role of the euro (Cohen 2008; Subacchi *et al.* 2008). While sound domestic policy and a credible central bank are integral to the successful exercise of monetary influence, they are not sufficient. Closer attention should also be paid both to the euro exchange rate and to the role of the euro zone in international monetary forums.

The external dimension of the euro

A decade after the EMU's birth, the international role of the euro has grown well beyond the legacy of the eleven currencies that joined together at the outset. For example, the share of the euro in global central-bank reserves is now some 26 percent—higher than the share of the sum of all its legacy currencies (including, most notably, the DM) at the end of 1998, which was about 18 percent (European Central Bank 2008a). The euro has also become the most popular currency in the world for international bond issues.

During the same decade, the dynamics of the world economy have changed as well. Ten years ago, when Europe's EMU was established, the emergence of China was more a possibility than a reality while the "Asian Tigers" were still coming to terms with a devastating financial crisis. Now the rise of the emerging market economies and the enlargement of the global economy's playing field pose significant challenges to the competitiveness of advanced economies such as Europe and the United States. These challenges particularly affect the labor market and the international division of labor, as well as income distribution, inflation, financial volatility, and the sustainability of current-account imbalances. They also affect the way the euro zone's adjustment process operates by altering both the typology of shocks and the available adjustment mechanisms.

The external dimension of a popular currency like the euro has two main components: one is its international use; the other, its external value. Though often conflated, the two components are not necessarily related. An international currency is the one that central banks and private market actors are happy to use for transaction purposes and to hold in their portfolios. On the other hand, the external value of a currency is related to a number of factors that surely include economic fundamentals and may also reflect transient trading conditions in foreign-exchange markets. An international currency may not always have a stable or rising external value. A strong or appreciating currency may not be widely used for international purposes.

The distinction is important to any discussion of reform of the EMU's governance structure. Too often in the past, debate about the role of the euro in the global system has been muddled by issues related to the currency's exchange rate rather than to its international use. In fact, the two issues are institutionally and logically distinct and therefore need to be addressed separately.

Exchange rates and EMU member states

Given the strengthening of the euro's external value since 2001—coupled with the persistently weak performance of the euro zone's real economy—it is hardly surprising that the exchange-rate issue has, by now, become central to EMU policy discussions. The question for policymakers is whether exchange-rate management and coordinated currency interventions should play a more prominent role in the bloc's macro-policy tool kit.

Modern economic theory contends that a floating exchange rate is best understood as a forward-looking asset price determined at a level that induces market agents to willingly hold the outstanding stock of a currency. This contrasts with the older view—no longer endorsed by most economists— that the exchange rate is determined by the flow demand and supply of foreign exchange (Williamson 2008). The exchange rate, accordingly, may be assumed to depend on expectations of future events rather than just on what is happening in the present or has happened in the past.[1] Given this theoretical framework, along with abundant empirical evidence, direct intervention in currency markets can be expected to have little scope and effect.[2] It may also risk sending wrong signals to the markets and setting unmanageable expectations. Central banks can still play a useful role, but mainly by helping market actors locate long-term equilibrium by signaling future changes in monetary policy and/or by changing the relative supplies of different assets.

In the case of the EMU, this suggests that the ECB should use its accumulated credibility to engage more proactively with the markets on the euro's exchange rate. In practice, this would mean focusing on the currency's long-term equilibrium rate as well as the short-term process of transition to equilibrium to counter the frequent tendency of market players to extrapolate recent exchange-rate changes into long-term future trends. In doing so, the ECB must remain credible about the goal of internal price stability.

Effective exchange-rate management will also require a concerted parallel effort by the EMU's member governments. Monetary policy alone cannot carry the load. Equally important is the role of fiscal policy as exercised by individual states, which can have a significant impact not only on the euro's external value but also on real rates of exchange within the EMU. Empirical evidence points to growing divergences of real exchange rates within the euro zone (Subacchi *et al.* 2008). At the root of these divergences are differences in national inflation rates. These are not only a function of cyclical positions, but are also determined by the shape of national institutions—above all, labor markets. Sound national policies aimed at strong productivity growth can help real exchange-rate readjustment for converging economies with a fixed nominal exchange rate, and therefore improve competitiveness. Better coordination and surveillance of policies, in turn, would ensure that separate national targets and instruments are consistent with each other and are integrated into a non-conflicting framework in order to avoid negative spillovers. This is one of the three pillars of the European Commission's policy agenda (European Commission 2008: 3).

The function of coordination would be best undertaken by the Eurogroup, the euro zone's informal committee of finance ministers, which, according to the European Commission (2008: 287), has become "a key body in the present EMU's system of economic governance." The main strength of the Eurogroup is its relatively small size and cohesiveness, which enables it to debate issues thoroughly and with candor. Currently it is charged with the surveillance of public finance and macroeconomic developments. Additionally in recent years, it has increasingly discussed microeconomic issues relevant to a better functioning of the EMU. The Eurogroup can play a bigger role in overseeing structural reforms and policy linkages among its members.

Speaking with one voice?

Even with more effective exchange-rate management, the euro zone will remain a political dwarf on the global stage so long as it continues to speak, as it currently does, with a so-called cacophony of voices. The disadvantages of the EMU's lack of coherence are by now well understood. In a report marking the ECB's tenth anniversary, the European Commission (2008: 279) explicitly identified the consolidation of the bloc's external representation as a policy target: "To be able to speak with a more coherent voice in global fora, the euro area needs to consolidate its external representation. ... [T]he time is ripe for launching this process of consolidation."

One possibility mooted by the Commission as a long-term objective would be the establishment of a single seat for all EMU members in relevant international bodies and forums such as the IMF and the G-7. Such a goal is easier to enunciate than to implement since those member states that now occupy individual seats are unlikely to relinquish their privileged positions without a struggle. Given the diffuse skepticism and increasing disillusionment toward the European project that seems rampant across Europe today— well demonstrated by the Irish public's rejection of the Lisbon Treaty in a referendum this past June—there is little appetite in Brussels for any move now that might seem to threaten such a key element of national sovereignty. Consolidation of representation in a single seat for the euro zone is simply not politically realistic under present circumstances.

More plausible is the possibility that a single EMU representative might be added to the EU's existing cast of characters to speak specifically for the euro zone on matters of critical interest to its members. Who might provide that representative? One possible candidate is the ECB. As the euro zone's only truly collective institution, the ECB seems to be the most natural candidate to speak for the EMU on global monetary issues. But that choice runs up against the tradition that, in most such settings, countries are usually represented not by central banks but by finance ministers with the political clout to speak for their respective governments. But the ECB cannot claim that kind of authority. Indeed, it is difficult to imagine the elected governments of Europe ever delegating such a fundamental power to an institution that was deliberately designed to be as free from political influence as possible.

The obvious alternative would be the Eurogroup, whose members have the necessary political clout. A start in this direction came in January 2005 when the position of Eurogroup president was created. Having improved the running of the Eurogroup's meetings, the president plays a key role in the economic governance of the EMU and is now expected to represent and articulate the views of finance ministers in the relevant international forums. The president participates on a regular basis in the G-7 finance ministers meetings, albeit with no specified responsibilities. Likewise, when issues relating to the euro are discussed at the IMF, the president is invited to make a statement on behalf of all EMU members.

Nevertheless, this is only a start and clearly falls short of what is needed to fully transform the EMU into a monetary heavyweight comparable to the United States. Because the Eurogroup remains an informal grouping within the EU, its president lacks any sort of formal mandate to negotiate on behalf of EMU members. Worse yet, the president's ability to speak authoritatively for the euro zone extends only to issues on which the members are able to agree, which are usually the least controversial. The ruling principle within the Eurogroup is consensus, which effectively gives each member a potential veto. As a result, the president's voice can be easily muffled by policy differences among governments. Given the EMU's present governance structure, a single official cannot ignore or override the preferences of diverse sovereign states.

Can the voice of the president be strengthened? It would help if the role of the Eurogroup were to be formally institutionalized within the EU's complex governance structure. Likewise, the president's legitimacy and credibility could be enhanced by the grant of an official mandate to represent the EMU in all international organizations and forums. There would also be great benefit if the finance ministers of the Eurogroup could be persuaded to look more often at the bigger picture, reflecting a genuine sense of community and common identity.

However, herein lies a difficult balancing act between the interests of the euro area as whole and those of member states. The euro's external representation and governance must fit within a framework in which member states pursue their own goals without conflicting with the EMU's overall interests (Pisani-Ferry *et al.* 2008).

Eventually, some way must be found around the de facto veto currently available to EMU members. One possibility is to make the Eurogroup's decision-making procedures more transparent, in hopes of reducing temptations for opportunistic behavior. Another is to take the ECB's Executive Board as a model to create a small inner council of no more than six elected members authorized to decide on policies after consultations with all EMU members. A third possibility is to introduce weighted majority voting in the Eurogroup, with appropriate safeguards for smaller states. With any of these options, there would be grounds for concern about a possible democratic deficit in the delegation of authority over potentially critical matters to such a small group of decision-makers. Notwithstanding, such worries could be alleviated by suitable provisions for accountability. For example, the Eurogroup president might be required to report regularly to the European Parliament, while finance ministers would continue to report, as they do now, to their respective national legislatures.

In the end, any step toward consolidation of euro-zone representation is bound to be accused of infringing on national sovereignty. Indeed, contestation over who speaks for the EMU is inevitable so long as the euro remains a currency without a country. The tradeoff is inherent in the interstate agreement that underlies the EMU. Still, if Europe really wishes to punch its true weight on monetary matters, there is no choice. Without the reforms needed to project power more effectively Europe will never be ready for prime time.

Conclusion

Throughout the decade since its birth, the euro has clearly established itself as the second most important international currency in the world. Nevertheless, contrary to expectations, the euro has not become a second pillar of the system on a par with the U.S. dollar. Though an economic giant, the EMU remains a political dwarf, unable to punch its weight in monetary affairs. The outcome can best be described as a one-and-a-half currency system— certainly not the two-pillar world that many anticipated.

The problem lies in the governance of the EMU, which structurally constrains the role that the bloc can play in monetary governance. Therefore, the solution lies in a reform of the bloc's rules and institutions that would put greater emphasis on the euro's external dimension. On one hand, this calls for more proactive management of the currency's exchange rate by the ECB in conjunction with an explicit commitment by the Eurogroup to undertake effective coordination of national fiscal policies. On the other hand, it would mean designating a single representative of the EMU with real authority to speak on behalf of members in international councils. Unless the euro zone can learn how to project power more successfully, dual leadership of monetary affairs at the global level will remain out of reach.

9 Toward a leaderless currency system

The dollar presently reigns supreme as an international currency. Can its dominance be challenged? Many observers foresee the rise of significant rivals for global currency leadership: the euro; possibly a revived yen; perhaps, in the longer run, even the Chinese yuan. My aim in this essay is to assess the prospects of the greenback's main competitors and implications for the broader monetary system.

Do any of the dollar's potential rivals represent a truly serious challenge? Like many others, I accept that the global position of the dollar is weakening. Essential to the greenback's dominance until now has been a widespread and remarkably durable faith in the currency's value and usefulness. Sooner or later, confidence in the dollar is bound to be undermined by the chronic payments deficits of the United States, which add persistently to the country's looming foreign debt. But that by itself will not ensure the success of some alternative. The decline of one currency does not automatically guarantee the ascendancy of another. In fact, potential challengers have considerable deficiencies of their own, which are likely to limit their appeal, too. There is no obvious new leader lurking in the wings, an understudy just waiting to take center stage.

So what, then, should we expect? We should anticipate something like the interregnum of the period between the two world wars, when Britain's pound sterling was in decline and the dollar on the rise, but neither was dominant. Coming years, I submit, will see the emergence of a similarly fragmented monetary system, with several currencies in contention and none clearly in the lead—an increasingly leaderless mix of currency relationships. We know that the absence of firm monetary leadership during the interwar period was a contributing factor to the financial crisis and Great Depression of the 1930s. The economic and political impacts of a leaderless monetary system in the twenty-first century could also be considerable.

I begin with a brief review of prospects for the dollar, setting the stage for the analysis to follow. Contrary to the more sanguine views of observers such as Harold James (2009) or Ronald McKinnon (2009), I do not consider the persistent buildup of America's foreign debt as sustainable for long. Unless reversed by significant policy reform in Washington, the U.S. economy's dependence on foreign capital must be expected in time to erode the advantages historically enjoyed by the greenback, creating an opportunity for possible challengers.

Three currencies are most frequently mentioned as potential contenders for the dollar's crown—the euro, yen, and yuan. Prospects for each are considered. Overall, my assessment is skeptical. None of the three candidates appears capable of mounting a serious challenge to the dollar; certainly none is likely to surpass the greenback in the foreseeable future. Rather, the more plausible outcome is one in which the dollar's supremacy is eroded but no other single money emerges to replace it. In the language of Jonathan Kirshner (2009), the dollar will become one of several "peer competitors" in a fragmented currency system, with no dominant leader.

I then turn, in conclusion, to the implications of a fragmented currency system for international monetary stability. A heightened struggle for leadership seems probable, threatening an increase of tension in currency affairs. Much will depend, however, on how aggressive policymakers choose to be in promoting their respective monies. The most likely battlegrounds are the Middle East, where the dollar and euro will contend for supremacy, and Asia, where the greenback can expect determined efforts on behalf of both the yen and the yuan. In both locales, the most likely outcome is intensified rivalry but not outright conflict.

Assumptions

I focus on the market role of the dollar and its potential challengers—that is, the extent to which alternative currencies are used by market actors as a medium of exchange, unit of account, or store of value in international transactions. Hence the competition for monetary leadership is treated here as primarily a function of economic constraints and incentives. Politics in this context enters only through what Eric Helleiner (2009) calls the "indirect" channel of political influence: the role that public policy may play in shaping economic constraints and incentives, thus helping to determine the relative attractiveness of alternative currencies for private market use. Only in the final section do I bring in what Helleiner calls the "direct" channel of political influence—the part that politics may play in seeking to sway the behavior of state actors in the currency system.

Underlying my analysis are four working assumptions, all well documented in practice. First is the assumption that for market actors international currency choice is shaped, above all, by a trio of essential attributes. (1) At least during the initial stages of a money's cross-border adoption, there must be widespread confidence in its future value backed by political stability in the economy of origin. No one is apt to be attracted to a currency that does not offer a reasonable promise of stable purchasing power. (2) The qualities of "exchange convenience" and "capital certainty"—a high degree of liquidity and predictability of asset prices—are essential to minimizing transactions costs.

The key to both qualities is a set of broad and efficient financial markets, exhibiting depth and resiliency. (3) A money must promise a wide transactional network, since nothing enhances a currency's acceptability more than the prospect of acceptability by others. Historically, this factor has usually meant an economy that is large in absolute size and well integrated into world markets. The greater the volume of transactions conducted in or with an economy, the greater will be the economies of scale to be derived from the use of its currency.

Second is the assumption that currencies in the global economy tend to be distributed hierarchically in what I have elsewhere called the Currency Pyramid (Cohen 1998, 2004). At issue is the geography of money—the spatial organization of currency relations. Driving the geography of money is the force of competition—the constraints and incentives that shape market demand for currencies for either foreign or domestic use. Under the force of competition, the monetary universe becomes stratified, assuming the appearance of a vast pyramid: narrow at the top, where the strongest currencies dominate, and increasingly broad below, reflecting various degrees of competitive inferiority. In the nineteenth century, sterling stood at the peak of the Currency Pyramid. Today, of course, the top currency is the dollar.

Third is the assumption that monetary preferences are "sticky," characterized above all by path dependence and a noticeable tendency toward inertia. Currencies derive their popularity, in part, from scale economies in use—what specialists call network externalities. Network externalities may be understood as a form of interdependence in which the choices of any one actor depend strategically on the practices adopted by others in the same network of interactions. The same scale economies that encourage use of a currency in the first place are also responsible for "hysteresis" or "ratchet effects"—a marked resistance to change reflecting the high cost of switching from one money to another. Stickiness of preferences gives leading currencies a natural advantage of incumbency. This does not mean that change in the hierarchy is impossible. But it implies that when change does occur it most likely will come relatively slowly. It took decades for the dollar to supplant sterling atop the Currency Pyramid.

Fourth—and following directly from the third—is the assumption that, at any given moment, more than one currency may be widely used for international purposes. There is a common view, as one recent commentary put it, that, "at any one point in time, there tends to be a single dominant currency in the financial world, not two or more. ... In the currency markets the spoils go to the victor, alone; they are not shared" (Persaud 2004: 1). But that scenario is patently inaccurate. It was certainly not the case during the interwar period, as the dollar gradually eclipsed the pound. Typically, it has not even been the case when one currency was clearly dominant, as during the decades before World War I. Though sterling was then the world's leading money, both the French franc and German mark also enjoyed widespread popularity, particularly on the European continent. Likewise, even as the dollar has dominated in more recent times, a considerable share of market activity has been accounted for by the Deutschmark (now the euro) and Japanese yen. Competition tends to be as keen at the peak of the Currency Pyramid as it is below. As Barry Eichengreen (2006: 145) writes, the "argument that competition for reserve-currency status is a winner-take-all game holds little water either analytically or historically."

The dollar

No one questions that the dollar today still enjoys top rank in the Currency Pyramid. In most categories of international market use, the greenback continues to dominate. In currency trading, the dollar remains the most favored vehicle, appearing on one side or the other of some 86 percent of all foreign-exchange transactions (Bank for International Settlements 2007). The dollar is also the most favored vehicle for the invoicing of world trade, used for just over half of all exports, and still accounts for some two-fifths of the international bond market, roughly one-half of the international banking market, and two-thirds of central-bank reserves. No other currency today comes close to matching the greenback's global reach.

The threat to the greenback's dominant status is obvious. In the short term it comes from the great financial crisis that started in America's sub-prime mortgage market in 2007, which has thrown the security of the entire U.S. financial structure into question. Over the longer term, the threat comes from America's chronic balance-of-payments deficits, which are unprecedented by historical standards. As measured by the current account of the balance of payments, the gap in recent years has widened markedly; in 2006 it surpassed $850 billion, equivalent to some 6.5 percent of gross domestic product (GDP). Every year, the United States spends considerably more than its income, relying on foreign capital to make up the difference. In effect, Americans have outsourced their saving to the rest of the world. Although now shrinking a bit, the shortfall continues to add to America's foreign debt, absorbing as much as two-thirds of the world's surplus savings. On a gross basis, external liabilities now exceed $20 trillion. Net of America's own assets abroad, the debt reached $2.5 trillion at the end of 2007, equal to nearly one-fifth of GDP.

Can the process be sustained? Many, optimistically, have tried to make a case for sustainability. One popular argument points to the attractiveness of the U.S. economy as a market for goods of all kinds. America's deficits, it is said, are the direct result of export-led development strategies promoted by governments in East Asia and elsewhere, which are unlikely to be abandoned anytime soon. A second argument stresses the attractiveness of the U.S. economy as a haven for investments. The growth of debt is said to be the direct result of a growing "global savings glut" seeking high returns in a secure environment—a long-term trend that *The Economist* (2005a) labeled the "great thrift shift." Either way, America's deficits are seen not as a sign of disequilibrium but rather as a form of equilibrium that we might expect to be sustained for a long time to come. James (2009) goes even further, suggesting that in these patterns can be found the conditions for a new preeminence of the dollar in global affairs.

Such optimism, however, hardly seems justified. James discounts the importance of market confidence as a factor underlying America's ability to persistently live beyond its means—what Charles de Gaulle had in mind years ago when he referred to America's "exorbitant privilege." For how long can the United States go on building up a mountain of debt before doubts finally begin to take over? Some amelioration is possible, of course. The rate of growth of net liabilities already appears to have slowed somewhat since 2006, as a result of exchange-rate shifts that have stimulated exports and discouraged imports; and further adjustments are no doubt possible given the celebrated flexibility of the U.S. economy. But not even the most sanguine observers expect to see America's deficits disappear completely under the influence of market forces alone. In the absence of significant policy reforms to raise the domestic savings rate, spending will continue to exceed income, sooner or later eroding the world's trust in the dollar. The exorbitant privilege obviously cannot endure forever.

The case for sustainability, in short, is not nearly as persuasive as optimists such as James would have us believe. In fact, the probability that the dollar can long avoid a significant loss of confidence is sadly low. A fall from grace is unlikely to happen suddenly, as Kirshner (2009) suggests; Kirshner seriously underestimates the stickiness of monetary preferences. Much more probable is a gradual, cumulative erosion of the greenback's appeal, opening the door to a possible challenge by others. Is any other currency capable of seizing the opportunity?

The euro

The most obvious candidate is, of course, the euro, the joint currency created in 1999 by Europe's Economic and Monetary Union (EMU). Many have predicted a bright future for the euro as an international currency. Europe is the equal of the United States in output and trade. Why should it not be America's equal in monetary matters, too? Typical is the cheerful enthusiasm of historian Marcello de Cecco (2009), who suggests that we are at a turning point in world monetary history. Europe's new currency, he avers, is a "rising star" that is destined to play a role in the twenty-first century comparable to that of gold in the nineteenth century.

In reality, however, such enthusiasm seems misplaced. De Cecco asserts that Europe's new currency will be attractive—especially as a store of value—because, like gold, it is not an expression of national sovereignty. But that is simply wrong. Europe's governments have not renounced monetary sovereignty, as de Cecco puts it. Rather, monetary sovereignty has been pooled—an important distinction. The euro is the expression of the joint sovereignty of a group of governments and therefore can be considered only as good as the political agreement underlying it—an example of what one scholar calls a "sovereignty bargain" (Litfin 1997). Because the euro zone lacks the clean lines of authority traditionally associated with the management of money by individual states, it will always be at a structural disadvantage in global markets. James (2009) is right when he contends that there are more uncertainties about the future of the euro than of the dollar.

Briefly updating a previous analysis (Cohen 2003), I argue that only in the immediate neighborhood of the European Union (EU), where trade and financial ties are especially close, does the euro enjoy any special advantages. That is EMU's natural hinterland—"the euro's turf," as Charles Wyplosz (1999: 89) calls it. Elsewhere, the joint currency's star lacks luster.

Critical shortcomings

Admittedly, the euro is blessed with many attributes necessary for competitive success, including a large economic base, political stability, and an enviably low rate of inflation, all backed by a joint monetary authority, the European Central Bank, that is fully committed to preserving confidence in the money's future value. Much room, therefore, does indeed exist for the euro's star to rise. But because of its base in a sovereignty bargain, the euro is also handicapped by several critical shortcomings, all structural in character, that limit the currency's attractiveness as a rival to the greenback. These include: relatively high transactions costs; a serious anti-growth bias; and, most important, ambiguities at the heart of the monetary union's governance structure.

Transactions costs

First is the cost of doing business in euros. Transactions costs directly affect a currency's attractiveness as a vehicle for exchange transactions or international trade. From the start, it was clear that the dollar would be favored by the natural advantage of incumbency unless euro transactions costs, which began high relative to the widely traded greenback, could be lowered to a more competitive level. That, in turn, would depend directly on what could be done to improve the structural efficiency of Europe's financial markets. In practical terms, much has been accomplished to knit together previously segmented national markets. Efficiency gains have been substantial. Yet, for all that effort, the dollar's cost advantage has persisted, discouraging wider use of the euro.

The core problem is evident. The euro is condemned to remain at a disadvantage vis-à-vis the dollar so long as the EMU is unable to offer a universal financial instrument that can match the U.S. Treasury bill for international investor liquidity and convenience. This is a deficiency that will be impossible to rectify so long as the euro zone, with its separate national governments, lacks a counterpart to the Federal government in Washington. The best the

Europeans could hope to do was encourage establishment of selected bench-mark securities for the public debt market. Gradually three euro benchmarks have emerged: the German Bund at ten years, the French bond at five years, and the Italian bond at two years. But such a piecemeal approach falls far short of creating a single market as large and liquid as that for U.S. govern-ment securities. The greater depth and convenience of the U.S. Treasury bill market continues to give an advantage to the greenback.

Anti-growth bias

Second is a serious anti-growth bias that appears to be built in to the institu-tional structure of the EMU. By impacting negatively on yields on euro-denominated assets, this bias directly affects the euro's appeal as a long-term investment medium.

When the EMU first came into existence, eliminating exchange risk within the European region, a massive shift was predicted in the allocation of global savings as compared with holdings of European assets in the past. But as the ECB (2008b) has ruefully noted, international portfolio managers have in fact been quite slow to commit to Europe's new money, despite some cyclical uptick of euro-zone growth in 2007. Liquid funds have been attracted when there was a prospect of short-term exchange-rate appreciation. But underlying investor preferences have barely budged, in good part because doubts persist about the longer-term growth prospects in EMU countries, which have been trending downward for decades. Many factors, as we know, contribute to the slowing of Europe's trend rate of expansion: aging populations, which limit manpower increases and stress old-age pension systems; rigid labor markets, which hinder economic adaptability; and extensive government regulation, which can constrain innovation and entrepreneurship. The EMU, regrettably, adds yet one more brake on growth.

The core problem here, as is well known, lies in the EMU's institutional provisions governing monetary and fiscal policy, two key determinants of macroeconomic performance. In neither policy domain is priority attached to promoting output. Rather, in each, the main emphasis is on other con-siderations that tend to tilt policy toward restraint, producing a distinct anti-growth bias for the euro zone as a whole. On the monetary policy side, the European Central Bank is mandated to focus exclusively on fighting inflation, even if over time this might be at the cost of stunting growth. Similarly, on the fiscal policy side, euro-zone governments have formally tied their hands with their controversial Stability and Growth Pact, which sets a strict cap on national budget deficits at 3 percent of GDP, inhibiting con-tracyclical stimulation. Though the pact is by no means airtight, empirical evidence suggests that overall it has in fact exercised a significant discipline, particularly on some of the EMU's smaller members (Annett 2006). Is it any wonder, then, that the anticipated shift of global savings has turned out to be illusory?

Governance

Finally, there is the governance structure of the EMU, which for the euro's prospects as an international currency may be the biggest handicap of all. The basic question is: Who is in charge? The answer, regrettably, has never been obvious. From the start, as is well known, uncertainty has reigned concerning the delegation of monetary authority among governments and EU institutions.

Who, for example, controls monetary policy? Practical operational control lies in the hands of the ECB's Executive Board, made up of the president, vice president, and four other members. Overall managerial authority, however, is formally lodged in the Governing Council which, in addition to the six-member Executive Board, includes the heads of the central banks of all the member states, each participating fully in discussions and sharing voting rights. The large size and mixed representation of the Governing Council are clearly inconsistent with efficient or transparent governance. No one really knows how critical decisions are arrived at.

Or consider the question of financial stability. Who, ultimately, is responsible for crisis prevention or the management of financial shocks? Under the Maastricht Treaty, the EMU's founding document, no specific tasks are assigned to the ECB to help forestall crises. Though linkages have grown among national financial markets, increasing the risk of contagion should troubles hit, the ruling principle remains decentralization, otherwise known as subsidiarity—the notion that the lowest level of government that can efficiently carry out a function should do so. Formal authority for prudential supervision and regulation continues to reside at the national level, as it did before the EMU. Each central bank is charged with responsibility for the financial institutions based within its own national borders. No one can be sure that such a decentralized arrangement can be counted on to assure the smooth operation of the overall system. The possibility that central banks might work at cross-purposes, provoking or aggravating a crisis, is certainly not outside the realm of possibility.

Finally, there is the issue of external representation. Who is to speak for the euro zone on broader macroeconomic issues such as policy coordination, crisis management, or reform of the international financial architecture? Here the Maastricht Treaty has no answer at all, leaving a vacuum at the heart of the EMU. At a minimum, the Treaty's silence compounds confusion about who is in charge. At worst, it condemns the euro zone to lasting second-class status, since it limits the group's ability to project power on monetary matters.

A regional destiny

For all these reasons, it should be no surprise to find that the euro's experience as an international currency to date has been underwhelming (even allowing for the characteristic stickiness of monetary preferences). In most categories of international market use, adjusting for the elimination of intra-EMU transactions, the euro has managed roughly to hold its own as compared with the past aggregate shares of the EMU's "legacy" currencies. This means that Europe's joint money has smoothly taken its place as the successor to Germany's old Deutschmark, which among international currencies had already attained a rank second only to the dollar. But that is about all. Evidence from the ECB (2008b) indicates that after an initial spurt of enthusiasm for the new currency, use in most market segments has leveled off or even declined in recent years. Moreover, since its birth the euro's only enduring gains have been in the EMU's natural hinterland, including the EU's newest members before they joined, as well as other actual or potential candidate countries. In the ECB's (2008b: 7) words, analysis "confirms the largely regional character of the euro." Beyond the European region, the euro remains very much in the dollar's shadow.

None of this, therefore, adds up to a serious challenge to the greenback. The dollar's appeal may be eroded by America's persistent payments deficits. But that by itself does not ensure success for the euro so long as the new currency's own deficiencies remain uncorrected. The euro clearly does have a future as an international currency. But its appeal is not unqualified and, worse, seems limited mainly to the EU's own backyard. The currency's destiny appears to be regional, not global.

The yen

Less need be said about Japan's yen—once thought to be the dollar's heir apparent, now looking more like a sad, faded also-ran. During the 1970s and 1980s, when the fast-growing Japanese economy seemed destined for superpower status, international use of the yen accelerated significantly. But then at the end of the 1980s came the bursting of Japan's "bubble economy," which abruptly halted the currency's upward trajectory. Years of domestic stagnation dampened foreign interest in the yen, despite some highly visible attempts by the government in Tokyo to promote internationalization. Today the yen appears to face a gradual erosion of market standing not unlike sterling's long decline in an earlier era.

The appeal of the yen in its heyday was obvious. Postwar recovery had transformed Japan into the second largest economy in the world, an exporting powerhouse with extensive trade ties in just about every corner of the globe. The potential for network externalities was considerable. Moreover, the country suffered from neither political instability nor high inflation; and its financial markets had come to rank among the largest anywhere. Most of the ingredients for success were present.

Yet even at the peak of its popularity, enthusiasm for the currency was limited. Internationalization was strongest in the banking and securities markets, where a record of seemingly endless exchange-rate appreciation made yen-denominated claims especially attractive to investors. But the yen never came close to surpassing the dollar, or even the Deutschmark, in trade invoicing or as a vehicle for exchange transactions. The central problem could be found in the Japanese financial system, which had long lagged behind the American and even many European markets in terms of openness or efficiency. Until the 1990s, Japan's capital markets remained the most tightly regulated and protected in the industrial world, preventing wider use of the yen. Strict controls were maintained on both inward and outward movements of funds; the development of a domestic securities industry was retarded by the historic reliance of Japanese enterprise on bank lending for capital investment; and financial institutions were rigidly segmented. Neither exchange convenience nor reasonable capital certainty could be assured.

Worse, since the end of the "bubble economy," foreign use of the yen has in relative terms actually decreased rather than increased. The currency's appeal has clearly waned, mirroring Japan's broader economic troubles. Challenges include not only anemic growth and a rapidly aging population but also a fragile banking system and a level of public debt, scaled to GDP, that is now the highest of any industrial nation. Japanese government bonds are scorned by rating agencies, discouraging investors and inhibiting the use of the yen in lending markets. In exchange markets, the percentage of transactions involving the yen has shrunk from a high of 27 percent of global turnover in 1989 to barely 20 percent in 2004. Overall, the yen's position near the peak of the Currency Pyramid has slipped dramatically vis-à-vis both the euro and the dollar.

Can the yen's appeal be revived? Belated efforts by the Japanese government to promote greater internationalization of the yen have largely proved futile. Today, even the most ardent of the currency's supporters appear to have lost their enthusiasm for the struggle. Like the euro, the yen might still realistically aspire to something of a regional destiny. But outside Asia it poses no serious threat to the dollar.

Ironically, a determined government interest in internationalization did not even emerge until the yen's popularity had already begun to wane. Intermittent discussions started as early as the mid-1970s, but for many years widespread foreign use was resisted on the grounds that it might destabilize the yen's exchange rate or compromise domestic monetary management. Official policy, as C.H. Kwan (2001: 110) puts it, could best be described as "neutral if not passive." It was only after the economy nose-dived that the authorities started to focus more on the potential advantages of an international currency. A greater role for the yen could help jump-start stalled growth. It might also enhance Japan's political standing in the global pecking order. In the words of one informed source (Castellano 1999: 5): "Success at internationalizing the yen would be tantamount to achieving greater political prominence. ... [It is] a bid to expand Japan's global political influence." Policy shifted from passive to active.

In substantive terms, most effort has been put into modernizing Japan's financial system, accelerating a modest program of liberalization that, under pressure from the United States, was initiated as long ago as the 1970s.

Capital controls have been loosened, new instruments and markets have been developed, and institutional segmentation has been relaxed. Most dramatic was a multiyear program announced in 1996, dubbed the Big Bang in imitation of the swift deregulation of financial markets that had taken place a decade earlier in Britain. Under the Big Bang all remaining capital controls were eliminated and a variety of other ambitious measures were set in motion to enhance the general attractiveness of the yen as a vehicle for exchange transactions or international investment. Further reforms were initiated in 1998–99.

In geographic terms, policy has taken on a distinctly regional cast. Any pretense that Japan's currency might challenge the dollar on a global scale has plainly been abandoned. But, officials hope, it might still be possible to cultivate Japan's neighbors in East Asia—what could be thought of as the yen's natural turf. The EU is bound to dominate financial relations in the European hinterland. So why not counter with an Asian strategy for the yen, to consolidate a region of its own? Particular impetus came from East Asia's financial crisis of 1997–98, which seemed to create an opportunity for broadening the yen's role in the area. Internationalization of the yen, comments one source (Green 2001: 260), "became a national cause célèbre for Japanese elites after the financial crisis." Most notable was Tokyo's proposal for a new Asian Monetary Fund (AMF), a regional financial facility that would have done much to institutionalize Japanese dominance in Asian currency relations. When the AMF initiative got shot down, owing mainly to opposition from Washington, the Japanese soon followed up with ideas for other regional schemes, culminating in the creation of a network of swap arrangements dubbed the Chiang Mai Initiative, after the town in Thailand where negotiations took place.

In practice, however, results have been discouraging. Asian governments prefer to hedge their bets as they watch China emerge as a rival to Japan for regional economic and political dominance. As Saori Katada (2002: 105) observes, "Asian countries still try to avoid any attempts by Japan that might result in locking those countries into power relations." These days, even Japan's own policy elites now seem resigned to a diminished future for the yen. Japanese aspirations today seem limited to little more than holding on to a piece of regional leadership.

The yuan

As the yen declines, could China's yuan rise? The notion that the yuan could one day become the key currency of Asia—or beyond—is widely shared. But is it justified? The renminbi (the "people's money," or RMB) certainly has much going for it and has already begun to step out onto the world stage. International use, however, remains rudimentary at best and is retarded by obstacles far more severe even than anything blocking the euro or yen. In time, the currency's handicaps might well be surmounted. But the time required is likely to be measured not in years but decades, if not generations. For the foreseeable future, the yuan poses no threat to the dollar.

The potential is there, of course. Years of double-digit growth have already made China's economy, in purchasing-power terms, the second largest in the world after the United States; as an exporter, China now ranks ahead of both the United States and Germany. With such a huge and well-connected economic base, the opportunity for network externalities is obvious. Few observers seem to doubt that international use of the yuan will eventually follow. As the *Financial Times* (June 2, 2003) puts it, "The emergence of the RMB as an international currency will be … a natural result of China's booming economy."

But that reckons without the other attributes essential for cross-border adoption—in particular, the qualities of exchange convenience and capital certainty that are so critical to the usability of a currency. China's financial sector is still at the very earliest stage of development, offering limited investment opportunities. The level of transparency and efficiency lags far behind that of all of the more established financial powers; markets are thin and liquid assets are few. Worse, the yuan itself remains tightly regulated, not easily accessible for international transactions. Convertibility for trade in goods and services was introduced only in 1996. Cumbersome capital controls are still nearly universal.

Not surprisingly, therefore, yuan internationalization to date has been negligible. A certain amount of Chinese paper currency has begun to show up in neighboring economies as a result of growing cross-border trade and tourism by Chinese citizens. But the totals remain small—no more than $2–3 billion at the end of 2004 according to one recent estimate (Zhang 2007), equivalent to roughly 1 percent of China's overall cash circulation. By comparison, as much as two-thirds of Federal Reserve notes are in permanent circulation outside the United States. Beyond the borders of China the RMB is rarely used for trade invoicing or as an investment vehicle.

To its credit, China's government acknowledges its currency's limitations and seems determined to do something about them. Unlike the Japanese prior to the 1990s, the Chinese have long welcomed prospective internationalization as a logical corollary to their country's reemergence as an economic superpower. As one prominent academic (Li 2006) in the authoritative *People's Daily* declared, "China has become a world economic power and the RMB has to be internationalized." But for reasons as much political as economic, nothing like Japan's Big Bang has ever been mooted. In their typically cautious manner, the authorities prefer to move only gradually to widen use of the yuan.

In 2005, for example, multilateral agencies such as the Asian Development Bank and International Finance Corporation (a subsidiary of the World Bank) were authorized for the first time to issue yuan-denominated bonds inside China. The so-called Panda bonds, it was hoped, would encourage greater use of the RMB as a borrowing vehicle. Two years later, domestic borrowers were given permission to issue RMB bonds in Hong Kong, with the aim of broadening the range of potential buyers as well. Steps like these are essential if the yuan is ever to attract significant international interest. At the present pace, however, it clearly will be many years before any kind of serious challenge to the dollar can be mounted.

Fragmentation

In short, prospects for the dollar may be discouraging (barring significant policy reforms in the United States), but the outlook for any of the green-back's main competitors appears little better. Neither the euro in Europe nor the yen or yuan in Asia seem ready to seize the dollar's mantle. Rather, a much more fragmented system appears in the offing, with much competition and no money clearly dominant. For years to come, the world will have to learn to live with a leadership vacuum at the peak of the Currency Pyramid.

Cooperation?

The dangers of fragmentation are clear. Without some form of leadership to assure a minimal degree of compatibility among national policies, the global monetary system will be at constant risk of instability or worse. Among public agencies there is no Invisible Hand to assure mutually beneficial outcomes. Decentralized decision-making among sovereign governments without some manner of coordination is potentially a recipe for disaster.

To be sure, a leaderless currency system would not necessarily be a bad thing. Some have argued it could even turn out be an improvement. Few knowledgeable observers doubt that the greatest threat to monetary stability today is to be found in America's mammoth payments deficits. As the supplier of the world's most popular currency, the United States is in the position of a monopolist that has grown complacent, abusing its "exorbitant privilege." But once the dollar's supremacy is eroded by emergent challengers, America would finally be forced to curb its appetite for foreign savings, lowering the risk of crisis. As Kwan (2001: 7) puts it, "The emergence of international currencies that compete with the dollar may help impose discipline on the economic policy of the United States by rendering the international environment less forgiving of its mistakes."

Much depends, however, on the kind of relationship that develops among the competitors. The last time that the world was obliged to live with a leaderless system, during the interwar period, the outcome was—to say the least—dismal. A lack of cooperation between the British, with their weakened pound, and a self-consciously isolationist United States was a critical cause of the financial calamities that followed the stock-market crash of 1929. As Charles Kindleberger (1973: 292) wrote in his classic *The World in Depression*, "The international economic system was rendered unstable by British inability and United States unwillingness to assume responsibility for stabilizing it." Can we expect better this time around?

Optimists might emphasize how much conditions have changed since the interwar period. In contrast to the years after World War I, an array of multilateral organizations and forums have developed to institutionalize cooperative practices, from the International Monetary Fund to the Group of Seven. Past experience has provided some pointed lessons about the costs of unbridled competition. Governments have a much better sense of where their enlightened self-interest lies. A system lacking a single dominant leader, therefore, might not lack effective leadership if the principal players can learn to work together for the common good.

Monetary cooperation, however, is notoriously difficult to sustain, as I have suggested previously (Cohen 1993). The issue is monetary autonomy, which governments greatly prize for its importance to domestic economic management. In times of crisis, when the benefits of coordination take precedence, governments may for a time be willing to enter into significant policy compromises. But once a sense of threat subsides, the desire to maintain control over domestic monetary conditions tends to reassert itself, encouraging defection. Despite the lessons of the past, cooperation among sovereign states tends to be episodic at best, with commitments ebbing and flowing like the tides.

Moreover, this time there are not just two major players involved, as there were after World War I, but as many as four. Worse, one of the four, the EMU, has still not resolved the issue of external representation; while two others, Japan and China, are in open contention for monetary influence in their regional neighborhood. In these circumstances, the probability that effective joint leadership could be successfully cultivated seems decidedly low.

Leadership struggle

Much more likely is a heightened struggle for leadership. Rational policymakers understand the benefits of widespread international use of a currency. The United States may be expected to resist any compromise of the greenback's historical dominance. The contenders in Europe and Asia may be expected to make every effort to defend or enhance the status of their own monies. Life at the peak of the Currency Pyramid will undoubtedly be tense.

But will it be dangerous? That depends on how aggressive policymakers choose to be in promoting their respective monies. As I have noted elsewhere (Cohen 2004), a critical distinction must be drawn between two different kinds of leadership aspirations: informal and formal. Much rides on the difference.

Informal leadership refers to dominance among market actors—the scope of a currency's use for private market purposes. At this level, a competitive struggle may be said already to exist, operating through what Helleiner (2009) calls the "indirect" channel of political influence. In the EMU, as well as in the two Asian contenders, public policy is already actively engaged in trying to improve the appeal of the dollar's rivals, particularly via financial-market reform; in defensive reaction, the United States will do what it can to sustain the popularity of the greenback. The consequences of an informal leadership struggle, however, are apt to be largely benign, since governments take this sort of contestation very much in their stride. Rivalry to promote or sustain each currency's competitiveness can be regarded as a natural feature of a decentralized monetary system based largely on market principles. The global community might even benefit if the result is lower transactions costs and more efficient capital markets.

But what if the players elect to go a step further, to seek to alter the behavior of state actors—what I term formal leadership? This option corresponds more closely to what Helleiner describes as the "direct" channel of influence. The aim here is to alter currency choices at the official level: to induce governments to switch to a different reserve currency or perhaps even to adopt the foreign currency domestically in place of their own national money ("dollarization"). The result, ultimately, would be the formation of organized currency blocs, not unlike the old sterling area that coalesced around Britain's pound in the interwar period. The world would face the "new geopolitical reality" of a "variety of regional systems" that David Calleo (2009) predicts.

As in interstate relations generally, tactics in a formal leadership struggle in monetary affairs may involve either coercion or persuasion, depending on circumstances. Currencies might be directly imposed on client states in a manner similar to what Susan Strange (1971a) meant by a "Master Currency." In Kirshner's (1995) terms, countries could be threatened with enforcement or expulsion if they do not align themselves monetarily—a threat of sanctions, say, or a withdrawal of past commercial or financial privileges. Alternatively, attractive inducements of an economic or political nature might be offered to reshape policy preferences in manner analogous to Strange's notion of a "Negotiated Currency"—what Kirshner (1995) describes as entrapment.

Whatever the tactics used, the consequences for the global monetary system could indeed be dangerous. In a formal leadership struggle, by definition, competition becomes more overtly politicized and hence less easy to contain. Economically, increasingly antagonistic relations could develop between mutually exclusive groupings, reversing decades of multilateral liberalization in trade and financial markets. Politically, currency rivalry could become transformed into serious geopolitical conflict.

Many observers discount the probability of a formal leadership struggle, pointing to the evident perils involved. Any efforts to alter currency choices at the state level would imply a cutback of dollar accumulations, which in turn could lead to a sharp depreciation of the greenback, causing massive losses on existing reserve holdings. Would governments truly risk such self-inflicted wounds? To avert a doomsday scenario, it makes more sense for state actors to support the greenback—or, at least, not undermine it—whether they like it or not. Optimists see this as nothing more than enlightened self-interest.

Others, however, see it as more like the notorious balance of terror that existed between the nuclear powers during the Cold War—a "balance of financial terror," as former treasury secretary Larry Summers (2004) has described it. A fear of mutually assured destruction is surely a powerful deterrent to overtly destabilizing behavior. But fear cannot rule out the possibility of miscalculation or even mischief by critical players. As Kirshner (2009) points out, today's challengers for currency supremacy, unlike in earlier years, are not all political allies of the United States bonded together by the glue of the cold war; indeed, one of them, China, is deemed America's greatest potential adversary. In fact, the balance of financial terror is inherently unstable and could conceivably break down at any time.

Battlegrounds?

Will the balance break down? Prediction is hazardous, of course (particularly, as the joke goes, when the future is involved), and a doomsday scenario can hardly be excluded. But I am less persuaded than some observers, such as Kirshner (2009), that the wolf is actually at the door, ready to wreak systemic havoc. Certainly the foundations for a confrontation over formal leadership are in place, suggesting that a threat somewhere, at some time, is possible. There seems little reason to worry in the Western Hemisphere, where a dollar bloc has effectively existed for some time; there, the greenback remains largely unchallenged. Nor do many question the euro's increasing dominance in the EMU's European hinterland as well as in much of Africa. But elsewhere room does indeed exist for serious clashes, though my expectation is that in the end most risks will be held in check by broader geopolitical considerations. The greatest dangers are to be found in the Middle East and East Asia.

Middle East

In the Middle East, where the greenback has long reigned supreme, Europe could be understandably tempted to seek a greater role for the euro. With its concentration of wealthy oil exporters, the region would seem a prize well worth fighting for. At the moment, the U.S. dollar is not only the standard for invoicing and payments in world energy markets; it also accounts for the vast majority of central-bank reserves and government-held investments in Middle Eastern countries. Overall, however, the region's commercial ties are far more oriented toward Europe—a disjunction that many Europeans find anomalous, even irrational. Repeatedly, the question is asked: Would it not make more sense for the area to do business with its largest trading partner, Europe, in Europe's own currency rather than the greenback? And if so, would it not then make sense to switch to the euro as a reserve currency as well? Europe is well placed to make the Middle East a currency battleground.

Certainly, the possibility of a switch to the euro is tempting from a European perspective. Displacement of the dollar might go far to restore a measure of

Europe's historically privileged position in the region. Arguably, the prospect might be tempting from the perspective of Middle Eastern governments, too, for sound economic reasons as well as to curb the presently overweening strategic influence of the United States. It is well known that from time to time oil-exporting states have actively explored alternatives to the dollar, only to be discouraged by the lack of a suitable substitute. Now, with the arrival of the euro, they see the possibility of a truly competitive rival for their affections. Talk of a switch to the euro (or to a currency basket heavily weighted toward the euro) has been particularly intense lately as a result of the greenback's most recent bout of weakness. Should Europe seek to capitalize on the dollar's travails, directly promoting use of the euro by regional governments, it might find itself pushing against an open door.

Any effort along these lines, however, would surely provoke determined opposition from the United States, which has long linked the region's use of the dollar to broader security concerns. For Washington, there is no higher politics than the Great Game being played out today in the energy-rich Middle East. America needs both the region's oil and continued support for the greenback; regional governments, in turn, need protection against enemies both within and without, which Washington has promised under a series of unwritten understandings dating back to the first oil shock in the 1970s. With so much at stake, the level of U.S. tolerance for a formal currency challenge from Europe would be correspondingly low, making geopolitical conflict a virtual certainty.

Indeed, for some observers, the conflict has already begun. Theories abound that America's 2003 attack on Iraq, following as it did shortly after Saddam Hussein's decision to demand payment in euros for Iraqi oil exports, was motivated above all by a desire to sustain the dollar's role in the region. Though the idea is wholly unsubstantiated by plausible evidence, one need not be a sensationalist to recognize the seeds of truth that it contains. A battle of currencies in the Middle East could get nasty.

Would Europe risk it? In the end, however strongly tempted, the Europeans are more likely to keep their aspirations in check, averting direct confrontation with Washington. Even after the Bush administration's decision to promote "regime change" in Iraq, there is no consensus among Europeans to risk the broader political and security relationship that they have long enjoyed with the United States. Beyond their currency's natural home in Europe's immediate neighborhood, therefore, they will most probably act with restraint. Maneuvering for advantage in the Middle Eastern region will undoubtedly persist. But the euro's challenge to the dollar is unlikely to be allowed to get out of control.

East Asia

In East Asia, where both Japan and China continue to aspire to regional leadership, it is easy to imagine a three-way contest developing between the greenback, still dominant for now, and its two regional counterparts, the yen and yuan. Here also the U.S. dollar still accounts for the vast majority of central-bank reserves and government-held investments. Hence here also there is much room for a vigorous campaign by either Tokyo or Beijing to promote a greater role for its currency at the greenback's expense. Japan, despite recent disappointments, has by no means given up on its Asian strategy for the yen, while China, taking the long view, clearly has committed itself to a policy of gradual internationalization of the RMB. These countries are well placed to make their neighborhood a currency battleground, too.

Determined opposition from the United States must be expected here as well, given America's long-standing security interests in the region. Much is at stake here, too. Washington has long enjoyed an impressive ability to project power in East Asia, based on an extensive network of military bases and alliances as well as deep commercial and financial ties. For decades America has in effect played the role of sheriff in the area, preserving a degree of stability among unfriendly, even hostile, neighbors. More recently, Washington has also aimed to contain the rise of China as a potential global rival. To a significant degree, all this has been made possible by the unquestioned acceptability of the dollar, which allows the United States to spend whatever it feels it needs to promote its policy ambitions. Washington is hardly likely to take any challenge from the yen or yuan lying down.

In the case of the yen the risk is actually quite modest. That is because of America's decades-old defense alliance with Japan, which neither Washington nor Tokyo would wish to jeopardize. Like the Europeans, the Japanese are most likely to keep their aspirations in check rather than confront the United States directly. Ever since World War II, Japan's foreign policy has involved a delicate balancing act, seeking to play a leadership role in East Asia while also keeping the United States engaged in the region as a counterweight to China. Tokyo has no interest in seriously alienating its most powerful ally for the sake of a putative yen bloc.

In the case of the yuan, by contrast, the risk is greater. That is because of China's evident superpower aspirations, which color every dimension of Beijing's relationship with Washington. China has already gained a great deal of clout throughout East Asia as a result of its rapid economic growth and shows every sign of intending to reclaim what it regards as its rightful place as the dominant power in the region—a strategy that we know includes a wider role for the RMB. Given its limitations, the yuan is clearly unready to replace the dollar as yet. On the other hand, with Beijing's enormous dollar accumulations that could be diversified at any time, the Chinese do have the means to undermine the greenback should they so desire. The question is: Would they so desire, knowing that they could themselves suffer massive losses in the process? The answer ultimately will depend on broader trends in Sino-American relations, which cannot be predicted in advance.

Prospects

Prospects for the future, therefore, are clouded at best. A weakening dollar is unlikely to be replaced by any other single currency. The outlook, rather, is for a more fragmented currency system, with three or four monies in direct competition in different parts of the world. Sustained cooperation among the major players is unlikely, except in the event of a serious crisis. Much more probable is a prolonged leadership struggle, particularly in such contested regions as the Middle East and East Asia, though for the most part there seems little risk of an escalation into outright geopolitical conflict. Once again, as during the long interregnum following the start of sterling's decline, it could be decades before the final outcome becomes clear.

10 The international monetary system
Diffusion and ambiguity

Ample evidence exists to suggest that the distribution of power in international monetary affairs is changing. But where does monetary power now reside, and what are the implications for governance of the international monetary system? On these questions, uncertainty reigns. The aim of this essay is to shed some new light on the dynamics of power and rule-setting in global finance today.

I will begin with a brief discussion of the meaning of power in international monetary relations, distinguishing between two critical dimensions of monetary power: autonomy and influence. The evolution of international monetary power in recent decades will then be examined. Major developments have dramatically shifted the distribution of power in the system. Many have noted that power is now more widely diffused, both among states and between states and societal actors. Finance is no longer dominated by a few national governments at the apex of the global order. Less frequently remarked is the fact that the diffusion of power has been mainly in the dimension of autonomy, rather than influence—a point of critical importance. While more actors have gained a degree of insulation from outside pressures, few as yet are able to exercise greater authority to shape events or outcomes. Leadership in the system thus has been dispersed rather than relocated—a pattern of change in the geopolitics of finance that might be called leaderless diffusion.

A pattern of leaderless diffusion generates greater ambiguity in prevailing governance structures. Rule-setting in monetary relations increasingly relies not on negotiations among a few powerful states but, rather, on the evolution of custom and usage among growing numbers of autonomous agents— regular patterns of behavior that develop from long-standing practice. Impacts on governance structures can be seen at two levels: the individual state and the global system. At the state level, the dispersion of power compels governments to rethink their commitment to national monetary sovereignty. At the systemic level, it compounds the difficulties of bargaining on monetary issues. Formal rules are increasingly being superseded by informal norms that emerge, like common law, not from legislation or statutes but from everyday conduct and social convention.

Monetary power

For the purposes of this article, the international monetary system may be understood to encompass all the main features of monetary relations across national frontiers—the processes and institutions of financial intermediation (mobilization of savings and allocation of credit) as well as the creation and management of money itself. As Susan Strange once wrote:

> The financial structure really has two inseparable aspects. It comprises not just the structures of the political economy through which credit is created but also the monetary system or systems which determine the relative values of the different moneys in which credit is denominated.
>
> (Strange 1994: 90)

Both aspects are influenced by the distribution of power among actors.

And what do we mean by power in monetary relations? To summarize briefly an argument that I have developed at greater length elsewhere (Cohen 2006b), I suggest that international monetary power may be understood to comprise two critical dimensions, autonomy and influence. The more familiar of the two is the dimension of influence, defined as the ability to shape events or outcomes. In operational terms, this dimension naturally equates with a capacity to control the behavior of actors—"letting others have your way," as diplomacy has jokingly been defined. An actor, in this sense, is powerful to the extent that it can effectively pressure or coerce others; in short, to the extent that it can exercise leverage or managerial authority. As a dimension of power, influence is the essential sine qua non of systemic leadership.

The second dimension, autonomy, corresponds to the dictionary definition of power as a capacity for action. An actor is also powerful to the extent that it is able to exercise operational independence: to act freely, insulated from outside pressure. In this sense, power does not mean influencing others; rather, it means not allowing others to influence you—others letting you have your way.

The distinction between the two dimensions of power is critical. Both are based in social relationships and can be observed in behavioral terms; the two are also unavoidably interrelated. But they are not of equal importance. Logically, power begins with autonomy. Influence is best thought of as functionally derivative—inconceivable in practical terms without a relatively high degree of operational independence first being attained and sustained. First and foremost, actors must be free to pursue their goals without outside constraint. Only then will an actor be in a position, in addition, to exercise authority elsewhere. Autonomy may not be sufficient to ensure a degree of influence, but it is manifestly necessary. It is possible to think of autonomy without influence; it is impossible to think of influence without autonomy.

For state actors in the monetary system, the key to autonomy lies in the uncertain distribution of the burden of adjustment to external imbalances. National economies are inescapably linked through the balance of payments—the flows of money generated by international trade and investment. One country's surplus is another country's deficit. The risk of unsustainable disequilibrium represents a persistent threat to policy independence. Excessive imbalances generate mutual pressures to adjust, which can be costly in both economic and political terms. Deficit economies may be forced to curtail domestic spending or devalue their currencies, at the expense of growth and jobs; surplus economies may experience unwanted inflation or an upward push on their exchange rates, which can threaten international competitiveness. No government likes being compelled to compromise key policy goals for the sake of restoring external balance. All, if given a choice, would prefer to see others make the necessary sacrifices. For states, therefore, the foundation of monetary power is the capacity to avoid the burden of adjustment required by a payments imbalance.

The capacity to avoid the burden of adjustment is fundamentally dual in nature, subdividing into what I have characterized as the two "hands" of monetary power (Cohen 2006b). These are the power to delay and the power to deflect, each corresponding to a different kind of adjustment burden. One burden is the continuing cost of adjustment, defined as the cost of the new payments equilibrium prevailing after all change has occurred. The power to delay is the capacity to avoid the continuing cost of adjustment by postponing the process of adjustment. The other burden is the transitional cost of adjustment, defined as the cost of the change itself. Where the process of adjustment cannot be put off, the power to deflect represents the capacity to avoid the transitional cost of adjustment by diverting as much as possible of that cost to others. The power to delay is largely a function of a country's international liquidity position relative to others, comprising both owned reserves and borrowing capacity. A particular advantage is enjoyed in this respect by the issuers of currencies that are widely used by others as reserve assets, since these can finance deficits simply by printing more of their own money. The power to deflect, by contrast, has its source in more fundamental structural variables that determine an economy's relative degree of openness and adaptability.

For societal actors in the monetary system, the key to autonomy lies in the uncertain relationship between relevant market domains and legal jurisdictions. In an increasingly globalized world, the reach of financial markets is persistently growing. Yet political authority remains rooted in individual states, each in principle sovereign within its own territorial frontiers. Hence a disjuncture prevails between market domains and legal jurisdictions that creates ample room for opportunistic behavior by enterprises or private individuals. The very policy independence that is so prized by governments tends to create differences in market constraints and incentives that may well be exploited to advantage. For societal actors, the foundation of monetary power is the ability to navigate successfully in these interstices between political regimes.

Autonomy, in turn, is the key to influence. Because monetary relations are inherently reciprocal, a potential for leverage is automatically created whenever operational independence is attained. The question is: Will that potential be actualized? Two modes are possible in the exercise of monetary influence: passive and active. Autonomy translates into influence in the accepted sense of the term—a dimension of power aiming to shape the actions of others—only when the capacity for control is deliberately activated.

The requirement of actualization is often overlooked. The potential for leverage that derives automatically from autonomy—the passive mode of influence—is another way of describing what economists call externalities. At best, it represents a contingent aspect of power, exerted without design and with impacts that tend to be dispersed and undirected. Only when the potential for leverage is put to use with self-conscious intent do we approach the more common understanding of influence: the active mode, involving sharper focus in terms of who is targeted and to what end. Unlike the passive mode, the active mode implies a "purposeful act." Both modes begin with monetary autonomy as a basic and necessary condition, and in both cases other actors may feel compelled to comply. But in the passive mode externalities are incidental and unpremeditated, whereas in the active mode pressure is applied directly and deliberately. The active mode, in effect, politicizes relationships, aiming to translate passive influence into practical control through the instrumental use of power. From a political economy point of view, as we shall see, the difference between the two modes is critical.

Diffusion

For both states and societal actors, the distribution of monetary power has shifted dramatically in recent decades. Not long ago the global system was dominated by a small handful of national governments, led by the United States. Most countries felt they had little choice but to play by rules laid down by America and, to a lesser extent, its partners in the Group of Seven (G-7); markets operated within strict limits established and maintained by states. Today, by contrast, power has become more widely diffused, both among governments and between governments and market agents. The diffusion of power, however, has been mainly in the dimension of autonomy, rather than influence—a pattern of leaderless diffusion in financial geopolitics. The days of concentrated power in a largely state-centric system are now over.

Three major developments share principal responsibility for this change: (1) the creation of the euro; (2) the widening of global payments imbalances; and (3) the globalization of financial markets. Each of these developments has effectively added to the population of actors with a significant degree of autonomy in monetary affairs.

The euro

The creation of the euro in 1999 was always expected to have a major impact on the geopolitics of finance. Even without the participation of Britain and some other EU members, Europe's Economic and Monetary Union (EMU) was destined to become one of the largest economic units in the world, rivaling even the United States in terms of output and share of foreign trade. A shift in the balance of power across the Atlantic thus seemed inevitable. Europe's new money, building on the widespread popularity of Germany's old Deutschmark, would pose a serious threat to the predominance of America's greenback as an international currency. The euro area—Euroland, as some call it—was bound to become a leading player on the monetary stage. Robert Mundell (2000: 57), a Nobel laureate in economics, voiced a widely held view when he expressed his conviction that EMU would "challenge the status of the dollar and alter the power configuration of the system."

To a significant degree, those early expectations have been realized. A decade on, Europe's monetary power has clearly been enhanced. The euro has smoothly taken over the Deutschmark's place as the second most widely used currency in the world. Euroland itself has grown from eleven members to fifteen, with as many as a dozen or more countries set to join in future years. Some measure of power has indeed shifted across the Atlantic.

Europe's gains, however, have been mainly in the dimension of autonomy, rather than influence. Currency union has manifestly reduced the area's vulnerability to foreign-exchange shocks. With a single joint money replacing a plethora of national currencies, participants no longer have to fear the risk of exchange-rate disturbances inside Europe and, in combination, are now better insulated against turmoil elsewhere. For a continent long plagued by currency instability, that is no small accomplishment. Moreover, with the widespread acceptability of the euro, EMU countries now enjoy a much improved international liquidity position. Deficits that previously required foreign currency may now be financed with Europe's own money, thus enhancing the group's power to delay. Operational independence plainly is greater now than it was before.

So far, though, Europe has conspicuously failed to convert its enhanced autonomy into a greater capacity for control in monetary affairs (Cohen 2008). Contrary to the predictions of many, the euro has yet to establish itself as a truly global currency, and this has deprived participants of an instrument that might have been used to help shape behavior or outcomes. Nor has membership in EMU yet enabled European governments to play a more assertive role in world monetary forums such as the International Monetary Fund (IMF) or G-7. Though freer now to pursue internal objectives without external constraint, Euroland has yet to actualize the potential for overt leverage that monetary union has created.

The euro's weaknesses as an international currency are by now familiar. The new money did start with many of the attributes necessary for competitive success, including a large economic base, unquestioned political stability and an enviably low rate of inflation, all backed by a joint monetary authority, the European Central Bank (ECB), fully committed to preserving confidence in the currency's value. But, as I have argued previously (Cohen 2003), the euro is also hampered by several critical deficiencies, all structural in character, that dim its attractiveness as a rival to the greenback. These include limited cost-effectiveness, a serious anti-growth bias and, most importantly, ambiguities at the heart of the monetary union's governance structure. Not surprisingly, therefore, experience to date has been underwhelming. Only in the EU's immediate neighborhood, where trade and financial ties are especially close, has the euro come to enjoy any special advantages as the natural heir to the Deutschmark. That is EMU's natural habitat—"the euro's turf," as economist Charles Wyplosz (1999: 89) calls it. Elsewhere, Europe's money remains at a distinct disadvantage in trying to overcome the incumbency advantages of the already well-established dollar.

Equally obvious by now are Euroland's weaknesses as a political actor. Joined together in EMU, one would have thought, European states would surely have more bargaining power than if each acted on its own. Europe's voice would be amplified on a broad range of macroeconomic issues, from policy coordination to crisis management. Yet here, too, experience to date has been underwhelming. In practice, membership of EMU has not enabled EU governments to play a more influential role in the IMF or other global forums, mainly because no one knows who, precisely, speaks for the group. Since no single body is formally designated to represent EMU in international discussions, the euro area's ability to project power on monetary matters is inherently constrained. Fred Bergsten (2005: 33), a euro enthusiast, laments that EMU "still speaks with a multiplicity, even a cacophony, of voices. ... Hence it dissipates much of the potential for realizing a key international role."

Overall, therefore, the power configuration of the system has been altered far less than Mundell or others anticipated. The Europeans clearly are now better placed to resist external pressures. Their collective autonomy has been enhanced. But Europe is still a long way from exercising the kind of leverage that monetary union might have been expected to give it. Influence has not been effectively actualized. Monetary power, on balance, has been dispersed rather than relocated from one side of the Atlantic to the other.

Global imbalances

A second major development in recent years has been the emergence of unprecedented global imbalances—most particularly, a wide gap in the balance of payments of the United States, matched by counterpart surpluses elsewhere, particularly in East Asia and among energy-exporting nations. (Notably missing is Euroland, which has maintained a rough balance in its external accounts.) In 2006 America's deficit swelled past $850 billion, equivalent to some 6.5 percent of U.S. gross domestic product (GDP). Although it is now shrinking a bit, the shortfall continues to add to an already record level of foreign debt. Net of assets abroad, U.S. liabilities reached $2.6 trillion at the end of 2006, equal to roughly one-fifth of GDP. Correspondingly, reserve holdings of dollars in surplus countries have soared, having risen to above $3 trillion by 2006. For many, imbalances on this scale seem certain to alter the balance of monetary power between the United States and the larger surplus countries. The only question is: How much?

In terms of the autonomy dimension of power, the impact is obvious. With their vastly improved international liquidity positions, countries in surplus are now much better placed to postpone the process of adjustment when they wish: Their power to delay is clearly enhanced. A decade ago, when financial crisis hit East Asia, governments in the region—under intense pressure from the United States and the IMF—felt they had little choice but to initiate radical economic reforms, backed by tight monetary and fiscal policies. Resentful of being forced to pay such a high transitional cost of adjustment, they were determined to insulate themselves as much as possible against similar pressures in the future. The result today is a greatly heightened capacity for operational independence.

The most notable example of this phenomenon is China, whose currency reserves are now above $1.4 trillion and continue to grow by as much as $20 billion each month. China has been the target of a determined campaign by the United States and others to allow a significant revaluation of its currency, the yuan (also known as the renminbi). Beijing, however, has stood firm, resisting all pleas. Since a well-publicized switch from a dollar peg to a basket peg in mid-2005, the yuan has appreciated, in small steps, by little more than 15 percent—far short of what most observers think is needed to make a real dent in China's trade surplus. Plainly, the world's largest stockpile of reserves gives China more room for maneuver than it might otherwise enjoy.

But does enhanced autonomy translate into greater influence? Certainly there is an increase of influence in the passive mode. Simply by exercising their power to delay, surplus countries have placed more pressure on the United States to do something—or, at least, to think about doing something—about its deficits. But are we witnessing an increase of influence in the active, purposive mode? There the outlook is more ambiguous.

Indirectly, influence might be increased through the operations of the newly fashionable sovereign wealth funds that many surplus countries have created to generate increased earnings on a portion of their reserves. Already there are more than thirty such funds controlling assets in excess of $2.5 trillion, a figure that could grow to as much as $15 trillion over the next decade. In principle, it is possible to imagine that at least some of these funds might be deployed strategically to gain a degree of leverage in recipient states. Investments might be carefully aimed towards institutions that are known to have privileged access to the corridors of governmental power—institutions like Citibank and Merrill Lynch in the United States, which in the midst of the recent credit crunch together attracted more than $20 billion from wealth funds in Asia and the Middle East. In practice, however, potential target states are not without means to monitor or limit politically risky investments within their borders. The balance of power has by no means tipped as much as it might appear.

Alternatively, influence might be increased directly through the use of newly acquired reserve stockpiles to threaten manipulation of the value or stability of a key currency such as the dollar. There is nothing complicated about the option. Indeed, as Jonathan Kirshner (1995: 8) reminds us, "currency manipulation is the simplest instrument of monetary power and ... can be used with varying degrees of intensity, ranging from mild signaling to the destabilization of national regimes." Yet the results could be devastating for the issuer of a key currency, such as the United States. If any nation is in a position to use its newly acquired influence in this manner, it is China. At any time, Beijing could undermine America's money by dumping greenbacks on the world's currency exchanges or even simply by declining to add dollars to China's reserves in the future. Such threats would take little effort on China's part and could be carefully calibrated for maximum effect. The advantages for China are enormous.

But there are also disadvantages, as the Chinese themselves well understand. Beijing's dollar hoard could hardly be sold all at once. Hence any depreciation of the greenback would impose costs on China as well, in the form of capital losses on its remaining holdings. China's dollar reserves today are equal to about one-third of the country's GDP. For every 10 percent depreciation of the greenback, therefore, China would lose something in excess of 3 percent of GDP—no small amount. In addition, dollar depreciation would greatly erode the competitiveness of the exports that are so vital to China's economic growth. In reality, currency manipulation is a two-edged sword that could end up doing China far more harm than good—a kind of "nuclear option," to be used only in extremis.

Here too, then, it is not at all clear that the balance of monetary power has tipped as much in favor of China and other surplus countries as might appear to be the case. Indeed, now that dollar holdings have grown so large, it actually makes more sense for China and others to support rather than threaten the greenback, whether they like it or not, in order to avert a doomsday scenario. Some see this as nothing more than enlightened self-interest. Others see it as more akin to the notorious balance of terror that existed between the nuclear powers during the Cold War—a "balance of financial terror," as former U.S. treasury secretary Lawrence Summers (2004) has described it. Neither side wants to risk a MAD (mutually assured destruction) outcome.

In short, global imbalances too have caused a shift in the balance of monetary power—but, as in the case of EMU, mainly in the dimension of autonomy. Reserve accumulations have not clearly amplified the influence, whether direct or indirect, of the large-surplus countries. Here too, power has been largely dispersed rather than relocated.

Financial globalization

Finally, there is the change in the international monetary environment that has been wrought by the globalization of financial markets. The story is familiar. Where once most financial markets were firmly controlled at the national level and insulated from one another, today across much of the globe barriers to the movement of money have been greatly reduced or effectively eliminated, resulting in a scale of financial flows unequalled since the glory days of the nineteenth-century gold standard. One consequence, observers agree, is a distinct shift in the balance of power between states and societal actors. By promoting capital mobility, financial globalization enhances the authority of market agents at the expense of sovereign governments.

Key to the shift is the wider range of options made available to privileged elements of the private sector with the integration of financial markets: a marked increase of autonomy for those societal actors in a position to take advantage of the opportunities now afforded them. In effect, financial globalization means more freedom for selected individuals and enterprises—more room for maneuver in response to actual or potential decisions of governments. Higher taxes or regulation may be evaded by moving investment funds offshore; tighter monetary policies may be circumvented by accessing external sources of finance. Ultimately, it means a fading of the strict dividing lines between separate national moneys, as weaker domestic currencies are traded in for more attractive foreign moneys like the dollar or euro—a phenomenon which I have previously referred to as the new geography of money (Cohen 1998). No longer, in many places, are societal actors restricted to a single currency, their own domestic money, as they go about their business. Now they have a choice in what amounts to growing competition among currencies. The functional domain of each money no longer corresponds precisely to the formal jurisdiction of its issuing authority. Currencies have become increasingly deterritorialized, their circulation determined not by law or politics but by the preferences of market agents.

Mirroring the increased autonomy of societal actors is a loss of some measure of operational independence by states. Financial globalization has forced governments into a tradeoff between exchange-rate stability and autonomy in monetary policy. Some still prioritize the external value of their currency, resigning themselves to a loss of control over domestic monetary aggregates and interest rates. Many others have moved towards some form of inflation targeting, substituting this for exchange-rate targeting as a monetary rule. Either way, state authority is compromised. The essence of the challenge has been captured by David Andrews (1994: 193, 204) in what he calls the capital mobility hypothesis: "The degree of international capital mobility systematically constrains state behavior by rewarding some actions and punishing others. ... Consequently, the nature of the choice set available to states ... becomes more constricted." Governments are compelled to tailor their policies, at least in part, to what is needed to avoid provoking massive or sudden financial movements. Market agents gain leverage in relation to public officials.

Here again, though, we must note that the influence gained is largely passive rather than active. Few knowledgeable observers of the decentralized decision processes of the marketplace would argue that the pressures now exerted on governments are somehow designed with conscious political intent. An informal kind of veto over state behavior has emerged. But it is a power that is exercised incidentally, through market processes, rather than directly in pursuit of a formal policy agenda. State autonomy is threatened, but not from a design that is purposive or hostile. Here too the pattern is essentially one of a leaderless diffusion of power.

Ambiguity

All these developments are having a profound impact on governance structures in the monetary system. The greater the population of actors with a significant degree of autonomy in monetary affairs, the harder it is to reach any sort of consensus on critical questions. By definition, autonomous agents can more easily resist pressures to conform. Hence a greater degree of ambiguity is introduced into the way the system is run. Increasingly, structures of governance are being remolded in an evolutionary fashion through the gradual accumulation of custom and usage. Formal rules (specific prescriptions or proscriptions for behavior) are being superseded by more informal norms (broad standards of behavior defined in terms of rights and obligations), in a manner not unlike that of English common law—unwritten law (lex non scripta) in lieu of written or statute law (lex scripta).

The impact on governance structures can be seen at two levels: the individual state and the global system. At the state level, the dispersion of power compels governments to rethink their historical commitment to national monetary sovereignty. At the systemic level, it compounds the difficulties of bargaining on international monetary issues.

National sovereignty

Tradition has long assigned the primary role in monetary governance to the sovereign state. As a matter of practice, governments have been assumed to enjoy a natural right of monopoly control over the issue and management of money within their borders. Ever since the seventeenth-century Peace of Westphalia, the conventions of standard political geography have celebrated the role of the nation-state, absolutely supreme within its own territory, as the basic unit of world politics. By the nineteenth century, the norm of national monetary sovereignty had become an integral part of the global governance structure. Just as political space was conceived in terms of those fixed and mutually exclusive entities we call states, currency spaces came to be identified with the separate sovereign jurisdictions where each money originated. With few exceptions, each state was expected to maintain its own exclusive territorial currency. I have labeled this the Westphalian model of monetary geography (Cohen 1998).

Though never written down anywhere, the norm of monetary sovereignty was of such long standing that by the mid- to late twentieth century it had taken on the legitimacy of a formal rule. Today, however, that old tradition has been shaken by the new growth of competition among currencies across national borders, resulting from financial globalization. As currencies become increasingly deterritorialized, governments find themselves driven to reconsider their historical attachment to the Westphalian model. The monetary sovereignty norm is gradually being eroded by changes of practice and circumstance.

National monetary sovereignty clearly does have its advantages, including the privilege of seigniorage (the ability to finance public spending via money creation) and the power to manage monetary conditions. But in a world where growing numbers of societal actors can now exercise choice among diverse currencies there are also distinct disadvantages. Most notable is the need to prioritize the goal of preserving market confidence in the value and usability of the nation's money—the "confidence game," to recall Paul Krugman's (1998) name for it. The label is ironic because, as in any con game, the effort to play may prove an exercise in futility.

The dilemma is simple. To preserve confidence in its currency, a government must above all make a credible commitment to "sound" macroeconomic management, meaning a strong emphasis on low inflation and financial stability. Monetary policy must not appear to be overused for expansionary purposes; fiscal policy must not be allowed to finance deficits via the printing press. Such policy discipline—what Krugman (2001) calls "root-canal economics"—is of course by no means undesirable, as any victim of past government excesses can attest. High inflation and financial instability can destroy savings, distort incentives, and suppress productive investment. Conversely, if sustained, "sound" management policies may indeed successfully enhance a currency's reputation. However, there is also a distinct downside. Root-canal economics can be extremely costly in terms of lost output or higher unemployment, owing to structural deficiencies that may inhibit an economy's ability to adjust to a constrained policy environment. Experience demonstrates that tight monetary and fiscal policies can in fact turn into dismal austerity policies, depressing growth for a prolonged period.

Faced with this dilemma, governments have three options. One is to continue playing the confidence game, whatever the cost. The other two would replace a country's national currency with a regional money of some kind (Cohen 2004). Currency regionalization occurs when two or more states formally share a single money or equivalent. In one variant of regionalization, countries can agree to merge their separate currencies into a new joint money, as members of EMU have done with the euro. This is currency unification, a strategy of "horizontal" regionalization. Alternatively, any single country may unilaterally or by agreement replace its own currency with the already existing money of another country, an approach typically described as full or formal dollarization ("vertical" regionalization). Both variants involve a delegation of traditional powers away from the individual state. Monetary sovereignty is either pooled in a partnership of some sort, shifting authority to a joint institution like the ECB, or else surrendered wholly or in part to a dominant foreign power such as the United States.

Already, under the pressure of currency competition, a number of governments have opted to abandon their traditional monetary sovereignty. In 2000 Ecuador adopted America's greenback as its exclusive legal tender; a year later El Salvador followed suit. In effect, both chose to become monetary dependencies of the United States rather than fight on to sustain a money of their own. Others have established currency boards—a more limited form of vertical regionalization—or have talked seriously about a monetary union of some kind. Tentative plans have already been drawn up for currency unification in West Africa and in the Gulf region of the Middle East and are under discussion elsewhere. In the opinion of many informed observers, it is only a matter of time before the universe of moneys will be radically shrunk (Beddoes 1999).

In reality, of course, it is easier to talk about currency regionalization than actually to do something about it. Giving up a national currency is not easy. As I have argued elsewhere, attachments to the tradition of monetary sovereignty remain strong in most parts of the world, however costly the confidence game may be (Cohen 2004). But there is no question that for many governments the stark choice must now be faced. The shift in the balance of power between states and societal actors has unquestionably undermined the foundations of the traditional Westphalian model. As a result, a previously clear norm is now increasingly clouded with uncertainty.

International bargaining

Much the same is happening at the systemic level, where prevailing governance structures have also been brought into question by continuing shifts in the distribution of power. As a corollary of the traditional norm of monetary sovereignty at the state level, governments have long relied on formal or informal negotiations among themselves to lay down the rules of the game at the systemic level. As far back as the Genoa Conference of 1922, the dynamics of rule-setting have centered on hard-won bargains struck among a few leading states with the capacity to cajole or coerce others into agreement. That was the scenario at the Bretton Woods Conference of 1944, which was dominated by the United States and Britain. The pattern could also be seen in the negotiations that led up to the earliest amendments of the charter of the IMF, providing for the creation of special drawing rights (negotiated in the 1960s by the Group of Ten) and ratifying a new system of flexible exchange rates (mainly the product of a 1975 agreement between France and the United States). In this respect, the geopolitics of finance were no different from the geopolitics of other issues, where power has always played a pivotal role.

But that was before so many more states gained a degree of autonomy in monetary affairs. The more governments feel insulated from outside pressure, the less likely it is that they will meekly accept the diktat of an inner circle of self-appointed leaders. Bargains made at the top will not be treated with the same respect as in the past. Existing or proposed new rules will no longer enjoy the same degree of legitimacy among states further down the hierarchy, unless these states too are incorporated into the decision-making process.

A diffusion of monetary power is nothing new, of course. The 1960s and 1970s, when U.S. hegemony seemed to be in decline, also saw the emergence of new powers in monetary affairs. Then, too, there was an increase of ambiguity in governance structures, especially after the breakdown of the Bretton Woods par value system in 1971–73. But even after those troubled decades the inner circle remained remarkably small, limited essentially to the United States and its partners in the G-7—as evident, for example, in the celebrated Plaza and Louvre Accords of the 1980s and the management of financial crises in Mexico and East Asia in the 1990s. What is distinctive about today, by contrast, is the sheer number of states that now feel entitled to seats at the high table.

That, of course, explains why recent years have seen a proliferation of new forums designed to widen participation in global discussions. A turning point came after the Asian crisis, when broad new interest was sparked in reform of what soon came to be called the "international financial architecture." One result was the Group of Twenty finance ministers' and central bank governors' forum (G-20), which was created in 1999 and now meets annually to discuss a range of economic and monetary issues. In addition to representatives of the G-7 and European Union, the G-20 brings to the table some dozen "systemically significant economies": Argentina, Australia, Brazil, China, India, Indonesia, Korea, Mexico, Russia, Saudi Arabia, South Africa, and Turkey. A second initiative was the Financial Stability Forum (FSF), also dating from 1999, which is charged with improving the functioning of financial markets and bringing about a reduction of systemic risk. Convened twice a year, the FSF includes some forty-three members representing twenty-six states and a variety of international financial institutions and supervisory bodies. Forums like the G-20 and FSF are obviously intended to enhance the legitimacy of current reform efforts.

The same concerns also explain why so much attention is now being paid to the allocation of quotas at the IMF which, inter alia, determine the distribution of voting power among the Fund's members. Many advanced economies—including especially the members of the EU—appear to be over-represented in the Fund's voting system, while some of the larger emerging market economies are clearly underrepresented. Past quota adjustments, it is generally agreed, simply have not kept up with the transformation of the world economy. In 2006 IMF governors agreed that it was time to implement a new, "simpler and more transparent" formula to guide adjustments in the future, generating a plethora of competing proposals (Cooper and Truman 2007). To date, consensus on any single approach has proved elusive—which is not at all surprising, given the zero-sum nature of the game. Any gain of voting shares for some countries must necessarily come at the expense of others. But some reallocation of quotas clearly does seem to be on the cards.

Wider participation, however, will not make rule-setting any easier. Quite the contrary, in fact. The efficiency of decision-making obviously suffers as more actors are given parts in the process. According to standard organization theory, the difficulties of negotiation actually increase exponentially, not just in proportion, with the number of parties involved. The more voices there are at the table, the greater is the temptation to smooth over unresolved differences with artful compromises and the deliberate obfuscations of classic diplomatic language. Clarity is sacrificed for the sake of avoiding the appearance of discord. Much room is left for creative interpretation.

Worse, even when some measure of agreement is achieved, little can be done about it. Apart from the IMF, none of the existing forums have any powers of direct enforcement. Bodies like the G-7, G-20, and FSF are essentially regularized procedures for consultation—little more than talking shops. Some advantage may be gained from the exchange of information and viewpoints that is facilitated. But wider participation, per se, does nothing to ensure that newly autonomous actors will feel obliged to compromise some part of their operational independence if it does not suit their interests. And even the enforcement powers of the IMF are limited today to just the poorest countries in the system, which remain the organization's only regular clients. The Fund's leverage rests largely on the conditions it may attach to its lending. But richer states, with their access to the global financial markets, no longer need the IMF for financing. Hence many are free to ignore Fund pronouncements, whatever the allocation of member quotas.

A case in point is provided by the Fund's recent effort to tighten up its rules for the management of exchange rates by member governments—the first revision since 1977 of the principles for what is called bilateral surveillance of currency practices (International Monetary Fund 2007b). Central to the revision is a new injunction urging states to avoid practices that cause "external instability." But there is little that the Fund can do if nations choose to resist. Some countries, like China (the obvious target of the new injunction), continue to maintain formal pegs that generate large trade imbalances. Others that have ostensibly abandoned pegging in favor of inflation targeting nonetheless intervene massively to manage their exchange rates, whatever the external consequences—a pattern of behavior known as "dirty" floating. The high reserve holdings generated by today's global imbalances make dirty floating feasible for many. Only governments that lack the requisite liquidity are susceptible to IMF blandishments.

Overall, therefore, the prospect is for growing ambiguity in the system's governance structures. Whether they are part of the bargaining process or not, newly autonomous states now have more leeway to follow their own instincts.

Some will undoubtedly continue to play the confidence game, at whatever cost in terms of "external stability." Others may well prefer to pool or surrender their monetary sovereignty in some degree. In effect, many governments have been freed to make up their own rules as they go along through practice and the gradual accumulation of experience.

In time, of course, patterns of behavior that originate in self-interest may lead to shared expectations (intersubjective understandings) and can eventually even become infused with normative significance. Often, what starts from a logic of consequences (a concern with material impacts) comes ultimately to rest on a logic of appropriateness (a concern with what is "right"). That kind of evolutionary process, relying on the development of informal norms rather than formal rules, is a hallmark of English common law. Increasingly, it is becoming central to international monetary governance as well.

Conclusion

The dynamics of power and governance in global finance today are indeed changing. A leaderless diffusion of power is generating greater uncertainty about the underlying rules of the game. At the state level, governments increasingly question the need for a strictly national currency. At the systemic level, governance now relies more on custom and usage, rather than intergovernmental negotiation, to define standards of behavior.

Greater ambiguity is not necessarily a bad thing, especially if it allows states and societal actors to get along without undue friction. But it does also have distinct disadvantages that cannot be ignored. Governance plainly is less tidy when effectuated through social conventions rather than formal agreements. Lex non scripta is inherently more opaque than lex scripta. Hence a wider latitude is afforded actors for strategic maneuvers that may be made at the expense of others. Outcomes may be neither as stable nor as equitable as we might wish. Crises could become more frequent or difficult to manage if more governments feel free to do their own thing, discounting disruptive externalities. Burdens of adjustment could fall disproportionately on the weakest members of the system, which have benefited least from the leaderless diffusion of power.

Can anything be done to lessen such risks? Since states remain the basic units of world politics, responsibility continues to reside with governments, which still have little choice but to try to resolve their differences through negotiation. What is needed, however, is a change of bargaining strategy to conform more comfortably to the new distribution of power. With autonomy spread more widely among actors, it is becoming increasingly fruitless to aim for specific prescriptions for behavior—what in biblical language might be called "thou shalt" types of rule. More governments are now in a position simply to ignore detailed injunctions when they wish. But it is not impractical to aim for the reverse—general "thou shalt not" types of rule that set outer limits to what might be considered acceptable. Even the most insular govern-ments are apt to recognize that there is a common interest in keeping potential externalities within bounds. If prevailing governance structures are to retain any practical influence at all, that is the direction in which the dynamics of rule-setting must now move.

Notes

2 The euro and transatlantic relations

1 Yarjani was head of OPEC's Petroleum Market Analysis Department.
2 For a direct critique of the oil-currency war theory, see Caffentzis (2003).

4 Global currency rivalry: can the euro ever challenge the dollar?

1 For some rare exceptions, see Feldstein (1997), Calomiris (1999), and Bush (2000).
2 This is in contrast to formal dollarization, which occurs when a foreign government officially adopts a currency such as the greenback in place of its own national money, as did Ecuador in 2000 and El Salvador in 2001. For more discussion of formal and informal dollarization, see Cohen (2004).
3 The term "legacy" currency, referring to the separate national monies replaced by the euro, was suggested by Detken and Hartmann (2002).
4 The figure of $1.2 trillion represented a significant drop, from nearly $1.5 trillion in 1998 (though still a considerable increase from $590 billion in 1989, the first year for which such data are available, and $820 million in 1992). The drop after 1998 was accounted for by several special factors, including, notably, the introduction of the euro in 1999, which eliminated trading among its constituent currencies.
5 Because each foreign-exchange transaction involves two currencies, the total of shares sums to 200 percent rather than 100 percent.
6 For more detail, see Cohen (1971).
7 The term "anti-growth bias" is used here in preference to "deflationary bias," as was once popular in the economics literature, because of the possibility that the latter might be mistakenly understood to mean a decline of prices rather than, as intended here, a decline or retardation of real output.
8 For some discussion, see Henning (1997: 7–9).
9 For an evaluation of alternative possible arrangements for ECB decision-making, see Berger (2002).
10 For an example of how this process has operated in the case of international trade organizations, see Cohn (2002).
11 In Russia, for example, where as much as $50 billion in greenbacks is believed to be hoarded away, euro banknotes are rapidly gaining in popularity (see *New York Times*, January 31, 2003).
12 For Henning, this was indeed a principal motivation of EMU. In his words: "Disturbances in the international system provided strong incentives for European governments to cooperate" (Henning 1998: 538).

8 A one-and-a-half currency system, *with Paola Subacchi*

1 Current-account outcomes also depend on saving and investment, with income flows and exchange rates both determined simultaneously in a general equilibrium setting. For a discussion of exchange-rate economics, see Williamson (2008: 1–24).
2 For a contrary view, see Williamson (2008: 15–16).

Bibliography

Ahearne, A. and Pisani-Ferry, J. (2006) "The Euro: Only for the Agile," Policy Brief 2006/01, Brussels: Bruegel.

Aliber, R.(1987) *The International Money Game*, 5th edn., New York: Basic Books.

Alogoskoufis, G. and Portes, R. (1997) "The Euro, the Dollar, and the International Monetary System," in Masson, P.R., Krueger, T.H., and Turtelboom, B.G. (eds.) *EMU and the International Monetary System*, Washington: International Monetary Fund.

Andrews, D.M. (1994) "Capital Mobility and State Autonomy: Toward a Structural Theory of International Relations," *International Studies Quarterly* 38: 193–218.

Androsch, H. (2007) "Wisdom from the Greybeards," *The International Economy* 21: 48–51, 62.

Annett, A. (2006) "Enforcement and the Stability and Growth Pact: How Fiscal Policy Did and Did Not Change under Europe's Fiscal Framework," Working Paper WP/06/116, Washington: International Monetary Fund.

Arestis, P. and Sawyer, M. (2003) "Making the Euro Work," *Challenge* 46: 80–96.

Baldwin, R. (2001) "The ECB's Numbers Problem," *Financial Times*, December 4.

Bank for International Settlements (1999) *Central Bank Survey of Foreign Exchange and Derivatives Market Activity 1998*, Basel: Bank for International Settlements.

——(2002) Triennial Central Bank Survey: Foreign Exchange and Derivatives Market Activity in 2001, Basel: Bank for International Settlements.

——(2005) Triennial Central Bank Survey: Foreign Exchange and Derivatives Market Activity in 2004, Basel: Bank for International Settlements.

——(2007) Triennial Central Bank Survey: Foreign Exchange and Derivatives Market Activity in 2007, Basel: Bank for International Settlements.

——(2008) *BIS Quarterly Review*, December, Basel: Bank for International Settlements.

Becker, W. (2008) "The Euro Turns Ten," EU Monitor 57, Frankfurt: Deutsche Bank.

Beddoes, Z.M. (1999) "From EMU to AMU? The Case for Regional Currencies," *Foreign Affairs* 78: 8–13.

Belke, A. (2003) "The Rotation Model Is Not Sustainable," *Intereconomics* 38: 119–24.

Bénassy-Quéré, A. and Lahrèche-Révil, A. (1999) "The Euro and Southern Mediterranean Countries," processed, Paris: Centre d'Études Prospectives et d'Informations Internationales.

Berger, H. (2002) "The ECB and Euro-Area Enlargement," Working Paper WP/02/175, Washington: International Monetary Fund.

Berger, H., de Haan, J., and Inklaar, R. (2004) "Restructuring the ECB," in Berger H. and Moutos, T. (eds.) Managing European Union Enlargement, Cambridge, MA: MIT Press.

Berglöf, E., Fulghieri, P., Gual, J., Mayer, C., Luis Pita Barros, P., and Vives, X. (2005) Integration of European Banking: The Way Forward, Monitoring European Deregulation 3, London: Centre for Economic Policy Research.

Bergsten, C.F. (1997) "The Impact of the Euro on Exchange Rates and International Policy Cooperation," in Masson, P.R., Krueger, T.H., and Turtelboom, B.G. (eds.) *EMU and the International Monetary System*, Washington: International Monetary Fund.

——(1998) "Missed Opportunity," *The International Economy* 12: 26–27.

——(2002) "The Euro Versus the Dollar: Will There Be a Struggle for Dominance?" paper prepared for a roundtable at the annual meeting of the American Economic Association, Atlanta, GA, January.

——(2005) "The Euro and the Dollar: Toward a Finance G-2'?" in Posen, A.S. (ed.) *The Euro at Five: Ready for a Global Role?* Washington: Institute for International Economics.

Bernanke, B. (2005) "The Euro at Five: An Assessment," in Posen, A.S. (ed.) *The Euro at Five: Ready for a Global Role?* Washington: Institute for International Economics.

Bertuch-Samuels, A. and Ramlogan, P. (2007) "The Euro: Ever More Global," *Finance and Development* 44: 46–49.

Biais, B., Declerc, F., Dow, J., Portes, R., and Thadden, E.-L. (2006) European Corporate Bond Markets: Transparency, Liquidity, Efficiency, London: Centre for Economic Policy Research.

Bieling, H.-J. (2006) "EMU, Financial Integration and Global Economic Governance," *Review of International Political Economy* 13: 420–48.

Bini Smaghi, L. (2004) "A Single EU Seat in the IMF?" *Journal of Common Market Studies* 42: 229–48.

Blinder, A.S. (1996) "The Role of the Dollar as an International Currency," *Eastern Economic Journal* 22: 127–36.

Branson, W.H. and Katseli-Papaefstratiou, L.T. (1980) "Income Instability, Terms of Trade, and the Choice of an Exchange Rate Regime," *Journal of Development Economics* 7: 49–69.

——(1982) "Currency Baskets and Real Effective Exchange Rates," in Gersovitz, M. (ed.) *The Theory and Experience of Economic Development: Essays in Honor of Sir Arthur Lewis*, London: Allen and Unwin.

Buiter, W.H. (1999) "Alice in Euroland," *Journal of Common Market Studies* 37: 181–209.

——(2000) "Optimal Currency Areas: Why Does the Exchange Rate Regime Matter?" Discussion Paper No. 2366, London: Centre for Economic Policy Research.

Bush, J. (2000) "Euro Blues?" *The International Economy* 22–23: 49.

Caffentzis, G. (2003) "A Note on the 'Euro' Explanation of the War" (Infoshop News), available at www.infoshop.org.

Calleo, D.P. (2009) "Twenty-First Century Geopolitics and the Erosion of the Dollar Order," in Helleiner, E. and Kirshner, J. (eds.) *The Future of the Dollar*, Ithaca, NY: Cornell University Press.

Calomiris, C.W. (1999) "The Impending Collapse of the European Monetary Union," *Cato Journal* 18: 445–52.

Castellano, M. (1999) "Internationalization of the Yen: A Ministry of Finance Pipe Dream?" *JEI Report* 23A: 1–10.

Chinn, M. and Frankel, J. (2007) "Will the Euro Eventually Surpass the Dollar as Leading International Reserve Currency?" in Clarida, R.H. (ed.) G7 Current Account Imbalances: Sustainability and Adjustment, Chicago: University of Chicago Press.

——(2008) "Why the Euro Will Rival the Dollar," *International Finance* 11: 49–73.

Clark, W. (2003) "The Real Reasons for the Upcoming War with Iraq: A Macroeconomic and Geostrategic Analysis of the Unspoken Truth" (Independent Media Center), available at www.indymedia.org.

Cobham, D. (2008) "Changing Currency Alignments: Euro versus Dollar," processed, Heriot-Watt University, Edinburgh, July.

Codogno, L., Favero, C., and Missale, A. (2003) "Yield Spreads on EMU Government Bonds," *Economic Policy* 37: 503–27.

Cohen, B.J. (1971) *The Future of Sterling as an International Currency*, London: Macmillan.

——(1986) *In Whose Interest? International Banking and American Foreign Policy*, New Haven, CT: Yale University Press.

——(1993) "The Triad and the Unholy Trinity: Lessons for the Pacific Region," in Higgot, R., Leaver, R., and Ravenhill, J. (eds.) *Pacific Economic Relations in the 1990s: Cooperation or Conflict?* Boulder, CO: Lynne Rienner.

——(1998) *The Geography of Money*, Ithaca, NY: Cornell University Press.

——(2000) "Beyond EMU: The Problem of Sustainability," in Eichengreen, B. and Frieden, J. (eds.) *The Political Economy of European Monetary Unification*, 2nd edn., Boulder, CO: Westview.

——(2003) "Global Currency Rivalry: Can the Euro Ever Challenge the Dollar?" *Journal of Common Market Studies* 42: 575–95.

——(2004) The Future of Money, Princeton: Princeton University Press.

——(2006a) "The Euro and Transatlantic Relations," in Ilgen, T.L. (ed.) Hard Power, Soft Power and the Future of Transatlantic Relations, Burlington, VT: Ashgate.

——(2006b) "The Macrofoundations of Monetary Power," in Andrews, D.M. (ed.) *International Monetary Power*, Ithaca, NY: Cornell University Press.

——(2007) "Enlargement and the International Role of the Euro," *Review of International Political Economy* 14: 746–73.

——(2008) "The Euro in a Global Context: Challenges and Capacities," in Dyson, K. (ed.) The Euro at Ten: Europeanization, Power, and Convergence, Oxford: Oxford University Press.

Cohen, B.J. and Subacchi, P. (2008) "A One-and-a-Half Currency System," *Journal of International Affairs* 62: 151–63.

Cohn, T.H. (2002) Governing Global Trade: International Institutions in Conflict and Convergence, Aldershot: Ashgate.

Collignon, S. (2003) The European Republic, London: Federal Trust for Education and Research.

Cooper, R.N. (1999) "Should Capital Controls Be Banished?" *Brookings Papers on Economic Activity* 1: 89–125.

——(2000) "Key Currencies after the Euro," in Mundell, R.A. and Cleese, A. (eds.) The Euro as a Stabilizer in the International Economic System, Boston: Kluwer Academic.

Cooper, R.N. and Truman, E.M. (2007) "The IMF Quota Formula: Linchpin of Fund Reform," Policy Brief PB07–1, Washington: Peterson Institute for International Economics.

Council of Economic Advisers (1999) *Annual Report*, Washington: Government Printing Office.

Cukierman, A. (2004) "Restructuring the ECB: Comments," in Berger, H. and Moutos, T. (eds.) Managing European Union Enlargement, Cambridge, MA: MIT Press.

Danthine, J.-P., Giavazzi, F., and von Thadden, E.-L. (2000) "European Financial Markets after EMU: A First Assessment," Discussion Paper 2413, London: Centre for Economic Policy Research.

de Boissieu, C. (1988) "Concurrence entre monnaies et polycentrisme monétaire," in Fair, D.E. and de Boissieu, C. (eds.) *International Monetary and Financial Integration—The European Dimension*, Boston: Kluwer.

de Cecco, M. (2009) "From Monopoly to Oligopoly: Lessons from the Pre-1914 Experience," in Helleiner, E. and Kirshner, J. (eds.) *The Future of the Dollar*, Ithaca, NY: Cornell University Press.

de Grauwe, P. (2004) "Challenges for Monetary Policy in Euroland," in Torres, F., Verdun, A., Zilioli, C., and Zimmermann, H. (eds.) Governing EMU: Economic, Political, Legal and Historical Perspectives, Florence: European University Institute.

de Haan, J., Berger, H., and Inklaar, R. (2004) "Is the ECB Too Decentralized?" in Sinn, H.-W., Widgren, M., and Kothenburger, M. (eds.) European Monetary Integration: Cambridge, MA: MIT Press.

de Larosiere, J. (2002) "The Euro: An Opportunity for Europe and for the International Monetary System," in Euro 50 Group (eds.) The Euro in the International Arena: The Euro 50 Group Roundtable, New York: Euro 50 Group.

Detken, C. and Hartmann, P. (2000) "The Euro and International Capital Markets," *International Finance* 3: 53–94.

——(2002) "Features of the Euro's Role in International Financial Markets," *Economic Policy* 35: 553–69.

Deutsche Bundesbank (1995) "The Circulation of Deutsche Marks Abroad," *Monthly Report of the Deutsche Bundesbank* 47: 65–71.

Dornbusch, R. (1999) "The Euro: Implications for Latin America," processed, Washington: World Bank.

Dornbusch, R., Sturzenegger, F.A., and Wolf, H. (1990) "Extreme Inflation: Dynamics and Stabilization," Brookings Papers on Economic Activity 2: 2–84.

Dowd, K. and Greenaway, D. (1993) "Currency Competition, Network Externalities and Switching Costs: Towards an Alternative View of Optimum Currency Areas," *Economic Journal* 103: 1180–89.

Dunne, P., Moore, M., and Portes, R. (2006) European Government Bond Markets: Transparency, Liquidity, Efficiency, London: Centre for Economic Policy Research.

Dyson, K. and Featherstone, K. (1999) *The Road to Maastricht: Negotiating Economic and Monetary Union*, Oxford: Oxford University Press.

Economist, The (1994) "Electronic Money: So Much for the Cashless Society," November 26: 21–23.

——(2000a) "Asian Currencies: Swapping Notes," May 13: 76–77.

——(2000b) "E-cash 2.0," February 19: 67–71.——(2005a) "The Great Thrift Shift: A Survey of the World Economy," supplement, September 24.

——(2005b) "Open Wider: A Survey of International Banking," supplement, May 21.

Eichengreen, B. (1994) *International Monetary Arrangements for the 21st Century*, Washington: Brookings Institution.

——(1997) "Comment on Bergsten," in Masson, P.R., Krueger, T.H., and Turtelboom, B.G. (eds.) EMU and the International Monetary System: Washington: International Monetary Fund.

——(1998) "The Euro as Reserve Currency," *Journal of the Japanese and International Economies* 12: 483–506.

——(2006) *Global Imbalances and the Lessons of Bretton Woods*, Cambridge, MA: MIT Press.

Eichengreen, B. and Bayoumi, T. (1999) "Is Asia an Optimum Currency Area? Can It Become One? Regional, Global, and Historical Perspectives on Asian Monetary Relations," in Collignon, S., Pisani-Ferry, J., and Park, Y.C. (eds.) *Exchange Rate Policies in Emerging Asian Countries*, London: Routledge.

European Central Bank (1999) "International Role of the Euro," *Monthly Bulletin*, August: 31–53.

——(2001) Review of the International Role of the Euro, Frankfurt: European Central Bank.

——(2002) Review of the International Role of the Euro, Frankfurt: European Central Bank.

——(2003a) "The Adjustment of Voting Modalities in the Governing Council," *Monthly Bulletin*, May: 73–83.

——(2003b) Review of the International Role of the Euro, Frankfurt: European Central Bank.

——(2007a) *Annual Report 2006*, Frankfurt: European Central Bank.

——(2007b) "The EU Arrangements for Financial Crisis Management," *Monthly Bulletin*, May: 61–74.

——(2007c) Review of the International Role of the Euro, Frankfurt: European Central Bank.

——(2008a) "The Euro's Impact on Trade and Capital Flows and Its International Role," *Monthly Bulletin*, May.

——(2008b) Review of the International Role of the Euro, Frankfurt: European Central Bank.

European Commission (2005) Second Report on the State of Practical Preparations for the Future Enlargement of the Euro Area, Brussels: European Commission.

——(2008) *EMU @ 10: Successes and Challenges after 10 Years of Economic and Monetary Union*, Brussels: European Commission.

European Union (2001) Final Report of the Committee of Wise Men on the Regulation of European Securities Markets, Brussels: European Commission.

Feldstein, M. (1997) "EMU and International Conflict," *Foreign Affairs* 76: 60–73.

Frankel, J.A. (1995) "Still the Lingua Franca: The Exaggerated Death of the Dollar," *Foreign Affairs* 74: 9–16.

——(1999) *No Single Currency Regime Is Right for All Countries or at All Times*, Essays in International Finance 215, Princeton: Princeton University, International Finance Section.

——(2000) "Impact of the Euro on Members and Non-Members," in Mundell, R.A. and Cleese, A. (eds.) The Euro as a Stabilizer in the International Economic System, Boston: Kluwer Academic.

Frankel, J.A. and Rose, A.K. (1997) "The Endogeneity of the Optimum Currency Area Criteria," *Economic Journal* 108: 1009–25.

Fratzscher, M. (2001) "Financial Market Integration in Europe: On the Effects of EMU on Stock Markets," Working Paper 48: Frankfurt: European Central Bank.

Frenkel, M. and Søndergaard, J. (2001) "How Does EMU Affect the Dollar and the Yen as International Reserve and Investment Currencies?" in Moser, T. and Schips, B. (eds.) EMU, Financial Markets and the World Economy, Boston: Kluwer Academic.

Frieden, J. (2004) "One Europe, One Vote? The Political Economy of European Union Representation in International Organizations," *European Union Politics* 5: 261–76.

Friedman, B.M. (1999) "The Future of Monetary Policy: The Central Bank as an Army with Only a Signal Corps?" *International Finance* 2: 321–38.

Galati, G. and Wooldridge, P. (2006) "The Euro as a Reserve Currency: A Challenge to the Pre-eminence of the Dollar?" Working Paper 218, Basel: Bank for International Settlements.

Geis, A., Mehl, A., and Wredenborg, S. (2004) The International Role of the Euro Evidence from Bonds Issued by Non-Euro Area Residents, Occasional Paper 18, Frankfurt: European Central Bank.

Giannetti, M., Guiso, L., Jappelli, T., Padula, M., and Pagano, M. (2002) Financial Market Integration, Corporate Financing and Economic Growth, Economic Papers 179, Brussels: European Commission.

Goldberg, L.S. and Tille, C. (2005) "Vehicle Currency Use in International Trade," Working Paper No. 11127, Cambridge, MA: National Bureau of Economic Research.

Goodhart, C.A.E. (1995) "The Political Economy of Monetary Union," in Kenen, P.B. (ed.) *Understanding Interdependence: The Macroeconomics of the Open Economy*, Princeton: Princeton University Press.

Goodhart, C.A.E., Love, R., Payne, R., and Rime, D. (2002) "Analysis of Spreads in the Dollar/Euro and Deutschemark/Dollar Foreign Exchange Markets," *Economic Policy* 35: 535–52.

Goodman, J.B. (1992) Monetary Sovereignty: The Politics of Central Banking in Western Europe, Ithaca, NY: Cornell University Press.

Green, M.J. (2001) *Japan's Reluctant Realism: Foreign Policy Challenges in an Era of Uncertain Power*, New York: Palgrave.

Gros, D. (2003) "An Opportunity Missed!," *Intereconomics* 38, May/June: 124–29.

Gros, D. and Thygesen, N. (1992) European Monetary Integration: From the European Monetary System to European Monetary Union, London: Longman.

——(1998) European Monetary Integration: From the European Monetary System to European Monetary Union, 2nd edn., London: Longman.

Gros, D., Mayer, T., and Ubide, A. (2005) *EMU at Risk*, 7th Annual Report of the CEPS Macroeconomic Policy Group, Brussels: Centre for European Policy Studies.

Guidotti, P.E. and Rodriguez, C.A. (1992) "Dollarization in Latin America: Gresham's Law in Reverse?" International Monetary Fund Staff Papers 39: 518–44.

Hale, D.D. (1995) "Is It a Yen or a Dollar Crisis in the Currency Market?" *Washington Quarterly* 18: 145–71.

Hall, S. and Hondroyiannis, G. (2006) "Measuring the Correlation of Shocks Between the EU-15 and the New Member Countries," Working Paper No. 31, Athens: Bank of Greece.

Hartmann, P. (1998) *Currency Competition and Foreign Exchange Markets: The Dollar, the Yen and the Euro*, Cambridge: Cambridge University Press.

Hau, H., Killeen, W., and Moore, M. (2002a) "The Euro as an International Currency: Explaining Puzzling First Evidence from the Foreign Exchange Markets," *Journal of International Money and Finance* 21: 351–83.

——(2002b) "How Has the Euro Changed the Foreign Exchange Market?" Economic Policy 34: 149–91.

Hausmann, R. (1999) "Should There Be Five Currencies or One Hundred and Five?" *Foreign Policy* 116: 65–79.

Hausmann, R., Gavin, M., Pages-Serra, C., and Stein, E. (1999) "Financial Turmoil and the Choice of Exchange Rate Regime," Working Paper 400, Washington: Inter-American Development Bank.

Hayek, F. von (1990) *Denationalisation of Money—The Argument Refined*, 3rd edn., London: Institute of Economic Affairs.

Heinemann, F. and Jopp, M. (2002) The Benefits of a Working European Retail Market for Financial Services, Report to the European Financial Services Round Table, Berlin: Institut für Europäische Politik.

Helleiner, E. (2009) "Enduring Top Currency, Fragile Negotiated Currency: Politics and the Dollar's International Role," in Helleiner, E. and Kirshner, J. (eds.) *The Future of the Dollar*, Ithaca, NY: Cornell University Press.

Henning, C.R. (1996) "Europe's Monetary Union and the United States," Foreign Policy 102: 83–100.

——(1997) Cooperating with Europe's Monetary Union, Washington: Institute for International Economics.

——(1998) "Systemic Conflict and Regional Monetary Integration: The Case of Europe," *International Organization* 52: 537–73.

——(2000) "U.S.–EU Relations after the Inception of the Monetary Union: Cooperation or Rivalry?" in Henning, C.R. and Padoan, P.C. Transatlantic Perspectives on the Euro, Washington: Brookings Institution.

Honohan, P. and Lane, P. (1999) "Will the Euro Trigger More Monetary Unions in Africa?" paper prepared for a World Institute for Development Economics Research (WIDER) Conference on EMU and Its Impact on Europe and the Developing Countries, Helsinki, Finland, November 11–12.

Hoshi, T. and Kashyap, A. (2000) "The Japanese Banking Crisis: Where Did It Come from and Where Will It End?" *NBER Macroeconomics Annual 1999*, Cambridge, MA: MIT Press.

Hüfner, M. (2000) "Give the Euro Greater Currency," *The International Economy*, November/December: 24–25, 50.

Hughes, C.W. (2000) "Japanese Policy and the East Asian Currency Crisis: Abject Defeat or Quiet Victory?" *Review of International Political Economy* 7: 219–53.

International Monetary Fund (1999) *Results of the 1997 Coordinated Portfolio Investment Survey*, Washington: International Monetary Fund.

——(2001) International Capital Markets: Developments, Prospects, and Key Policy Issues, Washington: International Monetary Fund.

——(2007a) Concluding Statement of the IMF Mission on Euro-Area Policies, Washington: International Monetary Fund.

——(2007b) "IMF Surveillance: The 2007 Decision on Bilateral Surveillance," fact sheet, Washington: International Monetary Fund.

Issing, O. (1999) "Hayek—Currency Competition and European Monetary Union," Annual Hayek Memorial Lecture, London: Institute of Economic Affairs.

Ito, T. and Melvin, M. (2000) "The Political Economy of Japan's Big Bang," in Blomstrom, M., Gangnes, B., and La Croix, S. (eds.) *Japan's New Economy: Continuity and Change in the Twenty-First Century*, New York: Oxford University Press.

James, H. (2009) "The Enduring International Preeminence of the Dollar," in Helleiner, E. and Kirshner, J. (eds.) *The Future of the Dollar*, Ithaca, NY: Cornell University Press.

Joint Economic Committee of the U.S. Congress (1999) *Joint Economic Report 1999*, Washington: Government Printing Office.

Kamps, A. (2006) "The Euro as Invoicing Currency in International Trade," Working Paper 665, Frankfurt: European Central Bank.

Katada, S. (2002) "Japan and Asian Monetary Regionalization: Cultivating a New Regional Leadership after the Asian Financial Crisis," *Geopolitics* 7: 85–112.

Kenen, P. and Meade, E. (2003) "EU Accession and the Euro: Close Together or Far Apart?" International Economic Policy Brief PBO3-9, October, Washington: Institute for International Economics.

Kindleberger, C.P. (1973) *The World in Depression, 1929–1939*, Berkeley: University of California Press.

Kirshner, J. (1995) Currency and Coercion: The Political Economy of International Monetary Power, Princeton: Princeton University Press.

——(2008) "Dollar Primacy and American Power: What's at Stake?" Review of International Political Economy 15: 418–38.

——(2009) "After the (Relative) Fall: Dollar Diminution and the Consequences for American Power," in Helleiner, E. and Kirshner, J. (eds.) *The Future of the Dollar*, Ithaca, NY: Cornell University Press.

Klaus, V. (2004) "The Future of the Euro: An Outsider's View," *Cato Journal* 24: 171–77.

Krueger, R. and Ha, J. (1996) "Measurement of Cocirculation of Currencies," in Mizen, P.D. and Pentecost, E.J. (eds.) *The Macroeconomics of International Currencies: Theory, Policy and Evidence*, Brookfield, VT: Edward Elgar.

Krugman, P.R. (1992) "The International Role of the Dollar," in *Currencies and Crises*, Cambridge, MA: MIT Press.

——(1998) "The Confidence Game," *New Republic*, October 5.

——(2001) "Other People's Money," *New York Times*, July 18.

Kwan, C.H. (2001) *Yen Bloc: Toward Economic Integration in Asia*, Washington: Brookings Institution.

Landler, M. (2004) "In Eastern Europe, Skepticism over the Euro," *New York Times*, December 6.

Lane, P.R. and Walti, S. (2007) "The Euro and Financial Integration," in Cobham, D.H. (ed.) The Travails of the Euro Area: Economic Policies, Economic Developments, New York: Palgrave Macmillan.

Lastra, R. (2003) "The Governance Structure for Financial Regulation and Supervision in Europe," *Columbia Journal of European Law* 10: 49–68.

Levy Yeyati, E. and Sturzenegger, F. (2000) "Is EMU a Blueprint for Mercosur?" *Latin American Journal of Economics* 110: 63–99.

Li, D. (2006) "Internationalization of the RMB to Be Accelerated," *People's Daily Online*, available at http://english.people.com.cn/other/archive.html.

Lim, E.-G. (2006) "The Euro's Challenge to the Dollar: Different Views from Economists and Evidence from COFER (Currency Composition of Foreign Exchange

Reserves) and Other Data," Working Paper WP/06/153, Washington: International Monetary Fund.

Litfin, K.T. (1997) "Sovereignty in World Ecopolitics," *Mershon International Studies Review* 41: 167–204.

London Economics (2002) *Quantification of the Marco-Economic Impact of Integration of EU Financial Markets*, Final Report to the European Commission, in association with PricewaterhouseCoopers and Oxford Economic Forecasting, London.

McCauley, R.N. (1997) The Euro and the Dollar, Essays in International Finance 205, Princeton: Princeton University, International Finance Section.

McCauley, R.N. and White, W.R. (1997) "The Euro and European Financial Markets," in Masson, P.R., Krueger, T.H., and Turtelboom, B.G. (eds.) EMU and the International Monetary System, Washington: International Monetary Fund.

McKinnon, R. (2009) "U.S. Current Account Deficits and the Dollar Standard's Sustainability: A Monetary Approach," in Helleiner, E. and Kirshner, J. (eds.) *The Future of the Dollar*, Ithaca, NY: Cornell University Press.

McNamara, K.R. and Meunier, S. (2002) "Between National Sovereignty and International Power: What External Voice for the Euro?" *International Affairs* 78: 849–68.

Makinen, G.E. (1998) "Euro Currency: How Much Could It Cost the United States?" CRS Report 98–998E, Washington: Congressional Research Service.

Masson, P.R., Krueger, T.H., and Turtelboom, B.G. (eds.) (1997) EMU and the International Monetary System, Washington: International Monetary Fund.

Meade, E. (2003) "A (Critical) Appraisal of the ECB's Voting Reform," Intereconomics 38: 129–31.

Momani, B. (2008) "Gulf Co-operation Council Oil Exporters and the Future of the Dollar," *New Political Economy* 13: 293–314.

Munchau, W. (2008) "This Crisis Could Bring the Euro Centre-Stage," *Financial Times*, March 23.

Mundell, R.A. (1993) "EMU and the International Monetary System: A Transatlantic Perspective," Working Paper 13, Vienna: Austrian National Bank.

——(1996) "European Monetary Union and the International Monetary System," in Baldassarri, A., Imbriani, C., and Salvatore, D. (eds.) *The International System between New Integration and Neo-Protectionism*, New York: St. Martin's.

——(1998) "The Case for the Euro," *Wall Street Journal*, March 24.

——(2000) "The Euro and the Stability of the International Monetary System," in Mundell, R.A. and Cleese, A. (eds.) The Euro as a Stabilizer in the International Economic System, Boston: Kluwer Academic.

Mundell, R.A. and Cleese, A. (eds.) (2000) The Euro as a Stabilizer in the International Economic System, Boston: Kluwer Academic.

Neaime, S. and Paschakis, J. (2002) "The Future of the Dollar-Euro Exchange Rate," *North American Journal of Economics and Finance* 13: 56–71.

Nye, J.S. Jr. (1990) "Soft Power," Foreign Policy 80: 153–71.

Orléan, A. (1989) "Mimetic Contagion and Speculative Bubbles," *Theory and Decision* 27: 63–92.

Padoan, P.C. (2000) "The Role of the Euro in the International System: A European View," in Henning, C.R. and Padoan, P.C. Transatlantic Perspectives on the Euro, Washington: Brookings Institution.

Papaioannou, E. and Portes, R. (2008) The International Role of the Euro: A Status Report, Economic Papers 317, Brussels: European Commission.

Papaioannou, E., Portes, R., and Siourounis, G. (2006) "Optimal Currency Shares in International Reserves: The Impact of the Euro and the Prospects for the Dollar," *Journal of the Japanese and International Economies* 20: 508–47.

Persaud, A. (2004) "When Currency Empires Fall," lecture presented at Gresham College, London, available at www.gresham.ac.uk.

Pisani-Ferry, J., Aghion, P., Belka, M., von Hagen, J., Heikensten, L., and Sapir, A. (2008) "Coming of Age: Report on the Euro Area," Blueprint Series IV, Brussels: Bruegel.

Porter, R.D. and Judson, R.A. (1996) "The Location of U.S. Currency: How Much Is Abroad?" *Federal Reserve Bulletin* 82: 883–903.

Portes, R. (1999) "Global Financial Markets and Financial Stability: Europe's Role," Discussion Paper 2298, London: Centre for Economic Policy Research.

Portes, R. and Rey, H. (1998) "The Emergence of the Euro as an International Currency," in Begg, D., von Hagen, J., Wyplosz, C., and Zimmermann, K.F. (eds.) EMU: Prospects and Challenges for the Euro, Oxford: Blackwell.

Posen, A. (2008) "Why the Euro Will Not Rival the Dollar," *International Finance* 11: 75–100.

Pramor, M. and Tamirisa, N.T. (2006) "Common Volatility Trends in the Central and Eastern European Currencies and the Euro, Working Paper WP/06/206, Washington: International Monetary Fund.

Prodi, R. (2004) "The Euro and Enlargement," in Deardorff, A.V. (ed.) The Past, Present and Future of the European Union, New York: Palgrave Macmillan.

Rey, H. (2005) "The Impact of a Five-Year-Old Euro on Financial Markets," in Posen, A.S. (ed.) The Euro at Five: Ready for a Global Role? Washington: Institute for International Economics.

Rogoff, K. (1998) "Blessing or Curse? Foreign and Underground Demand for Euro Notes," in Begg, D., von Hagen, J., Wyplosz, C., and Zimmerman, K.F. (eds.) EMU: Prospects and Challenges for the Euro, Oxford: Blackwell.

Rose, A.K. (2000) "One Money, One Market: The Effect of Common Currencies on Trade," *Economic Policy* 30: 7–45.

Rosecrance, R. (2000) "The International Political Implications of the Euro," in Mundell, R.A. and Cleese, A. (eds.) The Euro as a Stabilizer in the International Economic System, Boston: Kluwer Academic.

Sadeh, T. (2006) *Sustaining European Monetary Union: Confronting the Cost of Diversity*, Boulder, CO: Lynne Rienner.

Santillán, J., Bayle, M., and Thygesen, C. (2000) *The Impact of the Euro on Money and Bond Markets*, Occasional Paper 1, Frankfurt: European Central Bank.

Schadler, S., Drummond, P., Kuijs, L., Murgasova, Z., and van Elkan, R. (2005) Adopting the Euro in Central Europe: Challenges of the Next Step in European Integration, Occasional Paper 234, Washington: International Monetary Fund.

Schaede, U. (2000) "After the Bubble: Evaluating Financial Reform in Japan in the 1990s," processed, San Diego: University of California at San Diego.

Schinasi, G. (2003) "Responsibility of Central Banks for Stability in Financial Markets," Working Paper WP/03/121, Washington: International Monetary Fund.

——(2005) "Financial Architecture of the Eurozone at Five," in Posen, A.S. (ed.) The Euro at Five: Ready for a Global Role? Washington: Institute for International Economics.

Schwartz, A. (2004) "Global Order and the Future of the Euro," *Cato Journal* 24: 19–26.

Solomon, E.H. (1997) *Virtual Money: Understanding the Power and Risks of Money's High-Speed Journey into Electronic Space*, New York: Oxford University Press.

Solomon, L.D. (1996) *Rethinking Our Centralized Monetary System: The Case for a System of Local Currencies*, Westport, CT: Praeger.

Strange, S. (1971a) "The Politics of International Currencies," *World Politics* 23: 215–31.

——(1971b) Sterling and British Policy: A Political Study of an International Currency in Decline, London: Oxford University Press.

——(1994) *States and Markets*, 2nd edn., London: Pinter.

Subacchi, P., Marzinotto, B., and Rossi, V. (2008) "Exploiting Europe's Strong Potential: Governance, Institutions and Policies," briefing paper, London: Chatham House.

Summers, L.H. (2004) The US Current Account Deficit and the Global Economy, Washington: Per Jacobsson Foundation.

Thygesen, N. and the ECU Institute (1995) *International Currency Competition and the Future Role of the Single European Currency*, Final Report of the Working Group on "European Monetary Union—International Monetary System," London and Boston: Kluwer Law International.

Trichet, J.-C. (2008) "Hearing at the Economic and Monetary Affairs Committee of the European Parliament," speech, Brussels: European Parliament.

Truman, E.M. and Wong, A. (2006) "The Case for an International Reserve Diversification Standard," Working Paper WP 06–2, Washington: Institute for International Economics.

United States Treasury (2000) The Use and Counterfeiting of United States Currency Abroad, Washington: Government Printing Office.

——(2006) The Use and Counterfeiting of United States Currency Abroad, Washington: Government Printing Office.

Vaubel, R. (1977) "Free Currency Competition," *Weltwirtschaftliches Archiv* 113: 435–61.

Walter, N. (1998) "An Asian Prediction," *The International Economy* 12: 49.

——(2000) "The Euro and Its Consequences for Global Capital Markets," in Mundell, R.A. and Cleese, A. (eds.) The Euro as a Stabilizer in the International Economic System, Boston: Kluwer Academic.

Walter, N. and Becker, W. (2008) "The Euro Hits the Big Time," *EU Monitor* 58, Frankfurt: Deutsche Bank.

Weatherford, J. (1997) *The History of Money*, New York: Three Rivers Press.

——(1998) "Cash in a Cul-de-Sac," in "The Fiscal Frontier," *Discover* 19: 100.

Williamson, J. (1999) "The Case for a Common Basket Peg for East Asian Currencies," in Collignon, S., Pisani-Ferry, J., and Park, Y.C. (eds.) *Exchange Rate Policies in Emerging Asian Countries*, London: Routledge.

——(2008) "Exchange Rate Economics," Working Paper 2, Washington: Commission on Growth and Development.

Winkler, A., Mazzaferro, F., Nerlich, C., and Thimann, C. (2004) Official Dollarisation/Euroisation: Motives, Features and Policy Implications of Current Cases, Occasional Paper 11, Frankfurt: European Central Bank.

Wooldridge, P.D. (2006) "The Changing Composition of Official Reserves," *BIS Quarterly Review*, September: 25–38.

Woolley, J.T. (1984) Monetary Politics: The Federal Reserve and the Politics of Monetary Policy, Cambridge: Cambridge University Press.

Wriston, W.B. (1998) "Dumb Networks and Smart Capital," *Cato Journal* 17: 333–44.

Wyplosz, C. (1999) "An International Role for the Euro?" in Dermine, J. and Hillion, P. (eds.) *European Capital Markets with a Single Currency*, Oxford: Oxford University Press.

——(2002) "Fiscal Discipline in EMU: Rules or Institutions?" processed, Geneva: Graduate Institute for International Studies.

Yarjani, J. (2002) "The Choice of Currency for the Denomination of the Oil Bill," speech prepared for a meeting of European Union financial officials (April 14), available at http://www.opec.org/NewsInfo/Speeches.

Zestos, G. (2006) *European Monetary Integration: The Euro*, Mason, OH: Thomson South-Western.

Zhang, D. (2007) "Beyond Borders," *China Business Weekly*, May 16–22: 1–2.

Zimmermann, H. (2004) "Ever Challenging the Buck? The Euro and the Question of Power in International Monetary Governance," in Torres, F., Verdun, A., Zilioli, C., and Zimmermann, H. (eds.) Governing EMU: Economic, Political, Legal and Historical Perspectives, Florence: European University Institute.

Index

Africa 25, 42, 49, 59–60, 119, 178
Aliber, R. 20
Alogoskoufis, G. and Portes, R. 60,
     114, 115
anchor currency, euro as 125–6
Androsch, H. 86, 106
anti-growth bias 67–70, 85–8,
     105–7, 154
Argentina 25
"artificial currency units" (ACU) 30
Asia/East Asia 15–16, 23–4, 158, 164–5
Asian Monetary Fund (AMF) 23–4, 158
autonomy and influence 98–9, 138–41,
     168–70

Baldwin, R. 71, 89–90, 107–8
Bank for International Settlements (BIS)
     10, 62, 120, 123
banks: Deutsche 11, 101; Japan 11, 15,
     16; US Federal Reserve 11, 35, 38, 48,
     61, 91; see also European Central
     Bank (ECB)
bargaining 178–81
basket pegging 27–8, 48–9, 173
Becker, W. 128
Belke, A. 91
Bergsten, F. 24, 60, 73, 77, 81–2, 94,
     140, 172
Bernanke, B. 104
bias: anti-growth 67–70, 85–8, 105–7,
     154; conservative 14–15, 41, 56, 64
Big Three see Currency Pyramid (Big
     Three); dollar/US; euro/EMU; yen/
     Japan
bonds/bond markets 11, 63, 84, 104–5;
     Europe 17, 18, 23; Panda
     (yuan/RMB) 159–60
British pound 12, 13, 14, 41, 64–5
bystander, euro as 99–101

"capital certainty" 13, 40, 76, 149–50
Castellano, M. 157
Central and Eastern European countries
     48–9, 125; see also European Union
     (EU), enlargement
CFA franc zone 25, 49, 71, 97, 125
China see yuan/China
Chinn, M. and Frankel, J. 115,
     128, 129
Clark, W. 51
Cobham, D. 126
Cohen, B.J. 6, 9, 13, 21, 39, 41, 42, 46,
     65, 74, 98, 103, 116, 117, 129, 130,
     132, 138, 142, 150, 153, 161, 168, 169,
     171–2, 175, 176, 177, 178
conflict risks see leadership conflict
conservative bias 14–15, 41, 56, 64
Currency Pyramid (Big Three) 9–29
     passim, 150–1; implications of
     technological developments 34–5;
     see also dollar/US; euro/EMU;
     yen/Japan
currency reserves 126–9, 172–4
currency substitution 10, 11, 12;
     euro–dollar rivalry 124–5

de Gaulle, C. 1, 37, 59, 75, 152
de Larosiere, J. 81
decentralization 93–4, 102–3, 117
Delors, J. 42, 60, 77, 103
denationalization 29–30
deterritorialization 20, 25, 29–30
Deutsche Bank 11, 101
Deutschmark 12, 62, 78–9, 81–2, 119,
     137; currency exchange market 10, 63;
     currency substitution 11; euro as
     successor to 11, 12, 17, 22, 47, 78;
     international bonds 11
"dirty" floating 180

dollar/US 1, 2, 11, 12, 37; currency
    exchange market 10; depreciation
    39–40, 100–1; dominant status 55–6,
    151–2; and euro challenge 22–3
    (*see also* euro–dollar rivalry);
    Federal Reserve 38, 48, 61, 91;
    followership 25; payments deficit 97,
    151–2, 172–3;
    and pound sterling 12, 13, 14, 41, 64–5;
    and yen 24
dollarization 22, 23, 61
Dornbusch, R. 25
Dowd, K. and Greenaway, D. 14, 64

East Asia 23–4, 158, 164–5
Eichengreen, B. 25, 26, 82
"electronic money" *see* technological
    developments
euro/EMU 1–3, 16–18; diffusion of
    monetary power 170–2; disadvantages
    116–18, 153–6; external value of
    141–3; followership 25; global context
    98–113; internationalization 22–3,
    118–19 (*see also* euro–dollar rivalry);
    and monetary sovereignty 152–3;
    performance 62–4, 77–9; regional
    character of 78, 79, 108–9, 155–6; as
    successor to Deutschmark (DM) 11,
    12, 17, 22, 47, 78; usage details 120–9
euro–dollar rivalry 37–52, 55–8, 59–73,
    103–10, 114–34; EMU and member
    states 141–7; EU enlargement 79–82;
    and leaderless currency system
    148–56; one-and-a-half currency
    system 137–47; predictions and
    reality 115–19
Eurogroup 95, 144–7
European Central Bank (ECB): financial
    stability issues 92–3, 100, 101–2;
    governance 44–5, 71–2, 155;
    governance and EU enlargement
    89–92, 107–8; internationalization of
    euro 22, 119; limits of authority 116,
    117; monetary and fiscal policy 44,
    68–9, 86, 99, 106, 154; public debt
    market 83–4, 105; regional character
    of euro 78, 79, 109, 156;
    representative role 112; trade
    invoicing and settlement 122
European Commission 140, 144–5
European currency unit (ECU) 30
European mini-states 125
European Monetary Union (EMU)
    see euro/EMU; euro–dollar rivalry

European Union (EU): enlargement
    74–97, 107–8; Lamfalussy Report
    43, 66
"exchange convenience" 13, 40, 76,
    149–50
exchange markets 10, 62–3, 78, 109–10;
    euro usage 120–2, 125–6
exchange-rate: EMU policy 45, 72,
    143–5; euro 62, 77, 100, 171; floating
    vs fixed (basket pegging) 26, 27–8,
    48–9, 144, 173, 180; follower options
    26, 27–8; IMF surveillance 180
external representation 45, 72, 94–6,
    110–12; EMU member states 145–7

financial crisis (2007) 2, 115–16,
    117, 151
financial markets: euro usage 123–4;
    euro–dollar rivalry 63, 79; Europe 17,
    65–7, 83; globalization 174–6; Japan
    16; *see also entries beginning* exchange
    and market
Financial Stability Forum (FSF)
    179, 180
financial stability issues 99–103; EU
    enlargement 92–4
floating *vs* fixed (basket pegging)
    exchange-rate 26, 27–8, 48–9,
    144, 180
followership options 24–9
formal conflict 46, 48–9
Frankel, J.A. 26, 38; Chinn, M. and 115,
    128, 129; and Rose, A.K. 28
Frieden, J. 112
Friedman, B. 35

global imbalances 172–4
governance: euro 44–5, 70–3, 141–3,
    155; euro and EU enlargement 88–96,
    107–8; and international bargaining
    178–81; and national sovereignty
    176–8
government preferences 18–29
Gros, D. 90, 108; *et al.* 96; and
    Thygensen, N. 55, 60, 137
Group of Seven (G-7) 111, 112, 141,
    145, 146, 170, 179, 180
Group of Twenty (G-20) 179, 180
growth of international currencies 10–12

Hale, D. 24
Hayek, F. von 30, 31
Henning, R. 49, 61, 67–8, 72
Hüfner, M. 47

inertia 13–15, 40–1, 56, 64–5, 150
inflation: ECB policy 44, 68–9, 99;
new member states, EU 86–7
informal conflict 46–8
institutional participation *see* external
representation
International Monetary Fund (IMF) 2,
11, 67, 79, 93, 103, 117; allocation of
quotas and voting powers 179–80;
bloc and decision-making 140–1;
COFER data 126–7; exchange rate
surveillance 180; Special Drawing
Rights (SDRs) 30; US influence 21
internationalization 10–11, 12; euro
22–3, 118–19; *see also* euro-dollar
rivalry
Issing, O. 35

Japan *see* yen/Japan

Kirshner, J. 39, 131, 132, 149, 152, 162,
163, 174
Krugman, P. 13, 14, 41, 65, 142, 177
Kwan, C.H. 157, 158

Lamfalussy Report (EU) 43, 66
large denomination bills 22, 23, 47, 48
Latin America 25, 28, 178
leaderless currency system 148–66
leadership conflict 20–4, 161–5; *vs*
cooperation 160–1; euro-dollar 46–9,
57–8, 130–3

Maastricht Treaty (1992) 1, 44, 45, 60,
68, 69, 71, 72, 92–3, 94, 101–2;
convergence criteria 80, 87; *see also*
Stability and Growth Pact (SGP)
McNamara, K. and Meunier, S. 45, 72,
95, 96, 111, 112
macroeconomic flexibility 38–9, 61
market competition 12–18; attributes of
success 12–13, 40, 76, 149–51;
euro–dollar 40–5, 103–10
Mediterranean countries 25, 42, 49,
59–60, 119
Merkel, A. 3
Middle East 49–51, 129, 132–3, 163–4,
178
Momani, B. 129
monetary and national sovereignty
152–3, 176–8
monetary power: autonomy and
influence 98–9, 138–41, 168–70;
diffusion of 170–6;

euro 170–2; global imbalances 172–4;
globalization of financial markets
174–6; and monetary system
ambiguities 176–81; and state power
39, 61
monopoly and oligopoly 19–20
Mundell, R. 1, 21, 28, 39, 42, 60, 61,
76–7, 81, 103, 171

national and monetary sovereignty
152–3, 176–8
"network externalities" 56–7, 82, 150
network money 31, 32
network theory 34
networks *see* transactional networks

oil exports, Middle East 49–50, 51, 132,
133, 164
oligopoly and monopoly 19–20
OPEC 50, 51
optimum currency area (OCA)
theory 28
Orléan, A. 14, 64

Padoan, P.C. 49
Papaioannou, E.: *et al.* 121, 127–8; and
Portes, R. 122, 123, 126, 128;
Political instability 26–7, 40, 42; Middle
East 50, 129
Porter, R.D. and Judson, R.A. 11, 38
Portes, R. 23, 48; Alogoskoufis, G. and
60, 114, 115; Papaioannou, E. and
122, 123, 126, 128; and Rey, H. 17,
18, 38, 48, 50, 65, 82–3
Posen, A. 128, 129
pound sterling 12, 13, 14, 41, 64–5
public debt market 83–4, 105

regional character of euro 78, 79,
108–10, 155–6
regionalization 177–8
representation *see* external
representation
reserve currencies 126–9, 172–4
Rey, H. 78, 83
Rogoff, K. 22
Rose, A.K. 28

Schadler, S. *et al.* 84, 85
Schinasi, G. 93, 102, 103
seigniorage 19, 21, 27, 61; electronic
money 31–2; US 38, 48, 61
smart cards 31, 32
Solomon, E. 32

Stability and Growth Pact (SGP) 44, 69–70, 87, 88, 106–7, 154
status/prestige of market dominance 39, 61
Strange, S. 131, 162, 168
successful attributes of currencies 12–13, 40, 76, 149–51
Summers, L. 131, 163, 174

technological developments: deterritorialization to denationalization 29–30; electronic money 30–3; implications for Big Three 34–5; number of currencies 33–4
Thygesen, N.: and ECU Institute 10–11, 34; Gros, D. and 55, 60, 137
trade: invoicing and settlement 63, 78–9, 122–3; Middle East 50
transaction costs 14, 17; euro and EU enlargement 82–4; euro–dollar rivalry 42–3, 62–3, 65–7, 104–5, 153–4

transactional networks 13, 14–15, 40–1, 64, 76; EU enlargement 81–2
Truman, E. and Wong, A. 110, 127

United States (US) *see* dollar/US; euro–dollar rivalry

Volcker, P. 2–3

Weatherford, J. 32, 33
Wriston, W. 33
Wyplosz, C. 22, 42, 59–60, 70, 75, 76, 104, 119, 153, 172

Yarjani, J. 50
yen/Japan 10, 11, 12, 15–16, 156–8; and East Asia 15, 23–4, 158, 164–5
yuan/China 14–15, 163, 180; currency reserves 173, 174; and East Asia 164–5; Panda (RMB) bonds 159–60